THE REAL AMERICANS

Other books by A. Hyatt Verrill

ALONG NEW ENGLAND'S SHORES

THE SHELL COLLECTOR'S HANDBOOK

With Ruth Verrill

AMERICA'S ANCIENT CIVILIZATIONS

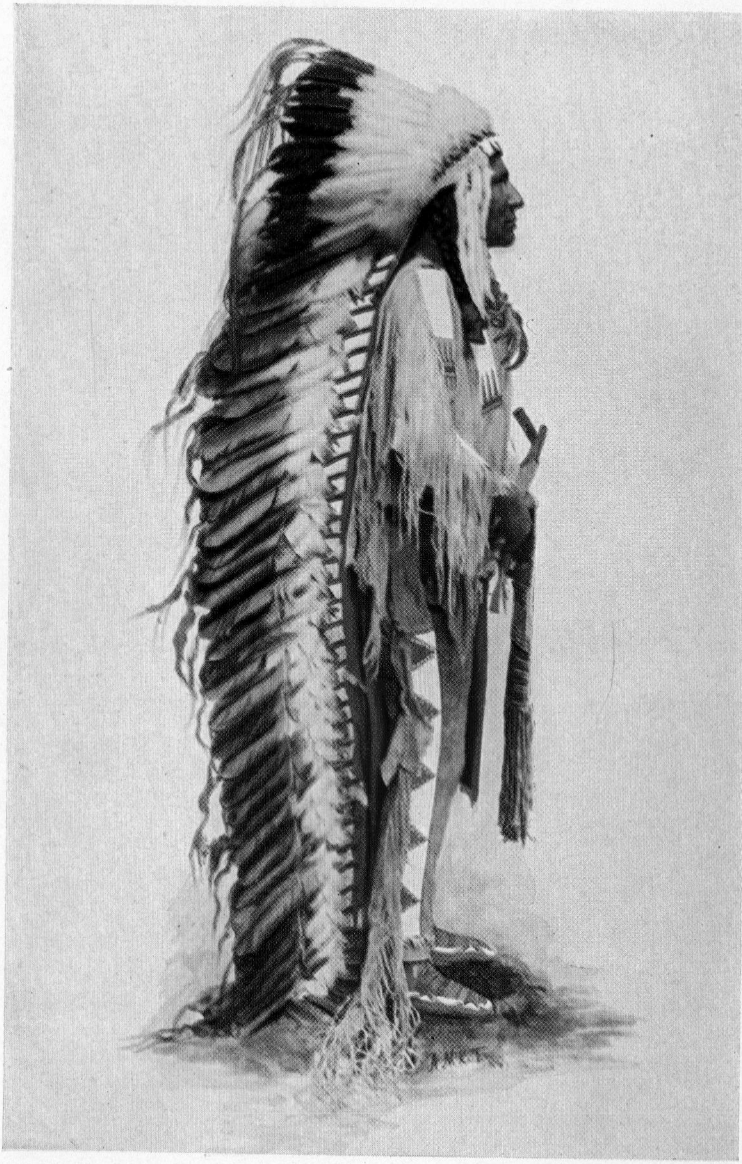

Sioux Indian warrior in full war costume, National Museum

THE
REAL AMERICANS

A. HYATT VERRILL

G. P. PUTNAM'S SONS
NEW YORK

Published on the same day in the Dominion of Canada by Thomas Allen, Ltd., Toronto.

Library of Congress Catalog Card Number: 54-5495

Manufactured in the United States of America

CONTENTS

Sixteen pages of illustrations will be found following page twenty-two.

INTRODUCTION

THIS BOOK is not intended to be a scientific ethnological work but is for the purpose of conveying a better knowledge and understanding of our Indians of the United States, to tell of their lives, customs, arts and industries, their psychology and mental reactions, their religious myths and their legends—in short their "human" characteristics, and not the shell they assume when in the presence of strange white men. For the Indian is in reality a most self-conscious person and dreads being regarded as a curiosity or a being apart or laughed at, and until his friendship and confidence are won he shuts up like the proverbial clam and appears to be a dour, austere, inarticulate personage. During more than an average lifetime I have visited and lived among innumerable tribes. I have become a blood brother of an Indian chief, a full-fledged "Medicine chief" of one tribe, an honorary member of a secret "medicine" cult of another tribe, and an adopted member of several tribes, and I flatter myself that I know my Indians about as well as it is possible for any white man to know them. Moreover, there is a goodly strain of Wabenaki blood in my veins while my wife is more than one-half Tuscarora which—officially and by Indian rules—makes both of us Indians.

In order to lighten the more technical portions of the book, as well as to convey a better idea of Indians' characters, I have included a few of my personal experiences among the Indians.

Many books have been written that deal with the Indians. Some are strictly ethnological and were written by scientists who not infrequently had no real or personal knowledge of the Indians. Others have been very superficial. And still others that are most excellent as far as they go deal only with one or two tribes or groups of Indians with whom the authors are familiar.

I do not think that any book hitherto published has covered the entire subject of our real Americans in a popular manner and as thoroughly as the present volume. Indians who have read portions of the manuscript have been most enthusiastic about it, and, after all, the Indians themselves should be the best judges of a book about themselves and their people. Moreover, in writing the book I have had the wholehearted assistance and co-operation of my many Indian friends, among them Chief Ho-To-Pi the Cheyenne opera singer and Lone Eagle Buckman; Chief Shup-She (H. L. LaHurreau) of the Pottawattomies; Aren Akweks (Ray Fadden) Councilor of the St. Regis Mohawks; Lone Bear (James Revey) of the New Jersey Delawares; Francois Burdette of the Caugnawgas; Johnny Whitehorse and Frank Young Antelope of the Pawnees; Will Taylor of the Osages; Fred Selsey of the Comanches; Francisco Colorado of the Cotero Apaches; Julio Longlance of the Jicarilla Apaches; Rafael Curo of the Hopis; Henry Whit of the Quapaws; Dick Redwing of the Chippewas; Walking Bear of the Crows; Lame Buffalo of the Nez Percés. John Saukolexis of the Tarratines; Chief White Eagle, Oglala Sioux and adopted son of Buffalo Bill Cody; Big Elk, Oglala Sioux and grandson of Crazy Horse and Red Cloud; Walks With the Wind of the Winnebagos; Joseph Walks his Horses of the Arikaras; Red Bear of the Mandans; Looks to the Moon, the aged Cherokee; James Orday of the Utes; Chief Bradbury of the Chickahominies; Black Eagle, Cray Badgor, Standing Elk of the Arapahos; Antonio Flores, a Yaqui; and many others who are thoroughly conversant with their tribal customs and costumes, their ancient religions and their legends despite the fact that they are outwardly thoroughly "civilized" and live, act and dress like white men. I feel therefore, that this book comes closer to being about our Indians by our Indians, than any work hitherto written. I have devoted considerable space to correcting a number of false ideas and misconceptions of the Indians, for the average white person has as much to unlearn as to learn when it comes to the real Americans.

Naturally there are good, bad and mediocre Indians just as among any race, but I have found that the more primitive they are the smaller the percentage of undesirables, for they seem to acquire the white man's faults along with his customs and garments. Moreover, the old tribal laws were very strict and punishment for their violations was swift and certain. On the whole I have found the Indians likable, honest, hospitable and thoroughly trustworthy once their friendship is won, and a jolly, talkative lot with a keen sense of humor and a great fondness for jokes. But one has to "get under the skin" of an Indian to really know and understand him and in this book I have tried to picture our Indians as they really are. In addition to the Indians I have known personally there are a great number of tribes and subtribes within our borders and it manifestly would be impossible to describe all of them in detail in a book of this size.

Fortunately many of the tribes are so closely related or are so similar in most respects that I have grouped them together in my descriptions. For much the same reason I have mentioned only a few of the Canadian tribes, for in most cases the Indians of Canada are similar to or identical with those of our northern states, so that a description of one will serve for the other, the only noteworthy exceptions being the tribes of Alaska and the far northwestern coasts who are a subject by themselves. However, in the Glossaries I have given brief condensed descriptions of every existing tribe in the United States and brief biographical accounts of the majority of Indians of history and fame or who have attained to noteworthy prominence. This never previously has been done as far as I can ascertain. It must be borne in mind, however, that my descriptions, as a rule, refer to the Indians as they were in earlier days for now the majority are throughly civilized—at least outwardly—and dress as do white persons, live in ordinary houses, own automobiles and are farmers, ranchers or are engaged in some white men's profession. Only on rare occasions, such as at ceremonial dances, at rodeos and pageants and tribal council meetings, do they don their tribal costumes and enact the ceremonies and dances of their ancestors that never are forgotten.

On the other hand, there are many tribes in the United States who still adhere to their tribal costumes and customs, who still dwell in the same types of houses as did their ancestors of old and who still carry on the same ancient arts and industries. Among these are the Pueblos (the Zuñis, Hopis and others), many of the Navajos, a number of the Seminoles of Florida, and some of the Blackfeet and other plains tribes. Unfortunately, however, the retention of tribal costumes and customs is all too often for purposes of publicity and to attract the tourist trade rather than the result of tribal pride and traditions. But there are a great many Indians who, despite their civilized manner of life, still adhere to the religions of the forefathers and who, like the members of the Kee-Way-Din Lodge association, are striving to reestablish the old beliefs. Many of these, as well as a great many devout Christian Indians, are outstanding men and women filling innumerable important positions and following countless trades and professions, and not only competing with but often excelling their white neighbors.

Considering the handicaps, the prejudices, the discriminations and the maltreatment the Indians have suffered and yet overcome, it is very doubtful if any race at any time has ever made such great and such rapid progress as the American Indians.

A. Hyatt Verrill

THE REAL AMERICANS

I

THE MYSTERY OF THE INDIAN

WHO ARE the Indians? Where did they originate? Are they a race apart, or a mixture of several races? How long have they inhabited America? These and many other questions regarding the true identity of the American aborigines we call "Indians" have never been answered. To be sure, innumerable opinions, theories, explanations, and suppositions have been advanced, but so far not one has been borne out by positive, incontrovertible proof. In fact, every theory advanced has about as much evidence against it as in favor of it.

We know that when the Europeans first reached America the entire western hemisphere, from the Atlantic to the Pacific and from the arctic circle to Tierra del Fuego, was inhabited by a great many tribes of Indians, some primitive nomads, others sedentary agriculturists; some warlike, others peaceful; some dwelling in large villages, while others had attained an extremely high state of civilization, with cultures superior in many ways to contemporary cultures of the Old World. We also know that man has inhabited America for a vast period of time—at least ten to twenty thousand years—and we also know that the most ancient Americans whose remains have been found were physically indistinguishable from the present-day Indian.

Finally, there are abundant evidences, in the form of inscribed records, that voyagers and colonists from the Old World reached South and Central America several thousand years B.C., and that they found the country inhabited. It has even been suggested, with no little confirmatory evidence, that some peoples of the Old World were themselves descendants of American aborigines who in the immeasurably distant past had crossed the Atlantic eastward, and that traditions pertaining to these migrations, handed down for countless centuries, led to the search for the "Land of the Sunset beyond the Western Sea."

From the time when I was a schoolboy until quite recently it has been the generally accepted idea that all American aborigines are descendants of a few immigrants from northeastern Asia who crossed to what is now Alaska via Bering Strait and the Aleutian Islands. Even after many ethnologists and archeologists began to question the validity of this theory, the majority accepted it. The principal and leading exponent of the Bering Strait migration theory was the late Dr. Alexander Hrdlicka, who claimed he had found indisputable evidence to prove it.

However, even if we admit that the ancestors of the northwestern and Pacific coast Indians—and possibly some in Canada—came by way of Bering Strait, there are many established facts to prove that the ancestors of most American Indians did *not* arrive by that route. If, as Dr. Hrdlicka claimed, the immigrants from Asia were primitive and brought no domestic animals and no food plants with them, how can the adherents of the theory explain the fact that some American Indians had reached a fairly high state of culture ages before the tentative date of immigrations from northeastern Asia? Also, it would have required a tremendous length of time for primitive people to have spread southward to southern Chile, and during that period they would unquestionably have advanced in crafts, tools, weapons, and many other ways; yet about Tal Tal and elsewhere in southern Chile we find stone implements of the crudest, most elementary type.

Arguments based upon skull structure—so-called long-headed or round-headed men—as proof of the Bering Sea theory must be discarded; among many tribes both skull types occur. (I have a photograph of three brothers belonging to an Indian tribe in Central America, one of whom is typically long-headed, another typically round-headed, and the third an intermediate type.) Even more conclusive evidence against the Bering Sea theory may be found in the artifacts that have come down to us. Beautifully made weapons of stone have been discovered in connection with the bones of long-extinct animals such as the woolly rhinoceros, shovel-jawed elephant, giant bison, and other. Some of these weapons are embedded in the bones, many of which had been cooked and broken open for the marrow, proving that man much further advanced in some ways than his Old World contemporaries had inhabited North America in glacial days—from 10,000 to 50,000 years ago. In Mexico, human remains have been found beneath lava flows 8500 years old; the skulls were in such good condition that some were restored, and restoration indicated that these ancient Mexicans were indistinguishable in appearance from Mexican Indians of today. In Canada, still more recently, great quantities of stone implements, various other artifacts, and a few human remains have been found that date back 17,000 years.

Until quite recently, estimating the antiquity of human remains and artifacts was largely guesswork, based on geology, strata of soil, existing conditions, and other matters. But with the discovery of the radioactive carbon method of determining the passage of time we can now definitely place the age of any carbonaceous material within limits of 1000 years. Some of the results thus obtained have been amazing. Charred giant bison bones associated with the Folsom Man stone weapons in Texas were found to date from 2000 to 3000 B.C. In Chile, bones of extinct horses and giant ground sloths, associated with human remains and showing evidences of having been cooked, proved that men inhabited the area as long ago as 6688 B.C. In Arizona, the Cochise (Apache) culture revealed a date of 4982 B.C. Remains from a Kentucky mound were fixed at 3352 B.C. In New York State, remains date back to 3432 B.C. In Nevada, human remains in a gypsum cave, associated with those of giant ground sloths, proved that men dwelt there in 8404 B.C., while woven rope sandals found in Oregon were used as long ago as 7002 B.C. The carbon test, with its margin for error limited to a few hundred years, destroys the old Bering Sea migration theory, for the oldest human remains found at Norton Bay, Alaska, proved to be comparatively recent, merely 490 B.C., while the oldest known pre-Aleut site on Uniak Island dates back only to 1067 B.C. With few exceptions, these tests seem to show that human beings inhabited America thousands of years before they inhabited Europe and Asia. Charred bones from the Belt cave in Iran were dated at 8609 B.C. At Jarmat, Mesopotamia, the oldest known village in western Asia, the tests gave the date as 4756 B.C. Wood from the tomb of the first dynasty of Egypt was dated 2932 B.C., and charred wood of Neolithic man in England dates to 3013 B.C., while the most ancient known remains in Europe, at the famous Lecaux Cave in France, were dated as 13,565 B.C.—antedated some 1500 years by the Canadian discovery previously mentioned.

All of these ancient carbon-dated American remains were those of people well advanced in culture. Since it must have required many centuries for truly primitive races to have attained such cultural states, we can feel sure that human beings inhabited America in extremely ancient times. In fact, there are a number of ethnologists who are beginning to think that the earliest ancestors of so-called American Indians were indigenous to this continent. If like conditions and like environment beget like results, as scientists claim, then there is no valid reason why man should not have originated in the western as well as in the eastern hemisphere. In the past, one of the strongest arguments against this theory was that no remains of any primate or anthropoid ape had ever been found in America, but now fossil lemur-like primates *have* been found.

Until recently, anyone who suggested that thousands of years ago men migrated to America via the Atlantic or across the Pacific Ocean would have been ridiculed. But today many eminent archeologists believe that voyagers from the Near East, China, India, and the Polynesian Islands did reach America several thousand years B.C. This shift in viewpoint is based upon the discovery that the wheel, rather than being introduced by Europeans, was known and used by the ancient inhabitants of Mexico and South America; wheels and wheeled toys have been found in the very ancient remains there (See *America's Ancient Civilizations.*[1]) Another argument once advanced against the theory of

[1] In much the same manner, archeologists once maintained that no American Indian tribe knew or used iron prior to the arrival of the white men. As a matter of fact, some of the tribes of the Middle West made and used tools, weapons, utensils, and ornaments of meteoric iron; more than two hundred of these artifacts have been found in mounds and graves that long antedate the arrival of Europeans. Among the objects found are hammers, hatchets, chisels, spear and

transoceanic migrants having reached America thousands of years ago was the claim that ancient peoples did not possess vessels capable of long ocean voyages, and that no Old World food plants were known in America and no American food plants known to Europeans prior to the so-called "discovery" of America. We know now, however, from records, carvings, and inscriptions, that several thousand years B.C. the Sumerians (Phoenicians) had large seagoing ships and that maize or Indian corn was known in Egypt and India ages before the coming of Columbus, while wheat has recently been found in extremely ancient cachés in caves in California.

The likelihood is that the Indians are a composite race, a mingling of migrants from Europe, Asia, the South Sea Islands, and, perhaps, indigenous Americans—which would explain their great variation in physical makeup and other respects. Little by little we are learning more and more about the origin and antiquity of man in America, and slowly but steadily the missing pieces of the jigsaw puzzle of the origin of the Indians are being found and fitted together. But we must bear in mind that there are vast areas in North, South, and Central America and Mexico that never have been searched for evidences of ancient man, while there are innumerable ruins of temples and cities, as well as enormous burial mounds and vast cemeteries, that never have been examined nor excavated. Archeologically speaking, the surface has only been scratched. At any time, anywhere, some epochal discovery may be made that will solve the mystery of the Indians. Until then the question: Who are the Indians? remains unanswered.

---

arrow points, knives, and beautifully embossed disks hammered to the thickness of tin plate and overlaid with a tin plating of copper. Many of these specimens are preserved in the Chicago Natural History Museum (formerly the Field-Columbia Museum), and scientists are generally becoming aware that some of our Indians did know and use meteoric iron, which they worked with consummate skill.

II

WHAT WE OWE THE INDIANS

FEW PERSONS realize how much we are indebted to the Indians. As a matter of fact, we owe them everything, for we owe them our country—which our people stole from them by conquest and chicanery and which has never been paid for. Nearly all the early discoverers and settlers owed their success and their lives to the Indians. Had it not been for the friendly Indians, the Pilgrims probably never could have survived their first winter in Massachusetts. The Lewis and Clark expedition might never have reached the far Northwest had it not been for the Indians' help. The settlements of Virginia, Pennsylvania, New York, and many other portions of North America were made possible by Indian friends and allies of the white man. Had it not been for the Indians' help, we might be living under the Spanish, French, or English flag. Quite aside from this, more than 80 per cent of our most important and valued food and medicinal plants are of American origin, used and cultivated by the Indians, although absolutely unknown to Europeans in pre-Columbian days.

When we celebrate our Thanksgiving we actually are celebrating the Indians' harvest feast, and the turkey and all the "fixin's" are purely Indian. Turkeys are strictly American, having been domesticated by the Mexican Indians for centuries before the days of Columbus, and sweet potatoes, roasting ears, popcorn, baked beans, brown bread, pumpkin puddings, corn bread and fritters, succotash, cranberry sauce, buckwheat cakes and maple syrup, as well as root beer, were all popular viands at the Indians' feasts. In addition, the Indians gave us lima beans, squashes, tomatoes, peppers, eggplant, peanuts, cassava and tapioca, watermelons, pineapples, strawberries, raspberries, blackberries, guavas, avocados, papayas, blueberries, sapodillas, vanilla, cocoa, chocolate, cashew nuts, butternuts, black walnuts, pecans, hickory nuts, Brazil nuts, and many tropical food plants and fruits. Besides turkeys, the Indians gave us muscovy ducks, alpacas, vicuñas, llamas, guinea pigs, and many other domesticated animals and birds. Indian medicines are in universal daily use; the Indians gave us quinine, arrowroot, calysaya, sarsaparilla, ipecacuanha, rhubarb, arnica, cocaine, boneset, aloes, jalap, snakeroot, wintergreen, and sassafras (the sources of aspirin and other medicines), viburnum, tansy, balsam of Peru, and scores of other medicinal plants, as well as tobacco, allspice, annatto (used for coloring margarine), gutta-percha, rubber, logwood, balsa wood, chicle (the basis of chewing gum) and other valuable products.

The most comfortable footwear ever devised is the Indian moccasin, and today moccasins and moccasin-type shoes have come into their own. Snowshoes and toboggans are both Indian inventions. Our finest canoes are patterned after the Indian birch-bark canoes, and Indian workmen are employed to build them. Moreover, the most seaworthy small boats ever built are really of Indian origin, for the famous whale boats of the old Yankee whalemen were modeled on the lines of the Indians' birch canoes.

Even many of our words in daily use are Indian—as, to give only a few examples, caucus, powwow, tuxedo, Tammany, sachem, chile (peppers), tobacco, cigar, tabasco, wampum, muskeg, hackamore. We use Indian names when we speak of potatoes, tomatoes, squash, maize, chocolate. Among fish which we know by their Indian names are menhaden, scup (a contraction of *Scuppaug*), tautog, cunner, squeteague (the weakfish or sea-trout), muscallonge, and tarpon. We call our round clams quohogs, and among the land animals known by their Indian names there are the skunk (corrupted from *Asa-kunkus*), puma, cougar, coyote, cayuse, mustang, woodchuck (a corruption of *Outa-chuga*), muskrat (corruption of *Musquash*), moose, wapiti, and caribou. We refer to the popular dish of corn and beans as "succotash," the name by which it was known to the Indians, and the term Yankee is merely the altered Indian word *Yamp-ag-oui* from *Yamp* (white), *Ag* (many or more than one), and *Oui* or *Awi* (race or people). Wigwam and tepee or tipi are Indian words, as are hammock, moccasin, canoe, coulee, and many more.

Even the handshake is Indian: among nearly all the tribes, to clasp another's hand was a sign of friendship and peace. The well-known greeting "How" is the incorrectly pronounced *"Hau"* or "Welcome" (literally "It is well" or "It is good") of the Indians. Most important of all, perhaps, is the fact that our own Constitution is said to have been influenced by the constitution of the Iroquois or Six Nations confederation. The Indians have also given us a great many notable and famous men and women. Among them have been the late Professor Charles Eastman, Vice-President Curtis, the athlete Jim Thorpe, the surgeon Carlos Montezuma, Governor Murray of Oklahoma, Dr. Frank La Flesche of the Smithsonian Institution, Sherman Coolidge, Canon of the Denver Cathedral, Vincent Natalish, the Apache Division engineer of the New York City elevated railway system, the wrestler Little Wolf, the grand opera tenor Hotopi, and hundreds of eminent lawyers, businessmen, executives, bankers and brokers, authors and actors, artists and educators, eminent physicians, and others, not forgetting the beloved Will Rogers, who was part Cherokee. Once when I asked Will—whom I knew well—how much Indian blood he had, he pushed his hat back on his head, ran his fingers along the angle of his jaw, and drawled, "I reckon you might say I'm a sort of Ivory Soap Indian: ninety-nine and forty-four one-hundredths pure."

It can hardly be said that the Indian has always been repaid with gratitude for his many contributions to our way of life. The early settlers in what is now the United States, the colonists and pioneers, the frontiersmen of the old West, all regarded Indians as little more than wild beasts unworthy of consideration or mercy, to be destroyed wherever and whenever possible. In fact John Winslow, the Puritan preacher, declared that, as the Indians were "sons of Satan" and had no souls, it should be the duty of all good Christians to destroy them. The slogan "The only good Indian is a dead Indian" was that of General Sheridan. President Grant ordered that all Indians who refused to be herded upon reservations should be annihilated—yet his own private secretary was a full-blooded Seneca Indian!

To many white men, treaties were merely bits of paper to deceive the Indians. Rarely in all our history were they the first to violate a promise or a treaty. Yet again and again we broke our promises, violated our treaties, or used a flag of truce to lure trusting Indians within reach, as was done in the case of Osceola and the Seminoles, and over and over again during our wars with the plains tribes. Falsehoods and anti-Indian propaganda were spread in order to justify our actions. When our cavalry raided a peaceful Indian village and slaughtered men, women, and children who never had been hostile, or when our troops defeated Indian warriors in battle, the events were hailed as "glorious victories"; but when the Indians were the victors or outfought or outgeneraled our Army officers, it always was a "massacre." Even when the Indian wars were a thing of the past, the "peace" that had been declared did not apply to the Indians, who, instead of being left in peace, were driven from their homes and lands and were treated like cattle or worse. If white men cast covetous eyes upon the Indians' lands, the "wards of the government" were again herded together and deported to reservations, often in the most barren and desolate areas. When irrigation made these deserts capable of cultivation or ranching, the Indians were again the ones to move on. If they protested at leaving the homes and farms they had managed to establish they were harried, imprisoned, or shot as malcontents. When the always friendly and peaceful Nez Percés, led by Chief Joseph, attempted to leave the United States and seek refuge in Canada, they were pursued by our cavalry, shot down, and forced as prisoners to return to the reservation allotted to them; yet they had committed no hostile acts, had not molested the whites, had destroyed no property, and had not taken a scalp.

Fortunately, within recent years great changes have taken place in our government's attitude toward the Indians. Most of the old maladministration, the graft, dishonesty, and abuses that made our Indian agencies a national scandal, have been eliminated, but there is yet a vast amount of room for improvement in our treatment of the Indians. Today in most states they have the right to vote, and to bring suit against the government for payment of lands under old treaties, in which connection they have been awarded millions of dollars. Yet there are many flagrant violations of the Indians' rights that would not be countenanced by white citizens. The government denies them the right to appoint their own lawyers, claiming they are being exploited and overcharged, and they are subject to many other irritating restrictions. But little by little our only real Americans are winning their centuries-old struggle for freedom and homes of their own. Indians have been elected or appointed to federal and state positions, and, although technically still "wards of the government," they may live and travel wherever they please. Within the past months a great change has taken place in the government's attitude regarding the Indians. By a presidential decree they have been granted entire freedom from government control and full citizenship, subject to the laws of the state in which they reside. Of course this will result in some hardship on the part of the Indians who have long been accustomed to depending upon government rations and kept on reservations; but on the whole it is the most progressive and just action that has been taken by the government in dealing with the Indians. There still are hotels, restaurants, and even Y.M.C.A.'s that will not admit an Indian if he is recognized as such, but, on the whole, racial prejudice and discrimination are becoming matters of the past. White persons with a strain of Indian blood who, a few years ago, made every effort to keep the fact hidden, now are proud of their Indian blood and regard it as an honor.

Partially the change for the better in our attitude toward the Indians is due to the fact that thousands of them were in the Army, the Navy, the Air Force, and the Marines, fighting shoulder to shoulder with other service men in two world wars and in Korea. As a result, soldiers of other races have learned to understand and respect their American Indian comrades and to cast aside their old prejudices and erroneous ideas. No fighters among all of the armed forces of the world have shown greater courage, endurance, heroism, and patriotism than the Indians. Considering the treatment they and their forefathers have received at the hands of the whites, it speaks volumes for Indian character to find them battling valiantly against our enemies and giving their lives for the preservation of a freedom that we are only now beginning to grant to them.

III

ERRONEOUS IDEAS

When Columbus landed in the Bahama Islands, thinking he had reached Asia, he called the natives "Indians." The belief that the aborigines were natives of India was the first of the white men's erroneous ideas. Although it was soon learned that the western hemisphere was not Asia, the error has never been corrected, and many of the present-day ideas of the only real Americans are fully as erroneous as the name bestowed upon them by Columbus. Unfortunately, no one has yet been able to coin any better name for these people, so we must still refer to them as "Indians"—although our British cousins call them "Red Indians" to differentiate them from the people of India.

We have been dealing with Indians—or fighting them—for the past three centuries. Thousands of tourists have seen thousands of Indians of the West and Southwest. Indians, as has just been noted, have fought in the two World Wars and in Korea; and hundreds of Indians dwell in our great cities, working at innumerable trades and professions, employed in many industries, and mingling freely with the "white skins." Yet the average white man does not recognize an Indian when he sees one.

His mental picture of an Indian is a hawk-nosed individual, grim-faced, red-skinned, attired in buckskin and wearing a so-called "war bonnet" or an upstanding "scalp lock." As a Maine Wabenaki declared when I criticized him for wearing a plains Indian headdress: "White men won't believe I'm an Indian unless I wear a war bonnet."

On one occasion, when I mentioned the fact that there was a large Indian population in New York City, a friend skeptically declared he never had seen a single Indian, whereupon I wagered a dinner that I could show him a dozen within two hours and that he would not recognize any of them as Indians. I won the bet easily. At the garage where I kept my car the elevator operator was a full-blooded Comanche, mistaken for an Italian by my skeptical friend. A mechanic whom I knew was a Delaware; a subway guard was an Ojibway. There was a Wabenaki clerk in a grocery; a Mikmak in a sporting goods shop; a Sioux dentist; and some Apache and Caugnawaga steelworkers helping to erect a new building. In this connection it is of interest to note that steelworkers of the Caugnawaga tribe, whose home is near Montreal, are considered the best in the world. Nearly all the younger men are engaged in this hazardous profession. Many have been employed on the New York skyscrapers, including the Empire State Building and on the various New York bridges and the Golden Gate bridge. Members of the tribe have carried on their trade in South America, Africa, Asia, and Europe; wherever there is structural steel work to be done, the probability is that there will be Caugnawaga Indians on the job. The next best group of steelworkers are the Apaches of the Southwest.

Many white steelworkers are unaware that the men working with them are Indians. Rarely does an Indian announce that he is an Indian, and when he uses his English name there is little to hint at his racial identity. One white steelworker told me he had been working among Indians for years, sharing the same bunkhouses with them when away from home, eating and drinking with them, and never suspected they were Indians. "I asked a lot of 'em what nationality they were," he told me, "and they always said 'American'—and damned if they ain't!"

But another Indian, or a person with a good percentage of Indian blood—or even a white man who has been long among the Indians—recognizes an Indian at once. My wife is more than half Indian, yet never have I known a white person to suspect her Indian blood, although Indians invariably recognize it at once. The majority of white persons, aside from those who live near the reservations or who are more or less in direct contact with Indians, know very little about them, and what they think they know is usually wrong.

One of the most prevalent, and I might say almost universal, misconceptions is that all Indians are red. They are referred to as Redmen, Redskins, or Red Indians, yet I have never seen an Indian with a skin that rightfully could be considered red unless he had been smeared with red ochre. The color of their skins varies with the tribe, as well as with the individual, just as the skin color of the white races varies. Some are much darker than others, and in the case of those whose parents are of different tribes the children may take after either parent. Moreover, Indians tan when exposed to the sun, and I have known many a full-blooded Sioux, Pawnee, Blackfoot, Cheyenne, Apache, Comanche, and various Eastern Indians, whose faces and hands were mahogany brown but whose bodies and legs were almost white. Normally many of our North American Indians are no darker than a rather swarthy white man or brunet woman; others are a rich olive or ochreous, but the majority are a pale-brown or dead-leaf color, with the unexposed portions of the body much paler. Neither is the Indian's hair always coarse, straight, and intensely black. Many tribes have fine, silky, somewhat wavy hair that may be black or dark brown. There are occasional full-blooded Indians who are true redheads or blonds, even though they are usually thought to be of mixed blood. Of course there are half- and quarter-blood Indians with blond or red hair, but there are many others who are either partial albinos or subject to erythrism. Albinism is the entire absence of pigment, and a true albino has colorless skin, white hair, and pink eyes. They are rare among white races, not uncommon among Negroes, and very numerous among some Indian tribes, particularly the San Blas of Panama, who regard these "moon children" as sacred. But there are all degrees of albinism. Among whites it is scarcely noticeable, but very pale platinum blonds, and the blond children of brunet parents, are usually partial albinos. More or less albinistic individuals of pure Indian blood have been reported by ethnologists in nearly every tribe in the United States, and it is a simple matter for a trained scientist to determine whether or not a blond or red-headed person is partially white, or is albinistic, or erythristic. These so-called blond Indians are much commoner among some tribes than among others and are most numerous among the Pueblos, who regard them with a great deal of respect.

Erythrism and melanism are totally different from albinism. Erythrism is a preponderance of red pigment and a lack of brown or black pigment, while melanism is an excess of black pigment and a lack of the red and yellow. Erythrism is a very common and widespread condition. It is common among four-footed animals, birds, insects, reptiles, fish, shells, and even plants. The red screech owls, red wolves, reddish-brown bears, red woodchucks, etc., are all examples of erythrism, as are all red-headed human beings. Unlike albinism, which is rarely inherited, erythrism is almost always inherited. In families where there are one or more red-headed ancestors there is rarely a generation without a red-headed member, while the children of red-headed persons are almost invariably red-haired. As a result, intermarriage of red-headed persons through many generations has produced races—such as the Irish—in which red hair is fairly common. Among Negroes cases of erythrism are not rare, and in some of the West Indian islands more than one-half of the colored population are redheads. Although rare among Indians, cases of erythrism occur from time to time. One of the sisters of White Eagle, a full-blooded Oglala Sioux, who teaches school in California, is a redhead. I know a full-blooded Wabenaki, an Osage, and one or two other full bloods who have red or reddish hair and freckled skins, and one of the most famous Shawnee chiefs during the time of the Revolutionary War was named "Fire Hair."

Melanism is very common among the lower animals. Black panthers, black leopards, black deer, black wolves, and many other creatures are examples of melanism. It is a rare condition among white people, but at times it may affect a white-skinned person and transform him to black. I know one man in Florida who is of pure English blood but whose skin is about the color of a dark-skinned Hindu or a Mulatto. Until he was in his twenties he was as white as any of his ancestors. To avoid being taken for a Negro in this section where racial discrimination unfortunately exists, he carries a medical certificate explaining his color. Melanism apparently is very rare among Indians, but I knew one pure-blooded Sioux who was as black as any African Negro, although with straight hair and typical Sioux features.

Just as the color of their skin and hair varies, so does the color of Indians' eyes. Although the majority have dark-brown or black eyes, many, especially among eastern Indians, have gray, hazel, or green eyes. That these variations in color of skin, hair, or eyes is not the result of any admixture of white blood seems to be proved by the fact that the earliest discoverers and explorers, whether Spanish, Dutch, French, or English, noted and wrote of the great variation in the physical characteristics of our Indians.

Most persons not thoroughly familiar with Indians picture them as tall, athletic, splendidly built, erect men, stoical and dignified; men with broad faces, square chins, high and prominent cheekbones, aquiline noses, thin lips, and narrow eyes; in other words, the Indian-head-nickel Indian. It is true that all of these characteristics may be found among members of some tribes, but they are by no means typical of the majority. As a rule Indians are not unusually tall; they actually average less in stature than white men. Also, as a rule, the Indian is neither powerfully built nor physically well-proportioned. In their youth most Indians are slender and sinewy rather than muscular, but as they grow older they usually become stocky, and often fat and paunchy. Many, especially among the plains tribes, have bandy legs from years on horseback, and because nearly all Indians place one foot before the other when walking they are usually pigeon-toed. Also, from constantly carrying packs or loads on their backs the majority of the forest-dwelling Indians habitually stoop and are far from erect. Environment plays a large part in the Indians' physical characteristics. Forest and mountain-dwelling tribes who walk a great deal usually have well-proportioned bodies and limbs, but in the case of river Indians constant paddling results in the chests and shoulders being developed out of proportion to the lower part of the body and the legs.

Indians' features vary as widely as the colors of their skins or other characteristics. Many North American tribes have aquiline noses, high cheekbones, and the other popularly accepted Indian features. But there are as many if not more who have low-bridged noses, full, rounded cheeks, rather thick lips, full eyes, and pointed chins. It would be as foolish and as impossible to attempt to describe the various European or Asiatic races as all alike in their physical appearance as to consider the American Indians in that manner. Moreover, Indians vary as much in their personal characteristics as in appearance. Indians as a whole are by no means stoical, taciturn, dignified, or lacking in a sense of humor. In the presence of strangers, especially white persons, Indians may be shy, suspicious and self-conscious; but among themselves, or when with whites who have won their confidence and friendship, they are talkative and full of fun, and laugh, chatter, "kid" one another and gossip as freely as anyone. I have yet to meet an Indian who does not possess a keen sense of humor. As a rule, they enjoy practical jokes. Very often, too, they will see the point of a humorous story much more quickly than a white man.

While among the Indians of Mexico I frequently told stories with subtle humor that quite often passed completely over the heads of white persons, yet in every case the Indians saw the point at once. One story in particular always delighted them. This was the story of a man who, entering a saloon, asked the bartender: "What is Jim's last name?"—whereupon the bartender demanded: "Jim who?" I have repeatedly seen white men look perfectly blank when I told them the story, but Indians, both in Mexico and here in the United States, invariably burst into hilarious laughter when they heard it. Sometimes, too, the Indians are unconsciously humorous. On one occasion when I was in Panama some of the San Blas Indians decided to start a revolt against the Panamanians, and the chief of one of the villages, whom I knew very well, came to Colon to ask me if I thought he should join the malcontents. "Why do you want to kill the Panamanians?" I asked him. "We don't want to be civilized." he replied. "We want to live like the Americans."

The old belief that Indian babies never cry is also wrong. Indian children as a rule are quieter and less addicted to squalling than are white youngsters, but among many tribes crying babies are almost as numerous and as exasperating as among white families. However, at a very early age they are trained not to cry, at least not audibly, and to be seen rather than heard.

A great deal of nonsense has been written and told as to the Indians' immunity to pain and suffering. An Indian may not show indications of pain or agony, for by a sort of self-hypnosis or autosuggestion he can place himself in a condition of semi-anesthesia during which he does not suffer as he would normally. But unless he is prepared for the ordeal and has time to place himself in this state he is as susceptible to pain as anyone. Many a time I have seen an Indian jump up and emit an agonized cry when he sat on a lively hornet or trod on a thorn, yet I have seen the same man stand knee-deep in a nest of voracious biting ants while gathering the female "honey ants" that are considered a great delicacy, and although the Indian's legs were covered with blood from the ants' bites he apparently was insensible to the pain. I have known an Indian to pry out an aching tooth from his jaw or permit fingers to be amputated without the use of an anesthetic and not even groan, while the same man would howl and jump about on one foot when a loose rock rolled on his toes.

Most of the popular ideas about Indians have been derived from stories of the more familiar tribes, from lurid Wild West literature, and, of course, the movies. Most persons speak of any Indian dwelling as a wigwam or tipi, and think at once of a conical tent of bark, skins, or painted canvas. But the bark wigwam was only the temporary summer home of the eastern and northern tribes, while the tipi or tepee was the home of the nomadic plains Indians. Neither the wigwam nor the tipi was universal. There were far more Indians who lived in log houses, or structures of sods, earth, or wattles, or under thatched roofs, than in conical tipis or wigwams. Many of the eastern tribes built really substantial houses of logs. The "long houses" or council halls of the Iroquois were of logs, and good-sized villages of log houses surrounded by palisades of logs were common. The Mandans and some other tribes of the West built beehivelike houses of poles covered with sods; the Navajos preferred their "hogans" of logs that are partially underground, or their "wickiups" of brush and sods; while the Pueblos erected adobe houses. The Seminoles and most of the tribes of the extreme southern states lived in open sheds roofed with palm-leaf thatch and with the floors raised a few feet above the earth. Some of the mountain tribes made houses of stones, while many of the eastern Indians preferred gable-roofed or arch-roofed homes of saplings covered with bark or with wattled walls.

There are also many erroneous ideas regarding the Indians' "war whoops," scalping, face-painting and "war bonnets." Many Indians never heard or uttered a "war whoop" and would not have known what it meant. The nearest approach to one is the *"Hopo—Hookahey,"* meaning "Charge," or "Let us go," of the Sioux and Cheyennes. Woodland Indians, such as those of New England and the eastern states, moved as silently as possible, and anything even faintly resembling a war whoop would have been fatal to them. They were led and guided by the counterfeited notes of birds, chirps of insects, the hooting of an owl or by other simulated forest sounds, and even when they attacked they did so silently, or at the most shouted taunts of defiance at their foes. When the plains Indians attacked they often yelled and shouted, but there was no typical recognized or universally used war whoop.

Scalping, with occasional exceptions, was restricted to a few tribes. Most tribes never scalped a fallen enemy until after the whites began paying bounties for scalps. When the white men paid more for a scalp than for a prime beaver skin, the Indians decided that scalps must possess some magical or "medicine" power, and commenced taking scalps on their own account. Moreover, it was fully as customary for a white man to take the scalp of an Indian as it was for an Indian to take the scalp of a white man, and in the early colonial days in New England organized groups of white scalp-hunters raided peaceful as well as hostile Indian villages, killed men, women, and children, and collected the bounties on their scalps. Scalps, after all, are merely trophies or "tallies," and many tribes preferred a war trophy in the shape of a dried hand or fingers or some other portion of a slain enemy's anatomy. The Cheyennes, for example, took the left-hand fingers or even the entire left hand as fetish trophies, and were known as "cut fingers": the sign for a Cheyenne in the sign language consisted of drawing one's right fingers across the left. They also took scalps, but these were taken to even scores for members of their own tribe who had been killed and scalped, and after the death chant had been sung the scalps were considered of no importance and were used for trimming and ornamenting clothing, weapons, etc. For that matter, few of the plains Indians considered scalps of any great value after they had been counted and dried, and they were almost universally used for ornamental purposes. A great many persons have the idea that when an Indian "lifted" a scalp he took the skin and hair of the entire head. Only a very few tribes did this; the majority took only a small portion of the scalp, and the portion taken varied with the tribe. Some took a strip along one side of the head, others a portion from the other side; some took an oval section from the crown, still others the back or the front of the entire scalp. An Indian could thus tell the tribal identity of the scalper. They were not always overparticular as to whether a man was dead or only wounded when they scalped him, and many a man has been scalped and has survived. In fact, one of my own uncles was scalped, yet lived to a ripe old age and died only a short time ago; there was always a hairless area of skin covering his skull where the scalp had been taken.

Neither did all the Indians wear "scalp locks." This was a custom of certain eastern tribes—a sort of "come and get it if you can" challenge—while a number of western Indians, such as the Blackfeet and Pawnees, wore short queues which doubtless served nicely as handles for the enemy who took the scalp. But far more numerous were the tribes who bobbed their hair or permitted it to grow, either braiding it in long plaits or brushing it back in a pompadour or into an upstanding comblike "roach." [1]

The "terror-inspiring hideous painting" of Indian tales was not intended to frighten the foe as much as to serve as a camouflage, the colors and designs blending with the lights and shadows and surroundings. Moreover, painting faces and bodies had both a symbolic and a "medicine" significance. Finally, it served

[1] It was not always necessary to kill an enemy in order to count coup. On one occasion a Sioux war party came upon some enemy scouts who were asleep by their fire. Without awakening or molesting them, the Sioux placed miniature coup sticks about the sleeping men and continued on their way. When the men awoke and saw the coup signs they realized what had happened and that, officially, they were dead and never could again take part in battles. Among their people they were regarded as being dead, and were referred to in the third person exactly as though they had actually been killed in battle.

as a means of identification. Each tribe and every individual had some particular designs and colors, which was very important, for when two war parties of Indians, often closely related, took part in a battle the painting served not only to distinguish friend from foe but to identify the tribes taking part. It was all an open book to the Indians but a meaningless lot of colored pigments and weird patterns to white men not thoroughly versed in the Indians' ways.

Rarely do we see a magazine or book illustration or a motion picture of an Indian battle where the braves are not shown wearing the so-called "war bonnets" with long, feathered "tails." As a matter of fact, no Indian in his senses would go to war wearing one of these showy contraptions. When about to attack an enemy an Indian tries to remain as inconspicuous as possible, and nothing is more conspicuous than the feather-tailed bonnet. Moreover, it is a cumbersome affair, and the long feather-bedecked tails would get in the wearer's way and interfere with his mounted activities. Imagine an Indian warrior clinging to one side of his pony and firing from beneath its neck with a long-tailed war bonnet on his head! At times some of the plains Indians did wear feathered headdresses during attacks on their enemies, but never the long-tailed war bonnet, which the public has come to associate with all Indians, although originally confined to the plains tribes. For that matter, "war bonnet" is a misnomer: as one of my Sioux friends declared, "It should be called 'peace bonnet.' " It was worn only during pageants, dances, ceremonials, councils, and similar affairs, or when an Indian wanted to "show off" and donned all his finery. Probably the most interesting feature of the war bonnet is its history, for it was derived from the age-old pleated cloth and lace headdress of the *huipile* costume of the Totenac (Tajin) women of Vera Cruz, Mexico, and the Zapotec Indian women of Chiapas and Oaxaca. As the *huipile* headdress spread northward where cotton cloth was not available, the pleated cotton was replaced by feathers, and was adopted by the nomadic Indians of northern Mexico. When some of these tribes moved into the American Southwest, the showy headdress gradually became popular with the Comanches, Kiowas, and other tribes, until it was universal among nearly all

INDIAN HOMES

1. Pole and bark house—Wabenaki 2. Pole and bark house—Wabenaki 3. Pole and bark house—Narraganset 4. Bark wigwam—Tarratine (Penobscot) 5. Posts and thatch—Seminole 6. Tipi made of buffalo hides—Sioux 7. Wattled walls, thatch roof—Creek 8. Wattled walls, bark roof—Powhatan 9. Poles and sod—Caddo 10. Stone walls, bark roof—Mohican

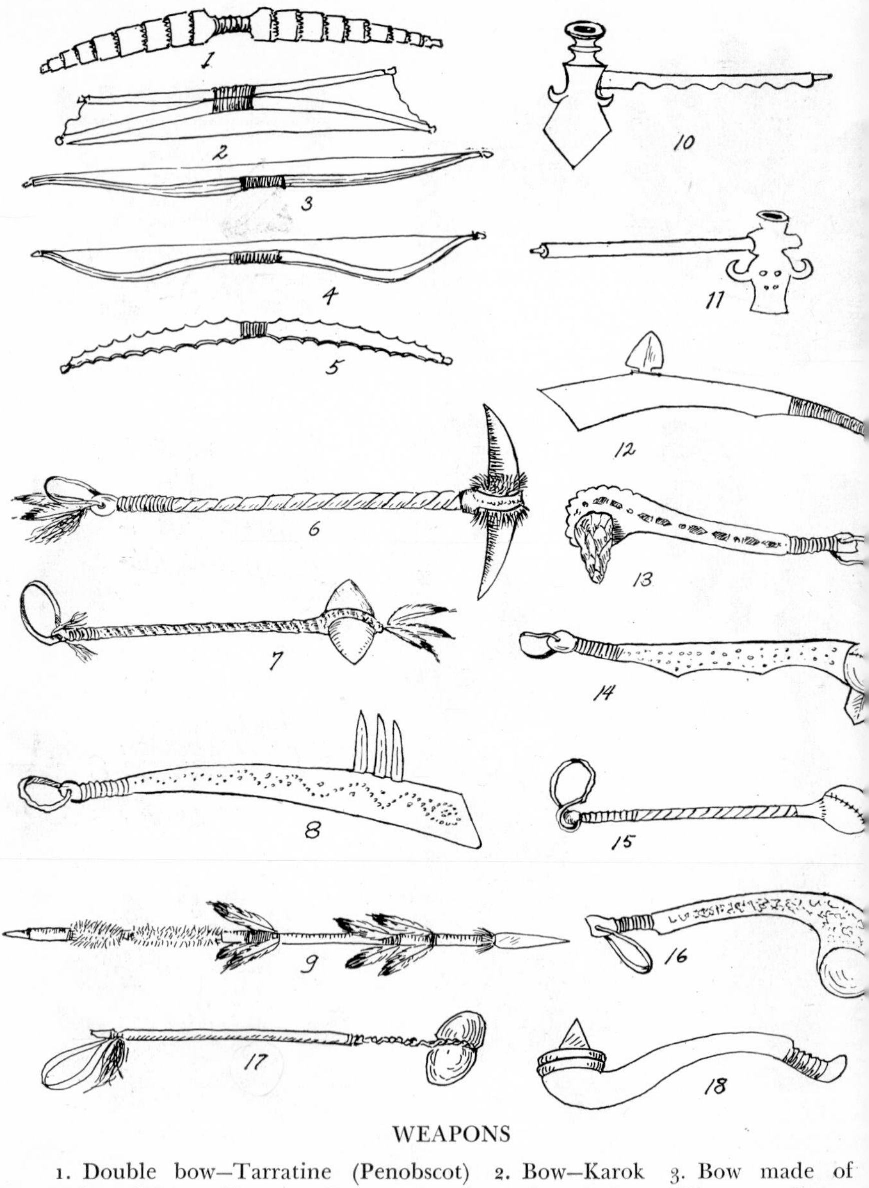

WEAPONS

1. Double bow—Tarratine (Penobscot) 2. Bow—Karok 3. Bow made of strips of horn—Sioux 4. Bow made of wood and sinew—Kiowa 5. Bow—Menominee 6. War club of horn—Cheyenne 7. Stone-headed skull cracker—Sioux 8. War club and knife blades—Sioux 9. Lance—Cheyenne 10. Pipe tomahawk—Miami 11. Pipe tomahawk—Assiniboin 12. War club—Cree 13. War club—Cree 14. War club—Caddo 15. Skull cracker—Apache 16. War club—Oto 17. Skull cracker—Apache 18. War club—Fox

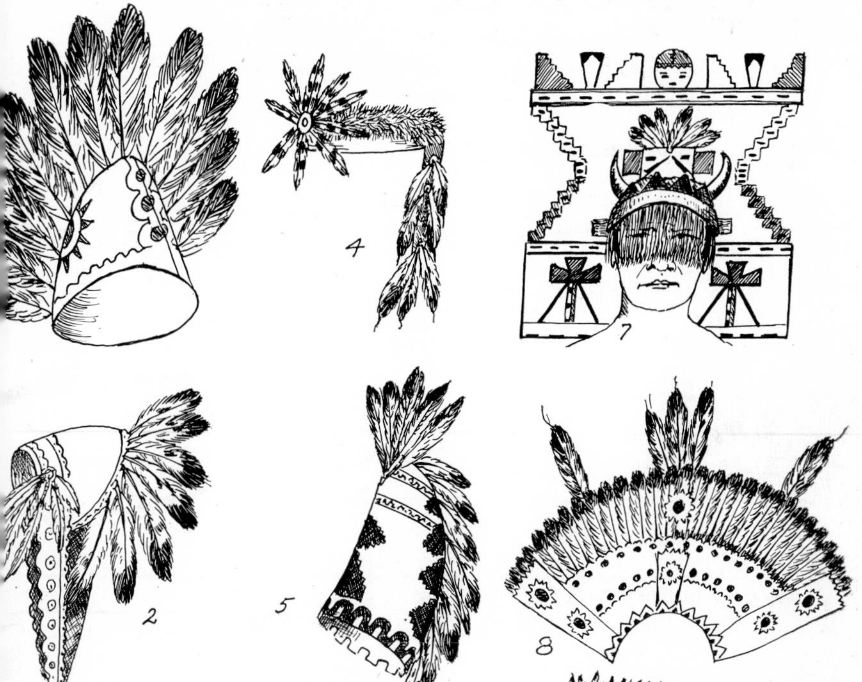

HEADDRESSES

1. Laguna (Pueblo) 2. Jicarilla (Apache) 3. Mescalero (Apache) 4. Comanche 5. Pueblo (Hopi) 6. Kiowa 7. Zuñi 8. Cotero 9. Pawnee 10. Taos (Pueblo)

1. Pretty Woman (wife of Big Elk–Sioux)–Passamaquoddy 2. Mrs. Florence Nicola Shay–Tarratine (Penobscot) 3. Little Smoky–Tarratine (Penobscot) 4. Bark wigwam–Tarratine (Penobscot) 5. Mohican chief 6. Chief Bradby–Chickahominy 7. Chickahominy 8. Niantic (Pequot) woman 9. Sherman Smokes–Mohawk 10. Hua-non-na (Ruth Verrill)–Tuscarora–Wabenaki 11. Seminoles 12. Tes Jacobs–Mohawk

1. Jack Harry (Waiawaknakuman: "Walking Eveywhere")—Delaware 2. Hopaegede ("Fish Carrier")—Cayuga 3. Winnebago chief 4. Creek chief 5 Shawnee woman 6. Delaware-Cherokee, Sand Hill Indians, New Jersey 7. Choctaw woman

1. Kiowa infant in carrier 2. Big Elk—Oglala Sioux—with wife Pretty Woman —Passamaquoddy 3. Lean Wolf—Hidatsa 4. Antelope—Caddo 5. Winnebago spearing fish 6. Fox chief 7. Oglala Sioux child (daughter of Red Cloud and mother of Big Elk) 8. John Grass—Oglala Sioux 9. Chippewa chief

1. Chief Ouray—Ute 2. Red Beaver—Ottawa 3. Strong Tree—Osage 4. Omaha man 5. Omaha woman 6. Chief George—Oto 7. Sauk woman 8. Kakebashna—Kansa 9. Pottawattomie

1. Running Crow—Piegan 2. Red Dog—Assiniboin 3. Black Heart—Blackfoot 4. Meraaparapa—Lance Mandan 5. Interior of a Blackfoot tipi 6. Rushing Bear—Arikara 7. Chief Joseph—Nez Percé 8. Scabby Bull—Arapaho 9. Paul Shoeway—Cayuse

1. Sauk 2. Uriewishi–Shoshone 3. Standing Bear–Ponca 4. Tonkawa man 5. Tonkawa woman 6. Joseph at time of famous retreat–Nez Percé 7. David Tohee–Iowa 8. George Gates–Missouri 9. Yellow Hawk–Sans Arc

1. Rain in the Face–Hunkpapa Sioux 2. David Yellow Elk–Oglala Sioux 3. Chief Gall–Hunkpapa-Teton Sioux 4. Sitting Bull–Hunkpapa Sioux 5. Two Strikes–Teton Sioux 6. Crow Dog–Brûlé Sioux 7. Red Cloud–Oglala-Teton Sioux 8. Midewakanton-Santee Sioux 9. Wife of Spotted Tail–Brûlé Sioux 10. Spotted Tail–Brûlé-Teton Sioux 11. Little Wolf–Cheyenne 12. Cheyenne 13. Cheyenne woman

1. Little Short Horn—Sisseton 2. Cohenompa—Two Kettle Sioux 3. Crow 4. Itashapa ("Dirty Face")—Oglala Sioux 5. Oglala Sioux woman 6. Eagle Track—Yankton 7. Crow chief 8. Other Day—Wahpeton

1. Navajo. 2. Manuelito—Navajo 3. Navajo 4. Navajo woman 5. Pima
6. Yuma

1. Westawana—Bannock 2. Winena (Toby Riddle)—Modoc 3. Klamath shaman 4. Yakutat priest 5. Kwakiutl chieftainess 6. Walla Walla 7. Washaki 8. Yuchi 9. Chinook 10. Kwakiutl 11. Salish

1. Copper plaque (plumed serpent motif) from Missouri 2. Shell plaque (Aztec motif) from Missouri 3. Copper ornament (Aztec wind-god, Ehecotl or Thunder Bird) Etowah Mound, Georgia 4. An Indian of 10,000 years ago. Restoration of Texpan (Mexico) man on skull dating back to about 7500 B.C. 5. Fetish necklace of human fingers—Cheyenne 6. A Florida Indian of the time of De Soto. From a very old cut 7. A Haida chief in ceremonial dress

1. Hatband, beads on horsehair—Winnebago 2. Pouch—Iroquois 3. Beadwork pouch—Yuma 4. Bead gorget—Pima 5. Moccasin—Caugnawaga

1. Basket with feathers woven in—Pomo 2. Basket—Apache 3. Basket—Apache
4. Pomo woman weaving a basket 5. Blanket—Navajo 6. Blanket—Navajo
7. Textile—Menominee

the plains Indians. If we delve more deeply into the war bonnet's history we find that the Totonac and Zapotec women's headdress appear to be derived from the extremely ancient headdresses of certain Old World races such as the Phoenicians and Egyptians. Stone sculptures, pottery figures, and carvings found in Mexico and dating back to the pre-Christian era show precisely the same headdresses as those of the present-day Zapotecs and Tehuanas, while sculptured figures, frescoes, and bas-reliefs from the Near East and Egypt show headdresses of exactly the same type. So strongly did the gorgeous and spectacular "war bonnets" appeal to both Indians and whites that they are now worn by even our eastern tribes when they dress up for special occasions. This is a great pity, for the feather headdresses of many of the tribes of the eastern and middle states were more artistic and more beautiful than the bonnets of the plains tribes. Many of these, such as the bonnets of the Wabenakis, were tight-fitting caps covered with the feathers of woodpeckers' scalps, the green feathers of heads of mallard ducks, or other bright-colored feathers, often arranged in artistic designs, and with a "bob" of feathers and ermine tails hanging at the back. Chiefs and leaders of many of the eastern tribes have used every effort to induce their fellows to discard the western type of headdresses and use only those of their ancestors. While some Indians have done so, there are many Iroquois, Delawares, Wabenakis and even Seminoles who don plains Indians' bonnets when they attend council meetings or dress for the purpose of attracting tourists.

There is a widespread belief that the plains Indians never used saddles but invariably rode bareback. While it is true that bareback riders were the usual thing, many Indians used saddles, either captured from the whites or made by the Indians. Many of the latter were excellent, although reduced to the minimum of size and weight. But many of the Indian-made women's saddles were ornate, heavy, and with very high pommels and cantles, practically horseback chairs.

Still another popular misconception regarding the Indians is the belief that they are beardless. It is quite true that with a few exceptions Indians did not permit any hair to appear upon their faces, but all North American Indians I have met have a natural growth of beard, which may be thin and sparse, or heavy and dense, just as in white men. Many pure-blooded Indians, both those of western and eastern tribes, shave daily and could raise luxuriant whiskers if they chose. My Sioux friend Big Elk, who was a full-blooded Oglala, shaved every day, but always preferred a bit of broken glass—especially a fragment of a beer bottle—to a razor. Ho-To-Pi, my Cheyenne friend, also shaves every day. My good friend Walks His Horses, an Arikara, is also a daily shaver, as are many other full-blooded Indians of many tribes whom I know quite intimately. At one time while on one of my trips I employed a pure-blooded Osage; after a few weeks in the woods and without shaving equipment he was as bearded as the proverbial pard. In the old days the Indians shaved, rubbed off, or pulled out the hairs on their faces, but now and then they allowed their mustaches or beards to grow. Many of the Navajos, some of the Pawnees, and a few others wore mustaches, and a photograph of Manuelito, the famous Navajo chief, taken about the time of the Civil War, shows him with quite a respectable mustache. During the War of 1812 the Choctaw chief Pushmataka was given a commission in the American Army; General Andrew Jackson in one of his reports wrote that "Pushmataka has grown a spade beard so he will not appear so different from the other officers." And there was no question of the purity of the chief's Indian blood. A famous Sioux chief was named Dewey Beard, so called because the white hairs in his head looked like dewdrops. Chief Tischcuhan of the Delaware's sported a goatee, and the Delaware chief Charles Journeycake had chin whiskers.

Another Indian myth is that Indian men were lazy and idle, and that the women performed all the labor. In reality, both sexes had their allotted duties and tasks. The men hunted, fished, trapped, fought, and made weapons, canoes, snowshoes and other things, but it was essential to the safety of the family and tribe that the men should not exhaust their strength by tasks which the women could do as well or better. Between battles and hunts the men rested and to the casual observer might indeed have appeared idle and lazy, but at such times they made their ceremonial dress ornaments, their fishhooks, bows and arrows, and performed tasks that were taboo to the women. The women, for their part, cared for the children, cleaned and tanned hides, made garments, beadwork, etc., cooked the meals and performed other household duties, and, in the case of agricultural tribes, cultivated their fields and garnered the crops. When nomadic tribes moved from one place to another the women attended to taking down and setting up the tipis and carried burdens, but this was essential in order that the men might protect the party from enemies, scout a trail and secure game—all duties that could not be carried out if the men were encumbered with burdens. And when an Indian man preceded his woman when entering their home or elsewhere, it was not because of his feeling of superiority but to safeguard her from harm. On the other hand, when the forest-dwelling Indians moved from one spot to another the men carried burdens, portaged the canoes, and did the paddling, as well as performing many tasks connected with making camp, in addition to hunting and providing food. Among almost all tribes there are certain tasks and occupations that are strictly those of the men, while others are as strictly confined to the women, just as it is among white persons. The man is, or at least should be, the provider or wage-earner, while the woman attends to the housekeeping, rearing the children, and necessary drudgery. From the Indian's point of view the average white man is much lazier and leaves more work to his woman than does the Indian.

Although we often hear or read of Indian "princesses," "princes," and even "kings," there never were kings, princes, princesses or royal families among the Indian tribes of North America. It was the exception rather than the rule when a chief inherited the leadership, for in most cases he was selected because of his bravery and prowess in battle and in hunting, or because of his oratorical ability, his wisdom, or other superior qualities. Even in cases where the chieftainship was inherited, the sons and daughters of the chief were not princes or princesses. They may have had a certain amount of social priority or superiority, but that was all, and even a hereditary chief could be deposed and another man elected as chief if the council so decided. In many tribes where the clan system or descent by the female line was in force, as among the Iroquois, the Delawares, and others, it was not unusual to have women chiefs or chieftainesses. A great many Indians who are erroneously referred to as chiefs were not chiefs at all. Osceola was never a Seminole chief. Sitting Bull was a medicine man or shaman but not a chief, and in many cases a man might be a war chief who led the braves in battle, yet had little or no say in other tribal matters.

The worst misconception of all is to judge the Indians of today by incidents that took place in the early days of our history or during the Indian wars. The ways and characteristics of the Indians have changed as much if not more than those of the pale faces. And that reminds me of yet another error on our part. The Indian term applied to white men when accurately and literally translated is not "paleface" but "whiteskin," which is much more appropriate. Neither is the proverbial "How" a query. The Indian greeting is *"A-Hau"*—"Peace be with you," or "All is well."

IV

SOME FACTS AND FIGURES

AMERICAN INDIANS are often referred to as "the vanishing race." But this description is entirely unwarranted: instead of "vanishing," these real Americans are increasing.

It is a very difficult, in fact an impossible, task to determine just how many Indians there are in the United States. Government census rolls include only those living on federal reservations or federal lands, or who are more or less under the jurisdiction of the Bureau of Indian Affairs. Many others live in states where there are state-controlled reservations, while a still greater number reside in states whose census rolls are not broken down by racial lines. Among these are several states where the Indian population is very large, among them California, Michigan, New York, and Washington, each with an estimated Indian population of fifty thousand or more. Still another difficulty in obtaining an accurate or even an approximately accurate census of our Indians is the question: Who is an Indian? Under the laws of descent of some tribes, only direct descendants of male members are considered to be members of the tribe, while under the rules of other tribes only descendants of female members are recognized. In a number of cases a child of a white mother and Indian father is considered white, whereas the child of an Indian mother and white father is accepted as Indian. Some tribes include in the tribal rolls members of other tribes (or even whites) who have been officially adopted into the tribe or have married members of the tribe, while other tribes do not include these individuals. Furthermore, some tribes consider anyone of one-half Indian blood or better as an Indian, others draw the line at three-quarter bloods, while others accept as Indian even one-quarter or one-eighth bloods. This may seem like stretching the term

"Indian" pretty far, but we must remember that anyone with even a slight trace of Negro blood is generally thought of as a Negro. Finally, when an Indian's parents are of two different tribes it often happens that he or she will be listed on the rolls of both tribes.

As a result of all this confusion the federal government's census of the Indians who come more or less under the jurisdiction of the Bureau of Indian Affairs is largely guesswork; the best estimate of that portion of the Indian population that comes into contact with the Bureau is about 400,000. When to this number is added Indians living on state reservations, and those who have completely lost their identities as Indians in so far as the census rolls are concerned, the total Indian population, if only those having at least three-fourths Indian blood are included, is undoubtedly at least 500,000. This is far in excess of the estimated Indian population of what is now the United States when the white man first reached these shores.

Moreover, on the basis of the figures available, it is obvious that the birth rate of the Indians is rapidly increasing, while the percentage of infant deaths is decreasing. In fact, the rate of increase of Indians' births far exceeds that of any other racial group. From 1940 until 1950 the recorded births of Indians more or less under federal jurisdiction increased 16.7 per cent. During the same period, births among the white population increased only 5 per cent, while the increase of births among non-whites, other than Indians, was 11.1 per cent. The tribe with the greatest increase (as far as figures are available) is the Navajo. In 1867, when they returned to their homes after their long exile (see Glossary) the Navajos numbered about six thousand. Today they number between forty and forty-five thousand, or nearly one-tenth of the total Indian population of the United States—by far the largest of all the tribes.

Very largely, the increase in the Indian population is due to the cessation of warfare and to control of epidemics, both of which in the past wiped out tens of thousands of Indians—sometimes entire tribes. Also, the Indians have gradually developed more or less immunity or resistance to common maladies of the white man which when originally encountered were fatal to the

Indians. Better living and housing conditions, proper medical attention, sanitation, and education have all played very important parts in the increase of the Indians. At the present time the Bureau of Indian Affairs maintains 327 schools, including day and boarding schools, forty of the schools being high schools offering vocational and college preparatory courses accepted by the state in which they are located. In addition, there are many schools maintained by various religious sects. During the fiscal year of 1952 approximately 38,000 Indian children were enrolled in federal schools.

Another perhaps surprising fact is that Indians own and utilize vast farm areas, as well as ranch and timber lands. As in the case of the census rolls, it is a difficult matter to obtain accurate figures on the total area of Indian-owned lands, since in many cases Land Office records are in the English names of the Indians and do not indicate that the owners are Indians. Furthermore, many Indians lease some or all of their lands to non-Indians. However, the total area of irrigated farm land known to be owned and cultivated by Indians amounts to 540,946 acres. Their non-irrigated farms total 3,255,784 acres, grazing lands 38,360,755 acres, timber lands total 10,349,955 acres—a grand total of 56,141,449 acres, not including hundreds of thousands of acres of nonarable desert and mountain land. In other words, the Indian today is apt to be a real landed proprietor. Neither can he be referred to as "Lo, the poor Indian," for, taken all in all, our Indians are quite well off financially. And as more and more mineral riches, notably oil and uranium, are being found on land owned by Indians, they bid fair to become really wealthy, as some of them are already. In fact, the Osage tribe is credited with being the richest community in the world.

According to the latest government reports, the per capita wealth of the Indians is about two hundred dollars. However, these figures are not very accurate; during the past year the Indians have been awarded many millions of dollars in payment of long-overdue debts for lands taken from them by force or trickery, while the oil deposits found in Nevada and the uranium mines in the Navajo country have added vastly to the Utes' and Navajos' incomes. The tribes under federal jurisdiction have on deposit with the United States Treasury nearly $100,000,000, but a great many of the more highly organized and wealthier tribes have enormous funds on deposit in various local banks, while there is no possibility of estimating the value of minerals, leases, options, royalties, etc., on Indian lands.

Today most Indians live under very much the same conditions as their white neighbors. Most of them dwell in well-built frame houses and dress like the white farmers, ranchers, and mechanics. Many, however, still wear their hair in two long braids—as do my good friend Ho-To-Pi the Cheyenne, my Arikara friend Joseph Walks His Horses, and others of the old-timers. Also, the majority of western Indians, and many eastern tribes as well, maintain the old tribal dances, ceremonials, and council meetings, and at such times—as well as at rodeos, pageants, and similar affairs—appear in full regalia of fringed and beaded buckskin and feather headdresses. Among a number of tribes the medicine man still holds a high place in tribal matters, while chiefs and council men are recognized as leaders.

Although many tribes were long ago completely exterminated by diseases or warfare, or both, and while others have merged with neighboring tribes and have practically lost their identities —as in the case of the Mandans, Arikaras, and Hidatsas—our Indians as a whole are far from becoming a "vanishing race." In fact, if their birth increase continues to be four or five times that of most other races, it will not be long before the majority of our population is more or less Indian. Perhaps, eventually, the real Americans may again own and dominate the country for which they fought so valiantly and so long.

V

ATROCITIES, TORTURES, AND MASSACRES

IN THEIR earliest contact with the Indians, the white men pictured them as cruel, inhuman, bloodthirsty savages who invariably tortured their prisoners and put them to lingering deaths. Much of this was propaganda spread as an excuse for exterminating the Indians, who were regarded by the early settlers as less than human. Not until the English colonists had raided and killed them did the Indians become hostile. War is always a cruel and bloody business, and acts that ordinarily would be considered inhuman atrocities are taken as a matter of course.

As far as the treatment of prisoners went, the white captives of the Indians were treated with far more consideration than Indians captured by the white men. Indian prisoners were either branded and sold as slaves in the West Indies, or were put to death by various methods. On the other hand, many white captives of the Indians were well treated. To be sure, the men, as a rule, were killed, but the women and children were merely carried off to the Indians' villages in Canada or elsewhere. There is no doubt that sometimes, when captives could not stand the rough going and became too exhausted to go on, they were killed, but this was far more merciful than to abandon them and leave them to die of exposure and starvation. On the other hand, there are numerous instances of the Indians allowing their female prisoners to ride the horses while the warriors went afoot, as well as cases where the Indians even carried young children in order to relieve the mothers. Of course, there was a more or less selfish motive in this, since the prisoners could usually be ransomed. However, a number of white women married their Indian captors and took to the Indian life in preference to returning to their friends and relatives, which would scarcely have been the case had they been badly or cruelly treated. One of these was Mary Jamison, who was captured by the Senecas in 1743 when she was ten years old. She married and lost two Indian husbands, lived with the tribe for eighty years, reared a large family, and stated that never had she been maltreated or insulted by an Indian, and never had known a white captive to be treated other than with kindness and respect. Another woman, Eunice Williams, who was captured in the raid on Deerfield, Massachusetts, and was carried to Canada, also married her captor. Although she often visited her childhood home and friends, she invariably lived in a wigwam, and refused to remain among the whites but always returned to her husband's village in Canada.

We must also remember that to great extent the tales of Indian cruelties and tortures date back to the very early days of the colonists in New England, to an era when legal punishments for even minor offenses were what we would today consider atrocities. Liars were branded or had their tongues nailed to a board. For the most trivial violations of the law, men were confined in the stocks or the pillory without food or water. For refusing to testify in court, men were pressed to death beneath huge stone slabs, petty thieves had ears or fingers cut off, and the death penalty was imposed for stealing anything valued at over five shillings. More serious crimes were punished by hanging in chains or in iron cages, where the condemned man died of starvation and his body was left to the crows as a warning to others. Tortures of the most fiendish type were legalized "third degrees," while burning at the stake was decreed for suspected witches.

There is no evidence of the New England Indians' having burned their prisoners at the stake until after they had seen their fellow tribesmen put to death in this manner. But they were not long in taking a leaf from the white man's book, so to speak, and more or less evening scores by burning their white prisoners. If we examine the matter with unbiased minds we will find that most of the Indians' atrocities and tortures were copied from the white men. The first record of a man being spread-eagled on a wagon wheel was when an Indian, captured during an attack on a wagon train, was lashed to a wheel of one of the wagons and died a lingering, awful death as the vehicle bumped and jolted over the desert under a fiery sun. In all probability, however, he lost consciousness very soon for no man could be constantly turned head over heels under such conditions and retain his senses for long. When eventually the Indians wiped out the emigrants and found their fellow tribesman's body lashed to the wheel, they decided that what was sauce for the gander was sauce for the goose and spread-eagled their white prisoners to their own wagon wheels. But as there were no vehicles left to which the wheels could be attached, the Indians merely left their victims exposed to the merciless sun and added a few fancy touches for good measure. Burying a man in an ant hill was an "old Spanish custom" that had been in vogue in Mexico since the days of Cortez. This was also the origin of the torture which consisted of binding a man's head with raw hide, or sewing him up in a rawhide and letting the sun shrink the skin until the victim was crushed to death. The Indians were only following the Spanish example when it came to lopping off hands and feet, cutting off eyelids, or tearing out tongues, for this was common practice among the dons in early colonial days. Valdivia boasted that on one occasion he had his soldiers chop off the hands or arms of over two hundred Indians merely because they had not surrended to become slaves.

I do not claim that all Indian atrocities and tortures were of white origin, but few if any of them were any more fiendish than those perpetrated by the whites. Neither were these outrages all matters of our early colonial days. Even during the western Indian wars, as recently as 1885-90, Indian captives were tortured by the whites, both civilians and the officers of the Army, in order to force them to betray the plans and whereabouts of their fellow tribesmen. A number died agonizingly rather than turn traitors, while others, who could not withstand the suffering, were crippled for life. Among the well-known leaders who were thus maltreated were Cochise and his comrades, who were seized when under a flag of truce. Cochise managed to escape, but when the others refused to confess to an alleged abduction of a white child they were hanged. Very largely this incident led to the long and bloody battles with Cochise and his Chiricahua Apaches.

Mangas Coloradas, the Mimbreño Apache chief, was taken prisoner by the Californians and was prodded with a red-hot bayonet, and when he tried to evade the torture he was shot down on the pretext that he was attempting to escape. Probably the most cruel punishment ever inflicted on the Indians by our government was sentencing them to imprisonment on the Dry Tortugas. To be incarcerated in gloomy Fort Jefferson on this malaria-ridden desert cay surrounded by shark-infested waters, and with nothing to occupy hands or mind, was torture almost unbearable. Quite a number of the prisoners committed suicide to escape their mental and bodily suffering, yet scores of Indians were sentenced to this living death for the most trivial offenses, and often with the flimsiest of evidence to convict them.

No Indian raid in the entire history of our country could equal the unprovoked murders and massacres of peaceful friendly Indians that time and time again were perpetrated by the whites. In the early days of New England, organized forces of white men killed hundreds of peaceful Christian Indian men, women, and children and even exterminated entire tribes merely to collect the bounty on Indian scalps. And when, as in their raid on the Norridgewocks, they found a priest in charge of the mission, they added his scalp to their collection. Under date of August 22, 1722, Jeremiah Bumpstead of Boston recorded in his diary: "This day 28 Indian scalps brought to Boston one of which was Bombazen's [the Norridgewock chief] and another was Fryer Rasle's."

No doubt many persons are under the impression that bounties on scalps were paid only in early colonial days. But until the close of the Indian wars in the west there were scalp bounties paid that made scalp-hunting a very profitable industry. The highest price paid for a scalp in Massachusetts was $400.00. In Pennsylvania, in 1764, a man's scalp was worth $134.00, the scalp of a boy under ten years of age brought $130.00, scalps of women and girls were worth only $50.00, while an infant's scalp had a value of $20.00. In Indiana the bounty on any scalp was $50.00, while in 1867 the bounty paid in Denver was only $10.00, and was paid on several hundred scalps. In Central City, Colorado, the bounty was $25.00, and was paid on more than two hundred scalps, while at Deadwood, Dakota, scalps were worth $200.00 each. Practically all the white men who killed Indians took their scalps. Even soldiers scalped the Indians they killed, when they had time to do so, and collected them as souvenirs or to obtain the bounties paid for them. To the frontiersmen a scalp was a scalp, and it made little if any difference whether they killed and scalped friendly or hostile Indians as long as they could get away with it. Over and over again such outrages committed upon the friendly, peaceful tribes transformed them to hostiles and led directly to long and bloody Indian wars.

In 1837, the miners of the Santa Rita copper mines in southwestern New Mexico invited the friendly Mimbreños to a feast and murdered them all, merely to obtain the bounty of $100.00 offered by the governor of Chihuahua, Mexico, for every Apache scalp. But they were dear at the price, for it cost the white settlers many times that amount in property alone lost in the long and bloody Apache wars that followed. The hostilities of the Comanches of New Mexico were the results of another atrocious act on the part of four white men. Coming upon the temporary camp of six Comanche hunters who were talking and laughing as they roasted buffalo steaks over a fire, the white men shot and killed three of the Indians. The others, unarmed, raced for their ponies, only to be shot down. Having scalped their victims, the white men proceeded to gorge themselves on the murdered Indians' food. Later on they displayed the scalps and boasted of their deed.

Massacres of peaceful Indians by the whites were not confined to civilians, for time and time again Army officers led attacks on friendly Indians, as when Custer attacked a village of Sioux and Cheyennes at daybreak and killed more than one hundred men, women, and children who were helpless and unarmed, and glorified his deed by recording it as "The Battle of the Washita," notwithstanding the fact that not a shot was fired or an arrow discharged by the Indians. Even worse was the raid led by Colonel Chivington at Sand Creek, Colorado, when very nearly one thousand troopers, equipped with howitzers, attacked the camp of White Antelope and Black Kettle, the Cheyenne chiefs who had just signed a peace treaty. Although the United States flag was flying over Black Kettle's tipi, together with a white flag of truce, nearly all of the Indians were shot down or sabered, the soldiers having been given orders that no Indian was to be spared. The soldiers scalped the fallen Indians, mutilated the bodies savagely, and rode their horses over the wounded until they died. Over one hundred of the scalps were taken to Denver, together with a few captured children, and placed on public exhibition as evidence of Chivington's "victory."

Wholesale massacres of Indians by whites were not confined to the military, nor to the later period of Indian wars, but had been taking place since colonial days. In 1782 Colonel Crawford, with a force of his fellow settlers, raided the peaceful Moravian Christian Indians at Guadenhutten. Having utterly destroyed them, he then swept down on the little band of Delawares under Chief Gelelemends, who, at the suggestion of the commandant of the Pittsburgh garrison, had sought refuge on an island in the Allegheny River. Practically every Indian was killed, and it seems fitting retribution for his deeds that when Crawford was later made a prisoner by the Indians he was put to a lingering and exceedingly painful death.

There are countless other similar instances of massacres of peaceful Indians by the white men. But for out-and-out fiendishness, none could equal that of the civilized, Christian Conestoga Indians at Pesheta, Pennsylvania. On a Christmas Day a party of the local settlers, led by an Indian-hater, attacked the little settlement of helpless Indians. Nearly all were killed, and were more fortunate than those who survived. The women were terribly mutilated, the young men had their hands or feet cut off or their eyes blinded, and the children and infants were decapitated and their heads kicked about like footballs. A pitiable few fled to the local jail for protection, only to be killed and scalped like their murdered comrades.

Considering how the whites hated and vilified the Indians, and regarded their leaders as fiends incarnate, it seems ironic indeed that over one-half of our states and hundreds of our cities are named after Indian tribes or Indian chiefs, and that numerous monuments have been erected in their honor!

VI

CANNIBALISM

A NUMBER OF the Indian tribes of the United States were once cannibals. Among these were the Iroquois, Assiniboins, Crees, Fox, Miamis, Ottawas, Wichitas, Chippewas, Illinois, Kickapoos, Sioux, Winnebagos, Kiowas, Caddoes, Utes, Pawnees, Nootkas, and Thilingits. The Mohawks were notoriously eaters of human flesh, and were called *Mohowauock* or man-eaters by the Narragansets, this name being later corrupted to Mohawk. The Senecas were also confirmed cannibals and were one of the last tribes to abandon eating human flesh. Also, among some tribes, a prisoner would be forced to eat his own flesh as a form of torture. On the whole, however, cannibalism among North American Indians was a ceremonial or religious rite, the heart, brains, or other portions of a slain enemy being eaten in the belief that the eater would be freed of some taboo or would acquire the bravery, intelligence, and other desirable attributes of the victim. Only the brave were eaten, and among the Iroquois, prisoners taken in battle expected to be eaten and regarded it as a religious duty. However, unfortunately, some of the tribes acquired a taste for human flesh and dined on their enemies irrespective of any symbolic, religious, or ceremonial purposes.

Among the Pawnees it was regarded as obligatory to burn or roast their prisoners. The practice, however, came to an abrupt end in a most unusual and spectacular manner. After a battle with the Comanches, one of the female prisoners was about to be sacrificed in the presence of the assembled tribesmen when a young warrior leaped up, dashed through the crowd, seized the woman in his arms, and, mounting one of two horses he had waiting, placed her on the other and rode away in the direction of the Comanche territory. The Pawnees, utterly astonished and bewildered by the sheer boldness of the deed, made no attempt to ride in pursuit, but, regarding the incident as what we would call an "Act of God," then and there it is said abolished human sacrifices and cannibalism. In the meantime, the Indian Lochinvar rode with the girl for three days. Nearing her home, he gave her the horse she rode and enough provisions to last until she reached her village, and returned to the Pawnees. Much to his surprise, he was not even censured for what he had done and no comment was made. Whether or not he eventually married the Comanche maiden history does not relate, but when, a few years later, he visited Washington, the young ladies of a seminary presented him with a silver medal to commemorate his deed and closed the presentation address as follows: "Brother, accept this token of our esteem. Always wear it for our sakes and when again you have the power to save a woman from death and torture, think of this and of us, and fly to her relief and her rescue."

Perhaps the most unusual and, in a way, grimly humorous, incidents in connection with cannibalism among the Indians was the murder of Father Juan de Padilla by the Wichitas. The earliest missionary work to be undertaken among the plains tribes was in 1541, when Father Padilla and a few other priests of the Coronado expedition remained among the Wichita Indians, who dwelt in permanent villages and cultivated small farms but were notorious cannibals for purely religious reasons. Always friendly toward the white men, they took readily to Christianity, and became greatly attached to Father Padilla and the other missionaries. Having converted practically all the Wichitas, the Padres turned their attentions to other tribes in the vicinity—but in a short time were killed by their Wichita disciples. When questioned as to why they had murdered their beloved Fathers, the Indians replied: "They were making Christians of our enemies. If they had become Christians, it would have been a mortal sin to kill and eat them!"

VII

ORGANIZATION AND HOME LIFE

WE OFTEN HEAR of the Indian clans, such as the Turtle Clan, Eagle Clan, Wolf Clan, etc., but very few persons understand just what this signifies. Practically all the tribes' social organization was based on either the clan or gens systems. These were intertribal groups of persons who might be either actually or theoretically related by blood. As a rule, each group took its name from some characteristic, such as its habitat, or from some patron creature or deity. In the clan system, ownership of property as well as descent and the right to public office is by the female line, whereas under the gens system it is by the male line. Neither totemism nor fetishes are essential features of the organizations. Blood relationship where the clan system is in vogue is traced through the female line, and membership in a clan constitutes membership in the tribe, with many rights and privileges that are denied aliens. Thus, among many tribes, a person with an Indian father and a white mother would be considered white, whereas if the father were white and the mother Indian the offspring would be accepted as an Indian. Likewise, a person whose parents were of two different tribes or two different clans would be regarded as belonging to the tribe or clan of the mother. In the gens system it would be the reverse: the person of mixed blood would be considered as belonging to the father's tribe or clan. Among some tribes the members of certain clans or gens were eligible as chiefs or subchiefs. Where the clan system ruled, the oldest woman of the clan was the ruler, whereas under the gens system the ruler would be the most elderly male member.

Among some tribes there were a great many of these groups; in other tribes there were only a few. The Mohawks and Oneidas had only three clans, three chieftainships, and three subchieftainships, whereas there were at least fifty clans among the Pottawattomies. It was not essential that a person should be born into a clan or a gens, since anyone could be adopted into one of the groups and become, theoretically, a member—although in many cases an exchange of blood with a true member, or "blood brothership," was required.

There were many rules and regulations governing the groups. As a rule the members were bound to purchase the life of any member who had killed one of his own tribe or an allied tribe, and the clan also had the right either to kill or to spare prisoners. The systems led to a great many taboos and rules and regulations in regard to marriage and other matters. Only an Indian and a member of the particular tribe could thoroughly understand the intricacies and ramifications governing such matters. Not infrequently hostilities and warfare between closely related or allied tribes or bands were the direct result of clans' or gens' disaffection and jealousies, while the division and subdivision of tribes into numerous bands, groups, and subtribes was due the clan and gens systems of organization.

All the Indian tribes had strict moral and ethical codes, and many maintained bands of police to enforce the tribal laws. Among all tribes truthfulnes was regarded as a paramount virtue, and breaking a promise was considered lying. Many tribes punished a liar by burning his home and all his property, while others banished a liar from the village. Honesty in all matters was expected and enforced, sometimes limited to members of the tribe but sometimes including all friends. (Among the plains tribes horse stealing was not considered dishonest, but was regarded as a legitimate part of hostility or warfare.) Theft was usually punished by flogging and ostracism and by compulsory compensation to the person robbed. Murder of a fellow tribesman or a friend of the tribe was punished by exile or by permitting the kindred of the slain person to avenge his death. Truthfulness, respect for property, and respect for the sacredness of life were the three cardinal virtues among nearly all Indians, but adultery and many other transgressions were also punished very severely.

Among many tribes, including some of the plains Indians, the lodges or tipis housed several families of relatives. The spaces occupied by each were not partitioned off, yet each member of the household held the allotted space inviolate, and the children confined their play to the spaces belonging to their mothers. There was also a space reserved for guests, usually at the back of the home, and etiquette decreed that a visitor when entering the lodge must not pass between the host and the fire. Haste in speaking was considered ill-bred, but no visitor left without parting words, usually expressing friendship and a wish that the host might "walk with God" or be guarded by the deities, or some equivalent that corresponded to the Spanish *"Adios."* Among some tribes a visitor was expected to ask: "Am I welcome?" before seating himself, and would be addressed as "friend," "my cousin," "clansman," or "brother." Among some tribes custom decreed that there could be no direct conversation between a woman and her son-in-law. As a general rule, the name of a dead person never was spoken, some other word symbol being substituted. Private and personal matters never were discussed, and it was deemed the height of discourtesy to interrupt another when speaking.

In case it became necessary to pass between the fire and some person, permission to do so was asked, and there were strict rules regarding the proper seating of visitors or members of the tribe in council. An apology was always expected if a person accidentally came in contact with another, and table manners were exacting. It was exceedingly bad taste to lean back when seated. If unable to eat all the food served him, a person was expected to apologize and offer some excuse so as not to show distaste, and when through dining he was obliged to return the dishes to the hostess and thank her for the meal. If a housewife borrowed a cooking utensil or vessel from another, custom decreed that it must be returned with some of the cooked food in it. Among the Delawares and many other tribes there was a code of etiquette to the effect that all knives, spoons, or other cutlery must be cleaned before being returned to the hostess, while other tribes expected visitors to provide their own eating utensils.

As all these rules and regulations varied according to the tribe, it was necessary for an outsider to be thoroughly familiar with the customs and etiquette if he were to avoid making some mistake that might brand him as an uncultured boor, although as a rule the Indians overlooked breaches of etiquette and decorum on the part of white men, whom, as a whole, they regarded as lacking most of the social amenities. Moreover, hospitality was an outstanding trait of the Indian, and all other matters took second place. Among some tribes hospitality was carried to extremes. Even an enemy, if he succeeded in entering a village, would be fed and housed like a friend, and as long as he remained within the area of the village or camp he was safe and treated like a guest. But once he left the area he became fair prey and it was up to him to escape if he could.

Today, with the majority of Indians living more or less like the whites and adopting many of their habits of life, many of the old-time customs have been abandoned or forgotten. But the majority of Indians still retain their high regard for truthfulness, honesty, and hospitality, and judge a man by the courtesy, respect, and proper manners he displays. I have many good friends among the Indians, and while nearly all are prosperous farmers or ranchers or businessmen and dwell in conventional houses, I invariably try to observe their tribal etiquette and social amenities when visiting them.

We read too often about "dirty Indians living in squalor and filth." As a general rule Indians are cleanly; unfortunately, when the Indian adopts the civilization and garments and habits of the white man, he sometimes includes the white man's vices as well as his virtues and, as a result, there *are* dirty Indians, just as there are dirty white men. But I have yet to see an Indian living in such squalor and filth as some white persons. There are no Indian slums. The great majority of Indian homes, both among the eastern and the western tribes, are as spick-and-span as the most exacting New England housewife could desire. Moreover, most Indians abhor disorder. They want a place for everything and everything in its place. Very often an Indian's home may seem lacking in comforts and almost bare of furnishings, but, unlike the tendency of some types of whites to fill their houses with a hodgepodge of knickknacks, the Indians prefer only essentials in the way of furnishings. There will often be vases or bowls of flowers, and bright-colored curtains and table covers, for Indians are passionately fond of flowers and brilliant colors. They are not, as a rule, addicted to carpets, preferring plain board floors with a few animal-skin or rag rugs, and they like a few large rooms better than a number of small ones. Neither are they given to painting their homes, usually preferring the mellow, weather-grayed wood that is in harmony with the natural surroundings—a fact that may prove misleading. But seldom will one find broken windowpanes stuffed with old rags or newspapers, doors and window blinds on broken or sagging hinges, or a litter of tin cans, broken bottles, and other trash. It is still rarer to find an Indian housewife going about in sloppy, slovenly dresses and with unkempt hair, or her husband wearing ragged or dirty garments, although they may be patched and repatched. Moreover, it is the rare Indian who will come tramping into his home with boots covered with mud or manure, or will sit down to a meal without washing his hands. In Mexico the Indians, no matter what their status or occupation, invariably stop and "wash up" at a basin provided for the purpose when entering a restaurant. How many white men do the same? On the other hand, it must be admitted that far too many Indians are opposed to modern methods of plumbing and sanitation and prefer out-of-doors latrines or "the wide open spaces" to accommodations indoors.

We may find an Indian farmer or rancher dwelling in an unpainted, meagerly furnished house, but the chances are ten to one that his tools and farming machinery will be well cared for, oiled, greased and under cover, instead of being left in the open to rust and deteriorate. Also, the chances are that his stock and poultry will be well housed and meticulously clean. In fact, I have seen many an Indian pigpen cleaner and better suited for human occupancy than the tumble-down shacks of his white neighbors. I have been in many Indian homes, both primitive lodges and conventional houses, with floors so clean one might eat a meal on them, and many white men who have lived long among Indians stress the cleanliness of their homes.

VIII

DANCES AND CEREMONIALS

ALL INDIANS are fond of dancing, ceremonies, and anything of a spectacular, pompous, or theatrical nature, but so are the white skins. The Masons, Odd Fellows, Shriners, and others, dress up and parade and carry on their elaborate ceremonies. Few are the women—and—men who do not enjoy masquerade balls and such carnivals as the Mardi Gras where they can don masks or falsefaces, disguise themselves in fancy costumes, and let themselves go; and when it comes to dancing, no Indian ever invented anything as weird, ludicrous, and primitive as some of the steps seen on the modern dance floor.

Few Indian dances are merely for pleasure; practically all have a mystical, symbolic, or religious significance, although their original meanings or purposes may have been long forgotten. Although there is a vast difference between Indian ceremonials and Indian dances, the two may be combined, the dances forming a part of the ceremonial and vice versa. Most persons, when they think of an Indian dance, picture a war dance in which the braves, attired in elaborate costumes and feather headdresses and with painted faces, prance around and around a fire, beating their chests, waving their weapons, and shouting war whoops to the accompaniment of tom-toms. In reality this form of so-called war dance is usually carried out for the benefit of tourists and the western "movies," and might better be classed as a side show than as a ceremonial dance. Moreover, the war dance in its true form is neither the most typical, the most common, nor the most spectacular of Indian dances. In fact, many tribes never held a war dance and would not know what it meant.

True war dances are merely one part of the ceremonial which the Indians believed gave them courage, protection, spiritual help, and victory, and in the case of some tribes, was supposed to render them invisible to their foes. This ceremonial has some similarities to the white man's custom of offering prayers or saying Mass just prior to a battle; in both cases faith in the ceremonies encourages and fortifies the warriors and gives them confidence in their ultimate victory. The white soldier, however, standing silently with bowed head, has neither the inclination nor the opportunity to work himself into a state of almost maniacal hate and blind fury, and a total disregard for his own fate. But the Indian, who invariably is a fatalist, by his dancing, chanting, and mystical ceremonies attains a semihypnotic state bordering on temporary insanity and a blind, unreasoning ferocity which, in combination with his disregard of death, frequently carries him to victory through the most desperate and seemingly hopeless battles. Not realizing that his success is the result of his own mental processes, he of course attributes it to the magic and "medicine" of the ceremonials. On the other hand, the Indian does not blame his deities or spirits if his "medicine" fails, but feels certain that for some reason or another his ceremonies failed to please the deities.

Moreover, the Indian, with his inherent love of the dramatic and the spectacular, finds intense satisfaction and pleasure in showing off before his women and his fellow tribesmen. Mimicking the actions of battle, chanting a war song consisting of boasts of his past deeds and what he plans to do, he uses every endeavor to impress his audience with his prowess and his bravery. Also, by some psychological process that no white man can fathom, the Indian believes that the war dance and its attendant ceremonies will terrify his enemies even if they are far away. This primitive idea of putting fear into the minds of his absent foes, who may have no idea of what is taking place, was especially prevalent among the plains Indians.

As I have mentioned, the war dance is not by any means the only ceremonial dance of the Indians and is not universal. Dances and ceremonies to test and prove their endurance, their fortitude, and their ability to withstand the most excruciating agonies were common. These usually embodied tortures, usually self-inflicted, which the young men had to endure without flinching in order to be regarded as braves.

But the great majority of Indian ceremonials and dances had nothing to do with warfare or bravery but were designed to insure full crops, to bring rain, give good hunting or fishing, or were celebrations or thanksgivings. Many of these are very similar among many widely separated tribes. The planting, harvesting, and rain dances take place at the proper seasons in North, Central, and South America, although the planting, harvesting, and rainy seasons are different in these various areas. In almost every case there are some features of these ceremonies that are very similar. But this resemblance is to be expected if we stop to consider that the ceremonies are extremely ancient in origin and undoubtedly date back to the earliest history of cultivated crops. Many of our own feasts, holidays, and dances are in reality survivals of such pagan ceremonials. Our May Day exercises and maypole dances are merely slightly altered forms of the ancient spring carnival of the pagans.

Indians' seasonal dances and ceremonials are numerous and of many kinds. There are the corn dances of many tribes, the rain dances of the Pueblo Indians, the snake dance of the Hopis, and many others. In the eastern states the Algonquin tribes, such as the Delawares, Shawnees, Iroquois, Mohicans, Massachusetts, Wabenaki and others, held a great autumnal or crop ceremonial or feast. A specially constructed "Great House" was erected where the Indians gathered to give thanks to the Great Spirit and their lesser deities for the abundant crops, the good hunting and fishing, and other blessings of the past year; to offer prayers for a continuation of the favors during the coming year, and to tell of the visions seen. Dances were held, the participants being masked and attired in animal skins; a bearskin represented a woodland spirit which was believed to be the guardian of wild creatures. Drums of a special and unusual form and turtle-shell rattles were used; a new fire, symbolic of a fresh start in life, was kindled with a ceremonial fire-bow drill, and there was a great feast with venison, roasting ears, wild turkey, squash, pumpkin pudding, stewed cranberries, wild plums, nuts, maple sugar, and other viands. It was from this ceremonial feast that we derive our own Thanksgiving Day. The Puritans were invited to the friendly Indians' feast, and copied it, even (as we have seen in an earlier chapter) to the foods when they held their first Thanksgiving. Each November when we gather together and feast to express, in this primitive manner, our gratitude for the blessings received, we are following the age-old Indian ceremonial custom, and are dining on the same foods that the Algonquin tribes served at their feasts.

Other types of thanksgiving ceremonials were held after battles, or on almost any occasion for rejoicing. The famous sun dance of the Poncas and some other tribes were of this type, although the sun dance is not so much a thanksgiving ceremonial as a fulfillment of vows made. The self-inflicted tortures, which included hanging suspended from a rope attached to a skewer through the back or chest muscles, are the fulfillment of promises made to the deities for benefits received during the year. They find a parallel in the practices common to all religions of doing penance, making presents, or undergoing fasts, hardships, and other forms of abnegation, in return for divine favors.

At times the Indians reversed the ceremonials: instead of making vows to be fulfilled later on, provided their prayers were answered, they went through their dances and attendant rites beforehand. One such ceremonial, common to many plains Indians in the days when they depended upon the bison for their existence, was the buffalo dance, whose purpose was to placate the spirits of the buffalo they hoped to kill, to bring success to the hunters, and to insure a plentiful supply of meat and hides.

Very different sorts of dances and ceremonials were held to exorcise evil spirits or "devils." These so-called devil-dances are common to a great many tribes throughout the Americas, and although they vary somewhat in detail all are very similar in purpose and general features. When taking part in these dances the Indians wear hideous or grotesque masks, partly to prevent the devils from recognizing the dancers and partly to frighten the evil spirits. It would certainly be a most courageous demon who would not be scared by the terrifying appearance of some of these masked Indians.

These devil dances are among the most persistent of all the

ceremonials of the Indians who, even after they have become so thoroughly civilized that they have discarded all their other primitive customs still carry out their traditional devil dances. Among the Senecas and Tuscaroras of New York State, who are highly civilized and who otherwise live exactly as do their white neighbors, the annual "false-face" ceremonies are carried out by a secret society known as the False-Face Company. The masks, carved from living trees, are weird, grotesque, and terrifying. They are supposed to represent the faces of woodland spirits or hobgoblins who are believed to have the power to prevent or to cure diseases. During the time the Indians are carrying out the false-face ceremonies, they appear to acquire some inexplicable power; they handle red-hot coals and hot ashes and unhesitatingly plunge their hands into the fires as the others dance and prance, shaking turtle-shell rattles and thumping their drums. Rushing about, they enter the houses, chanting and shouting and driving off any lurking devils and diseases from the houses and their occupants.

In nearly every case, Indian dances are followed by a feast—a custom that appears to be universal and world-wide. Very often all objects used in an Indian dance or ceremony are made especially for the event. On the other hand, they may be the ordinary weapons, costumes, or other objects that have been made sacred or ceremonial by the medicine man or by symbolical painting or other means. No white man and no one Indian has a complete and definite knowledge or understanding of all the innumerable intricate and involved details of Indian ceremonials. Frequently the true significance of the ceremonies, and of the objects and costumes used, is known only to the medicine men of the tribe. Just as many laymen of other races and religions leave an understanding of the deeper meaning of their rituals to their spiritual leaders, so the Indians take part in these rites and ceremonies just as their ancestors have done for ages, never asking the whys and wherefores.

IX

RELIGIONS AND BELIEFS

MOST PERSONS have an idea that all of North America Indians believed in a Great Spirit called Manitou, and believed that after death they would go to the Happy Hunting Grounds. However, this is not the case. Although practically all Indians believed in a Creator or Great Spirit, he was called Manitou only by a few of the Algonquin tribes. Neither did all Indians believe in the Happy Hunting Grounds. To a great many, a hunting ground was not nearly as important and not so idealistic as a rich land and abundant crops. Moreover, among the North American tribes there were so-called sun-worshipers, fire-worshipers, etc. Their mythologies were usually very involved and complex; many had a number of deities, but even those who believed in a rain-god, a war-god, a crop-god, and other deities still believed in one Supreme God or Great Spirit. Some tribes believed in immortality of the soul or spirit, others believed in a Hell as well as a Heaven; some believed in bodily resurrection, others believed in some form of reincarnation. Also, some regarded certain lakes, rivers, mountains, trees, or animals as sacred, and made offerings and prayers to them, just as other religions regard certain places and shrines as sacred.

In addition to numerous good spirits, the Indians believed in a multiplicity of evil spirits or "devils." As they reasoned that good spirits would not harm them, they devoted a great deal of time and effort to propitiating the evil spirits. It was this which led many persons, especially missionaries, to assume that the Indians were devil-worshipers.

Most of the Indians considered the devil or chief evil spirit, as well as the lesser ones, to be rather stupid and easily hoodwinked, and often employed the simplest means to keep them at a distance. Among a great many tribes the children were given a secret name known only to the shaman or witch doctor and to the child's godmother. This name was never used or spoken, the Indians believing that in this way they could prevent devils from learning the child's real name and hence could not enter into him. Another widespread custom was to fashion a charm, such as a crudely carved or modeled figure, which served as a proxy to attract the evil spirits, who would enter the figure instead of the maker. It was also an almost universal custom to interrupt or "break" the design or pattern on a textile, a basket, or other object. It might be merely an interruption in the design, it might be a slight variation of the pattern, or it might be nothing more than a change of color. The Indians believed that when this was done the devil could not find his way into the object. It was such a widely used method of befuddling the evil spirits that the "break" is one of the most infallible means of distinguishing a genuine Indian-made object from an imitation.

As a general rule, the Indians believed that the Great Spirit resided in the sky and that his visual manifestation was the sun. Some tribes believed that the Supreme Being had his abode in some lake or mountain. When they prayed to or made offerings to the sun, to a sacred lake, or to a mountain, they were not actually worshiping the sun or the natural formation but the deity who resided there. For that matter, the great majority of the so-called "idols" of the Indians are not idols in the true sense, but merely representations—"proxies," in other words.

Among many tribes the Supreme God was believed to have a wife, whose visual manifestation was the moon. They pointed out that the planets appeared to move, and explained that by so doing the god and his goddess were watching over all races everywhere on earth. Some believed that during the days when no moon is visible, the goddess came to earth and wandered about in human guise among the people, or in invisible spirit form, and that during the night the sun descended to earth. As they saw the sun "rising" from the earth in the morning and "descending" to earth at night, while the moon reversed the process, they have some logical basis for their belief. Other tribes believed that both sun and moon remained always in the sky, but were visible only when tenanted by the deities.

Thus, the Indians, like all mankind, conceived their gods as beings to whom they owed the most, and imagined their abode to be the spot whence came man's greatest blessings. Even the Hebraic and Christian idea of a God in the sky or celestial Heaven is derived from similar reasoning, for from the sky comes the life-giving rain, the sunshine, and the warmth necessary to life on earth. With a few exceptions, the Indians' supreme deity was regarded as a most kindly and beneficent deity who watched over them, helped them and guided them, and left punishments for transgressions to the evil spirits or devils. Their god might be called a sun-god, a serpent-god, or by some other name, but such appellations were merely symbolical, the sun being the source of heat and light while the serpent was symbolical of wisdom. As has been stated, many Indians believed in a resurrection, either bodily or spiritual, nearly all believed in a soul or spirit and immortality, and in some of their religions there was a Son of God in human form who was born of a lowly virgin.

In addition to their true religions, the Indians had innumerable beliefs or superstitions which, although not actually sacred, were so inextricably interwoven with religion that it is next to impossible to separate the two. The Indian was prone to see some occult or supernatural meaning or manifestation in anything he could not explain or understand, and hence he attributed it to spirits either good or evil, as the case might be. In this he was in no wise different from the rest of mankind, as witness the residue of superstition in the white man's world today. Many of us carry "lucky pieces" or "lucky coins," and dread breaking a mirror. Very few of us will willingly walk under a ladder, and we are obsessed with the idea that thirteen is an unlucky number. Many of the largest hotels, apartment houses, and office buildings have no thirteenth floor, the numbers jumping from twelve to fourteen, and having not a room, office, or apartment with thirteen in its number.

A number of Indian tribes, especially in North America, believed in visions and spirit communications. When an Indian wanted advice on some matter that he could not decide for himself, or wished to make some potent charm or talisman, he would go to a remote spot and there fast and pray until he had a vision and the spirit gave him explicit directions as to what he must do. Many a man of whatever race who has suffered hardships and privations has had visions, even though he has not been truly delirious, and the Indian is far more susceptible than most to such hallucinations. In his exalted state, and implicitly believing in the efficacy of his prayers and fasting, his visions will be far more vivid and realistic than would normally be the case. Neither can we, or dare we, state that any such visions are purely imaginary. Much of so-called "revealed religion" is based upon experiences of the world's great spiritual leaders during visions inexplicable by the voice of reason. Moreover, the Indian was at heart a true spiritualist, and when he isolated himself with fasting and prayer he was actually conducting a séance. He invariably followed the dictates of his vision to the most minute detail —not infrequently with amazing results.

In fact I think faith was—and to less extent still is—the most outstanding feature of Indian psychology. I have never yet met a primitive Indian, or one who has not been ruined by civilization, who knowingly lied, who intentionally broke his word or a promise, or who was dishonest. As a result, the Indians judged others by themselves, and had faith in the white men's words and treaties. Once this faith was destroyed, they lost confidence in all white men, and withdrew into a shell of suspicion and aloofness. However, those Indians who have not been converted to the white man's religions have never lost their essential faith in their own religions and their own deities. They reason that their gods are infallible, and when anything goes wrong they blame themselves or the evil spirits. And their faith in prayer is sublime, especially if their prayers are agumented by fasting, dancing, elaborate ceremonials, or some form of self-sacrifice.

On one occasion, after a prolonged drought during which the Zuñis had prayed and made offerings and had gone through impressive ceremonies to their rain-god, there was a torrential downpour over a small area that completely washed away the fields of an old Indian.

"I guess you'll stop praying for rain now," a white man remarked as he saw the ruined crops.

"Me pray," replied the Indian. "Rain-god make mistake, send too much water one place, must send water other place now."

In addition to their innumerable charms, fetishes, and proxies, the Indians had absolute faith in their good and bad "medicine." In its broadest term "medicine" was anything that had either a beneficial or a detrimental power or influence. A "medicine" might be anything; either animate or inanimate, natural or artificial. It might be a true medicine or cure, but the term we translate as "medicine" includes witchcraft, dreams, spiritualism, prophecies, visions, unusual or peculiar objects—in fact, anything the Indian considers lucky or unlucky, or just plain mysterious.

Thus, Indians have their medicine dances, medicine moccasins, medicine houses, medicine bundles, medicine weapons, and so forth, as well as their medicine societies and medicine clans. One popular form of medicine is the use of medicine sticks. These are of many designs and are used for numerous purposes. They may be offerings to spirits designed to bring about some particular result, they may serve to repel undesirable spirits or affect persons at a distance, or they may even serve as invitations. Among the Sioux and other plains tribes these medicine sticks are very common. They usually consist of a wand of some tree sprout, preferably the wild plum, peeled and painted or left bare. When painted, the designs and colors are symbolic. A red stick, for example, indicates an offering to some supernatural being. Near one end of the stick is fastened a tiny bundle of something the Indian thinks will be pleasing to the spirits. It may be tobacco, food, cloth, beads, trinkets, fur; a bit of skin or feathers or some medicinal seed, root, or tuber, for the offering is a proxy or representation of gifts and expresses the Indian's desire to please his deities. No matter how small the offering is, it contains the spirit or immaterial self of a true offering. Provided the sticks are prepared with the proper ceremonies, anyone may make and use them, but as a rule they are made and used to cure sickness. Often twenty or more may be seen outside a home where someone is ill. The Huicholes of Mexico employ medicine arrows in much the same way, and the Mapuches and Tuelches of Chile use medicine stones. One very popular form of medicine used by the plains Indians is found in the so-called "buffalo stones," (species of fossil mollusks) which the Indians believed called or attracted the buffalos. These stones were neatly covered with buckskin or rawhide, often painted or beaded, but always with a small opening in the leather to enable the stones to "look out."

Also, among our western Indian tribes, the medicine bundle was almost universal. This had innumerable forms; no two were just alike, as each contained the medicines of its owner. It might be an actual bundle, containing all sorts of odds and ends, such as scalp locks, herbs, roots, teeth, fur, gum, bones or even a human jawbone or skull, but almost always buffalo stones would be found among its contents. Other bundles consisted mainly of wearing apparel, such as shirts, beaded vests, feather headdresses, medicine moccasins, etc., often in miniature sizes but sometimes full-sized. Often an Indian's medicine bundles were so numerous and voluminous that special "shrines" were constructed to hold them. In addition to the private medicine bundles there were the clan and tribal bundles. Some of these were so sacred and highly prized that the Indians would go to any extremes to protect them. Very often these were war bundles, and contained amulets that were attached to a warrior's person in battle, each symbolic of some desired power. A bison's tail was believed to impart strength, the skin of a hawk insured ferocity, a swallow's skin gave speed; a miniature war club symbolized lightning and the power of the thunder-god, and a stone ball was the symbol of the lightning's destruction. To insure success in taking prisoners, a decorated thong or rope was included, while a miniature human figure made of buckskin represented a foe in the power of the bundle's owner. Finally, there would be true medicines to be chewed or eaten or rubbed on the body for healing wounds and to safeguard the owner from any evil effects of his own bundle.

In addition to such war bundles, there were love bundles, tattooing bundles, hunting bundles, horse-breeding and horse-stealing bundles, etc. Very often, in fact more often than not, a medicine bundle would be handed down from father to son or from one chief or medicine man to another, and many were extremely old. Quite frequently these sacred bundles were kept in medicine lodges or houses, where mystical rites and ceremonies were held. (Such ceremonies, incidentally, were taboo to women, as were the medicine musical instruments used only for such ceremonies, which no woman was ever permitted to see.)

Mystical or medicine painting and tattooing of the face or body was common to a great many tribes, although among the majority painting was preferred to tattooing, since it could be changed to suit conditions. When plains Indians painted their war ponies, the various figures and designs were largely "medicine," not merely decorative.

Among the plains Indians, the use of medicine shields was almost universal. These were ordinary shields which were prepared in accordance with instructions imparted by visions. They were decorated with mystical designs that were supposed to attract or draw the enemy's weapons away from the shield-carrier's body, as well as to be impervious to arrows and spears. When the Indians found that these medicine shields were no protection from the white men's bullets, did they lose faith in their medicine? Not a bit of it. They reasoned that the medicine had failed because of some fault or omission on their own part—the wrong symbols, the wrong rituals, or some minor mistake in the preparation of the shield. Eventually, of course, they discovered that their medicine had no power to stop bullets, no matter how well it was prepared, and medicine shields were discarded.

Practically every tribe of American Indians has or had its "medicine men," shamans, witch doctors, machis, neles, leles, peaimen, or whatever they were called: men who in most instances embody a variety of professions or positions and usually are a powerful factor in their tribe. Many of these men or women (for there are medicine women as well as medicine men) possess hypnotic powers, others have an uncanny gift of mind-reading or mental telepathy, and with few exceptions they are past masters at concocting drugs, medicines in the white man's meaning of the word, and poisons, and are experts at sleight of hand. Very often they have a profound knowledge of medicinal plants and act as true doctors when occasion arises. To be sure, many of their "cures" are either charms or nostrums, for most Indians believed that illness resulted from some evil spirit entering the body and that this must be driven out. But irrespective of whether or not the shaman believed that an evil spirit entered the patient's body, many of their true medicines were highly efficacious and are in universal daily use today. (Chapter II lists some of these remedies.) Invariably the witch doctors or shamans or peaimen are men of superior intelligence, whose advice is sound, and quite frequently they hold greater power and influence than the chief. Sitting Bull was not a chief but a shaman, and several other famous Indians were both shamans and chiefs, among them Corn Planter, Chief Gall, Chief Joseph of the Nez Percés, Cochise, and others.

There is a distinction if not a difference between an out-and-out medicine man and a medicine chief. Just as a war chief must be a warrior, so a medicine chief must be a medicine man, but a medicine man was not necessarily a chief any more than a prominent warrior was of necessity a war chief. Among many tribes there was an official shaman or witch doctor as well as the medicine chief. The advice and decisions of the latter were sought only on most important matters, or in times of necessity, just as the war chief was called upon only in case of impending hostilities. Also, among many tribes, the medicine chief was the titular head of one or more of the medicine clans or societies.

It is not surprising that Indians should regard their shamans or peaimen with a great deal of awe and respect, for, as I have already stated, many were skilled hypnotists and sleight of hand experts, and there is no question that some possessed a remarkable ability to accurately foretell forthcoming events. That certain persons do seem to have the power to describe happenings taking place elsewhere, and are even seemingly able to fortell events, has been indicated by scientific tests, and on several occasions I have had incontrovertible evidence of certain Indians' seemingly occult power in such matters. On one occasion while in British Guiana I traveled through uninhabited jungle for nearly thirty miles. No Indian was met or seen, yet when we arrived at the village that was my objective I found that the Indians not only knew we were coming but had advance knowledge of the number in my party and full details of our equipment.

In Peru, some of the Andean Indians have an amazing ability to report events transpiring many miles distant. I have known them to state that soldiers were arriving at a distant village and they even told how many were mounted, how many afoot, and described their equipment. When, later on, we reached the village we found matters exactly as had been stated. I could mention several other similar experiences, but I think the most remarkable was the case of the peaiman in British Guiana who declared we would be killed or injured by a falling tree if we made camp where we had planned.

There were no dead trees near and no sign of a tree having reason to fall. Personally, I would have paid no heed to the fellow's warning, but my Indians insisted upon camping at another spot. During the night there was a violent thunderstorm and in the morning we found that the upper portion of a huge tree, thickly overgrown with air plants and other parasitic growths and weighing many tons, had been splintered by lightning and had fallen on the precise spot we originally had selected for our camp. I cannot explain such things and I do not attempt to. I leave that to the scientists studying such phenomena. The great trouble is that it sometimes is practically impossible to be sure how much is hocus-pocus and how much is genuine.

At present the majority of the North American Indians are, nominally at least, Christians. But in a great many cases their Christianity is a very thin veneer, and at heart they still have faith in their ancient tribal religions and deities. They are, figuratively, "on the fence," and are not quite certain whether the white men's or their own religion is the true faith. We cannot blame them for this. As one Indian complained to me, "The missionaries come to us, but each tells us that his religion is the only true religion. If the Christians cannot agree, how can we Indians feel sure which is the true religion? How can we be sure whether the religion of our Old Ones should be followed or whether we should become Christians?" As a result, the Indians, just to be on the safe side, often worship their ancestral deities as well as the Christians' God.

Perhaps the most peculiar and interesting of such religious combinations is the Peote Cult, very popular among the Dakotas and other western tribes. The Peote is the "button" or fruit of a cactus and is slightly narcotic. It is regarded by the Indians as a mystical thing and most powerful "medicine." The ceremonies of the members of a Peote Cult are held in a special tipi or house, surrounded by much secrecy and mysticism. Visions and spiritual manifestations are claimed to take place, and there is no doubt that the members of the cult—with the aid of the Peote narcotic—work themselves up into a state of self-hypnosis or auto-suggestion during which they certainly possess inexplicable powers. During the ceremonies special "medicine" drums and utensils are employed. While the whole affair savors of paganism, yet a crucifix or a statue of Christ is always displayed in a conspicuous spot, and fully as many prayers and offerings are made to the Christian God as to the Peote spirit. Whatever else we may think of this strange cult, it has one feature that is most laudable and is lacking in the majority of religions. Only strict teetotalers can become members of the sect, and any member caught using alcoholic liquor is blackballed for life.

X

WHEN THE WHITE MEN CAME

When Europeans first reached the shores of what is now the United States, they found the entire country inhabited by hundreds of tribes of the people they called Indians. Today no one knows how many tribes there were or their names at that time, for many tribes have died out, or have been exterminated by warfare with the white men or with other tribes, while many more have joined with other tribes and have completely lost their original identity and even their languages. But there are still about two hundred tribes, with the majority of their members of pure or nearly pure Indian blood, still living within the boundaries of the United States.

To describe or even to mention all of these, to describe the arts, crafts, weapons, musical instruments, houses, costumes, headdresses, religions, beliefs, customs, languages, and other details of each, would require volumes. As many tribes are closely related and as even more are similar in most respects, they may be divided into groups and treated as such. (In the "Glossary" at the back of this book, every tribe is briefly described.) Ethnologists divide the Indians into sixteen groups, based mainly on the original areas inhabited by the tribes. In a great many cases, however, Indians classed as tribes of the far west were originally living in the eastern or central areas of our country, while others classed as tribes of the north-central states migrated northward from the far south. To my mind, therefore, it is much better, as well as less confusing, to treat the Indians in groups of tribes with more or less similar characteristics.

Where they inhabited wooded areas or where there were fertile valleys and prairie lands, the tribes were usually sedentary, with permanent villages of well-built houses. They cultivated crops of maize, pumpkins, beans, squash, tobacco and other plants. Even in the most densely forested areas, in New England, New York, and in the Alleghenies, the Indians had their kitchen gardens to provide them with food, in addition to fish and game. Where tribes were near the coast or in the vicinity of lakes or large rivers, fish and shellfish were among the most important foods, and many tribes made long journeys from the interior of the country to the coast or to the lakes in order to gather, dry, and smoke vast quantities of seafoods or fresh-water foods, such as clams, oysters, fish, crabs, mussels and lobsters. In the vicinity of the Great Lakes many tribes depended largely upon wild rice which they harvested and stored. In the deep south most of the Indians cultivated crops to some extent, but as game of all kinds was abundant and fish swarmed in the streams and sea, food was seldom a problem there.

Far different were the Indians of the far western plains. Although some of these tribes carried on agriculture in a small way and even had permanent villages, yet all relied mainly upon the buffalo for a livelihood, and the majority were nomads, moving from place to place, bag and baggage, and setting up their skin tipis wherever they found water and buffalos. All of these plains tribes were "horse Indians" with large herds of ponies and were born fighters, almost constantly at war among themselves, whereas the majority of eastern and southern tribes were inclined to be peaceful.

Beyond the Great Plains, in the mountainous areas, there were still other tribes, some of whom were nomadic, others sedentary, and semiagricultural, although they had no permanent settlements. In what is now California there were a great number of tribes, nearly all of whom were quiet peaceful Indians of the sedentary agricultural type, while in the far northwest, in Oregon, Washington, and Alaska, were still other tribes, the majority of whom had large permanent villages and depended upon salmon and other fish, whales, seals and game, for a living. Finally, in the desert areas of the far southwest there were a number of tribes who differed greatly from all others. Here were the Pueblo Indians, who dwelt in fortresslike towns of solidly built adobe structures and who were thoroughly agricultural. In sharp contrast were their neighbors, the Navajos and so-called Apaches, the Comanches, Kiowas, Yaquis, and others, all of whom were horse Indians and, with the exception of the Navajos, desert nomads. All these relied upon the buffalo and other game, and were hereditary enemies of the Pueblos.

In addition to dividing the tribes into various geographical groups, ethnologists and anthropologists classify the Indians by linguistic groups, such as the Athabascan, Siouan, Shoshonean, Keresan, etc. But because an Apache belongs in the Athabascan linguistic group it does not mean he can converse with the Hupas of northern California, the Kaiyhkhotanas of Alaska, or the Kutchins of British Columbia, who are also included in tribes of Athabascan linguistic stock. In our eastern states the Indians from Virginia to Canada were nearly all of Algonquin stock and could readily converse with one another, as was also the case with most of the tribes of the middle west in the vicinity of the Great Lakes. This was also true of the Cherokees, Chickasaws, and Choctaws, all of Muskhogean stock, in our southern states. However, in the far west there were a number of tribes of various linguistic stocks with very similar habits who roamed the plains and were constantly meeting others who spoke totally different dialects. In order to converse, some common medium of expression had to be devised, and the problem was solved by the invention of sign language. It might be supposed that only a very limited number of thoughts or ideas could be expressed by gestures and the positions of hands and fingers. In reality, those familiar with the sign language of the plains tribes can converse as readily, as fluently, and as comprehensively, as well as almost as rapidly, as by word of mouth. It is not a very difficult matter to learn to use sign language. Largely it is a question of memorizing the meanings of gestures and hand positions, and basically these are comparatively few. Once the signs for various nouns and pronouns and verbs, and the gestures or signs for various tribes, for queries and occupations, are mastered, the rest is easy.

Theoretically, according to ethnological classification, all tribes belonging to one linguistic stock are supposedly related. Perhaps once upon a time they were; we know, for example, that the Catawbas of the Carolinas and Georgia, who are of Siouan linguistic stock, are closely related to the Dakota or Sioux tribes of the plains. But in a great many cases widely separated tribes with no similarities in habits, religions, or other respects will belong to the same linguistic group, whereas in other localities we may find a number of tribes, almost identical in customs, religions, and characteristics, who belong to a number of linguistic stocks. Thus in California there were large numbers of very similar tribes but each speaking a totally distinct language of its own, over one hundred different dialects having been in use within a small area. In fact, there were more tribal languages in use than in any other portion of the world of equal size. Also, it often happened that a tribe belonging to one linguistic group, but whose neighbors or allies belonged to another group, would abandon their own language and adopt that of their neighbors. Thus the Cheyennes, who are classed as members of the Algonquin group, now speak a Siouan dialect, and can thus converse readily with their friends the Sioux. Another example is that of the Pottawattomies, who have completely lost their own language and use that of the Chippewas, except for ceremonial purposes.

If such changes have taken place within comparatively recent years, there is every reason to assume that they have been taking place since the earliest times, hence it does not follow that because two tribes speak languages of the same stock that they are related. As no one knows the truth as to the origin or arrival of the Indian in the United States, no one knows what language or languages they spoke or how the various dialects originated. The chances are that in the dim and distant past, some five or ten thousand years ago, only one tongue was spoken by the primitive men of the continent and that, through the ages, the various dialects were evolved and developed through necessity and the changes in life and conditions. Even in England today there are a great number of quite distinct dialects, such as the Norfolk, Yorkshire, Devonshire, Cornish, Lancashire, etc., although all are English. Within our own borders we find very much the same condition for the local dialects of the down-East Yankee, the Cracker of the deep south, the native of the middle west, the Texan, and the "hillbilly" differ greatly. In other words, the classification of Indians by linguistic groups may be all very well for ethnologists and anthropologists, but is of no real value or interest to the average person who is not interested in acquiring a knowledge of Indian tongues. When it comes to a white man learning to speak Indian, I very much doubt if any white man—unless reared and brought up among Indians as a member of the tribe—can ever acquire a complete knowledge of any Indian language. Even the simplest dialects are exceedingly complex, with shades of pronunciation and inflection regulating the meanings of words and often with endless forms of verbs. In fact, the dialect of one tribe of California Indians has over 100,000 verb forms!

Because some interpreters lack a complete mastery of either the Indian or English languages, a great many Indian names have been incorrectly translated and are actually quite different from those by which they are commonly known. Thus Tashunkekokipapa, the name of a Sioux chief, became "Man Afraid of His Horses," although in reality it means "Men of the Enemy Fear His Horses." The Sioux name of chief Crazy Horse was Tashunkewitko, which literally means "A Man Like a Wild Horse." Red Cloud's name, Makhpiya Luta, if correctly interpreted would have been "Red Tempest." Sitting Bull was really "The Bull Who Waits." The Indian name of Leather Lips, the Wyandotte chief, meant "Twin Clouds." Little Crow's name, Chetan-wakan-mani means "Sacred Hawk Who Comes Walking." Hosa, the name of an Arapaho chief, means "Young Crow," although the whites knew him as Little Raven. Two Strikes' real name, Nomkopa, meant "He Killed Two." In fact, very few Indian names have been literally translated into English.

XI

WEAPONS, MOCCASINS, HEADDRESSES, ETC.

BEFORE THE COMING of the white men and the introduction of firearms, the most important and universal weapon of the North American tribes was the bow and arrow. These varied greatly according to the tribe. Among most of the eastern and middle western Indians the favorite bow was of hickory, osage orange, or ash, flat on both sides, fairly wide, and about four feet in length, but the exact shape varied greatly. The Iroquois used bows with the hand hold narrower than the portions above and below, and usually with the ends somewhat recurved. For use in warfare, the Wabenaki Indians of Maine used a unique double bow in which the supplementary bow doubled the power of the regular bow, while some of the more southerly tribes, such as the Creeks, Chickasaws, and Choctaws, used long slender bows flat on one side and rounded on the other. The tribes of the far western plains used bows of a very different type. Wood suitable for bows was scarce until the white men left hickory wagon bows, ox yokes, and other equipment which supplied the Indians with seasoned hickory and ash. In order to add power to their bows, the buffalo-hunting Indians bound sinews or strips of horn to their wooden bows and wrapped them with rawhide. They also made bows of horn carefully fitted together and wrapped with rawhide, for to these tribes the power of the bow rather than its accuracy counted most, and many of their bows would drive an arrow completely through a buffalo. Beyond the plains, in the Sierras and on the Pacific coast, the Indians as a rule used very broad flat bows with a narrow rounded grip and often with strongly recurved ends. Although the arrows varied somewhat among the many tribes, the differences were mainly in the method of feathering, the form of the finger grip, and the method of attaching the head. Some tribes used two, some three, feathers. Some fastened the feathers to the shaft for their full length, while others attached them only at the ends. Some placed the feathers straight and parallel with the shaft, while others attached them at an angle or at a curve. Some tribes preferred a flattened finger grip above the notch, others used arrows with the notch end slightly larger than the shaft. In order to allow the blood of a wounded creature or a man to flow freely, the arrows were often made with grooves or shallow gutters, sometimes straight and sometimes wavy or spiral, extending the length of the shafts. This was an almost universal custom among the plains tribes. Before the arrival of Europeans the Indians used stone, horn, bone, tooth or wooden heads for their arrows, but these were quickly discarded in favor of iron or steel once the metals were obtainable.

Another weapon rarely mentioned in accounts of our Indians but quite popular was the blow gun. This was used by practically all of the more southerly tribes, and even by the Iroquois, although as far as known the Indians of the United States did not use poisoned darts as do the Indians of tropical America. Spears or javelins were important weapons of many of the eastern woodland tribes, and after the plains Indians had acquired horses the long lance became a favorite and was almost universally used in warfare and in hunting buffalo. It will doubtless surprise a great many people to learn that our North American Indians used both the bolas and the boomerang. Even the tribes of New England used a form of the bolas with three round stones enclosed in rawhide connected by buckskin or rawhide thongs for hunting certain kinds of game. The Indians of New Mexico and Arizona, such as the Zuñis, Yumas, Pimas, Navajos, Hopis, and others, used, and still use, a crude type of boomerang for killing rabbits.

It is almost impossible to find a story in which Indians are mentioned that does not refer to their use of tomahawks (the name is a corruption of the old English "tammi-axe" or little ax). Short-handled hatchets or axes with stone heads were favorite weapons of practically all the eastern, the southern, and the middle western tribes before the coming of the white men, and the iron- or steel-headed hatchets brought by the Europeans became very widespread and popular weapons. Although the majority were plain hatchets, some were carved and cut into highly ornate forms. Combination tomahawks and pipes became common, although as a rule these were used only for ceremonial purposes and not as weapons.

All of the tribes also had their war clubs. These varied greatly in design. Some were mere bludgeons of heavy wood, others were of wood with a stone attached to the end by rawhide, while others had sharp stone or metal blades inserted at the striking end. In fact, the number of forms of war clubs was almost endless, since they varied not only according to the tribe but with the individual taste or ideas of the owner. With the acquisition of horses the lives, customs, and weapons of the plains Indians were greatly altered to suit conditions. They still used the short-handled hatchet or tomahawk to some extent, but came to prefer their own long war clubs and long-handled stone-headed skull-crackers. The short-handled tomahawk was effective only at close quarters and in hand-to-hand fighting and it could not be used to split the skull of a fallen enemy as a warrior dashed by on horseback. But the four-foot wooden war club with its stone-weighted tip or with sharp steel blades, or the skull-crackers with their round or ovoid stone heads and long flexible handles of buffalo sinew or twisted rawhide, were terrible and most effective weapons with which a warrior could bash in the head of an enemy at a distance of seven or eight feet. We often read of the plains Indians throwing a tomahawk at an enemy with deadly accuracy while at full gallop. This is pure fiction, for no man, white or red, no matter how skillful, can throw a hatchet—or even a knife—with accuracy when mounted and in motion. In order to hit his mark with the blade the thrower must know the exact distance of his target, for a variation of even three feet will make all the difference between a weapon striking blade-on or handle-on. Every thrown weapon makes a certain number of turns in a certain distance. In fact, the art or skill in knife- or hatchet-throwing depends very largely upon the thrower's ability to judge distance accurately, which is manifestly impossible when a man is charging forward on horseback or afoot.

Another fallacy that frequently occurs in tales of Indians is that a skilled tracker could identify the tribe of an Indian by the imprints of his moccasins. Many eastern and middle western Indian tribes used soft buckskin or moosehide moccasins, and, while each tribe had its own particular method of fitting the tongue to the uppers, the imprint would be that of the wearer's foot, with no indication of how the moccasins were made. The majority of the eastern and central tribes gathered or puckered the uppers to the tongue. While the latter might be narrow, broad, oval or wedge-shaped the imprint left by the wearer would still be the same. Even the Seminole moccasin, which is a very distinctive and unique type without a tongue but with the two sides of the uppers gathered together over the instep, leaves an imprint of the wearer's foot exactly like that of a man wearing a Tarratine, an Iroquois, or a Delaware moccasin. There are, however, certain types of soft moccasins that *do* leave identifiable imprints, such for example, as those of the Quapaws, with a seam along the sole. With the moccasins of the plains Indians it was a different matter, for while with one or two exceptions all were made with thick rawhide or parfleche soles, and soft buckskin uppers the shape of the soles varied with the different tribes. Also, a skilled tracker, familiar with the moccasins used by the various so-called Apache tribes, the Comanches, Kiowas, and others, could usually identify the tribe of an Indian by his moccasin tracks, for most of these desert Indians used moccasins of rawhide that did not conform to the shape of the wearers' feet as did the soft buckskin footgear of the woodland tribes.

Very much the same is true about Indian headdresses. Certain tribes *did* have distinctive feather headdresses or wore their hair or the feather plumes in a certain easily recognized manner: for example, the hornlike tufts of hair of the Pawnees, which gave the tribe its name of *Piriki* or "little horns," the queue and drooping feather plume of the Blackfoot brave, or the low, diagonally placed plume of the Cheyennes, were unmistakable means of identification; on the other hand, each of the various tribes also wore a great many forms of elaborate headdresses.

Although the "bonnet" of the Blackfeet, with its vertical feathers, was very different from the bonnets of the Sioux and Cheyennes with the feathers lying almost flat over the head, yet for certain ceremonies and under certain conditions a Blackfoot might wear the Sioux type of headdress or vice versa. In fact, the types and designs of headdresses were innumerable, for special forms were required for various ceremonials. Some were symbolical, others told of the brave or noteworthy deeds of the wearer, others denoted rank or social status, others were clan or "medicine" headdresses, and in addition to all of these the individual taste of the maker resulted in endless forms and variations of headgear and hair-dos. It seems to be a popular idea that the larger and more spectacular the Indian's feather headdress, the more important and famous the wearer. This, however, is not the case. Many of the most showy war bonnets with double tails and hundreds of feathers are purely ornamental, whereas, on the other hand, one or two eagle feathers with coup marks may identify the wearer as a doer of brave deeds, a mighty warrior, or a high-ranking chieftain. And if we see a war bonnet with its plumes tipped with smaller coup feathers or notched in a certain manner, we may be sure the wearer is a veteran of many battles and a mighty man in the land.

To the Indian, coup marks were what service ribbons or buttons are to the soldier today. And just as those who know may interpret the significance of a veteran's multicolored ribbons, so the Indian read in the coup marks the story of the wearer's deeds. Very often coups might be recorded by feathers attached to lances, war clubs, shields, or more frequently to coup sticks, which resemble shepherds' crooks in form. I have a coup stick that once belonged to Crazy Horse; it is completely covered with prime minkskins and bears eleven coup feathers won in the Battle of the Little Big Horn. Very often headdresses, coup sticks, and other objects were decorated with scalps, but to the plains Indians the scalp itself was of less importance than the coup itself, which meant being first to touch a dead or wounded enemy, for once a foe was touched by coup he was considered dead and was treated as if nonexistent. The scalp, once taken, dried, and displayed, was of little value other than as an ornament or to be used in fringes for garments. In fact, among most of the western tribes taking the scalp was more an act of vengeance or retribution than of obtaining a souvenir, each scalp taken being regarded as payment for the death of a tribesman of the taker. In somewhat the same manner, the so-called "scalp dance" was not in reality a dance at all, but a chant or dirge of mourning for members of the tribe lost in battle, carried out with the participants standing almost motionless.

Another matter regarding which there is a deal of popular misconception is the so-called peace pipe. The true peace pipe or calumet was a very symbolical, elaborate affair with both a male and a female pipe, brought forth from their wrappings only on momentous occasions, and surrounded by symbolism and ceremonies incomprehensible to the average white man. The ordinary commonly called peace pipe had merely a friendly or companionable meaning, and was smoked on practically all occasions of councils, discussions, or with visitors. On ceremonial occasions tobacco was used, the Indians regarding the tobacco as a sacred gift from the Great Spirit, whereas on ordinary occasions or when smoking for pleasure the Indians used various other substances, such as red willow bark or dried leaves, sometimes with a little tobacco added.

Although we usually think of the Indians' musical instruments as consisting of drums and rattles only, they also had numerous forms of fifes, flutes, whistle, trumpets, etc. However, the drums and rattles were the most important, as they were particularly adapted to the Indian types of dancing, music, and ceremonies. Each tribe had its own favorite or popular type of drum, and in addition each had a number of forms of drums, each designed for a certain purpose. There were deep slender drums, short broad drums, drums with double heads and those with single heads. Many had the heads attached permanently to the barrel, while others had devices for tightening the head. Although none of the North American Indians could transmit drum "talk" for such long distances as did the Negroes of Africa and the Indians of South America, yet the sounds of a large buffalo-hide drum are clearly audible for fifteen to twenty miles on a still night. The Koroks of the far northwest used a square drum; the Zuñis had bowl-shaped pottery drums that were beaten with a peculiar light scroll-shaped "stick." Several tribes had drums no deeper than barrel hoops. Many "medicine" drums were the size of tambourines, with heads permanently attached. The Pottawattomies had a remarkable water drum that was filled with water when in use. The rattles varied even more than the drums, for aside from certain forms restricted to definite ceremonial and dance use, each tribe had typical forms while, in addition, individual ideas and taste resulted in rattles of every conceivable form, size, and material. There were gourd rattles, wooden rattles, rattles of rawhide and of turtle shells. Very often rawhide rattles would be made in the forms of frogs, turtles, or birds, and entire turtles, with the head and neck forming the handles, were used. A special form of ring-shaped rawhide rattle was used solely during the sun dance of the Poncas, and rattles containing sacred or "medicine" seeds were restricted to certain ceremonial and "medicine" uses.

Although most persons visualize an Indian's home as a conical "wigwam" of bark or a "tipi" of skins, yet the Indians used a great many other kinds of houses. Many of the eastern tribes lived in well-built log houses, usually banked with dead leaves and grass during the winter. Some made huts of stones and clay, and many used houses of bark slabs lashed or sewn to a framework of poles. The form varied, some being cylindrical and dome-roofed, others rectangular with an arched roof and others with gabled roofs. The Indians of the middle west also used permanent houses of wood, thatch, or other material that were rectangular in form, as well as sod houses. The nomadic plains tribes were partial to the conventional tipi, for it was readily set up or taken down, it could be transported easily from place to place, it was commodious, comfortable, and weatherproof, even in the most severe winter weather. However, tipis were not universally used by all the far western tribes. The Navajos and some of the other desert tribes of the southwest dwelt in partially dugout homes with an "upper story" of timbers covered with sods.

The Pueblos, of course, had their adobe dwellings, and quite a number of tribes used regular sod huts. In fact, there was almost as much diversity among Indian homes as among Indian weapons, moccasins, or other artifacts.

Although to a person not versed in Indian lore a Sioux in full costume might be indistinguishable from a Blackfoot, an Arapaho, a Pawnee, or a Crow, a Ute, a Cheyenne, or any one of a dozen plains tribes, yet to another Indian or to a person familiar with the Indians there would be certain details of dress that would instantly identify the tribe of the wearer: the cut of the garments, the length and type of fringes, the style of breech cloth, and, perhaps most important of all, the type and designs of the ornamental bead and quill ornamentation. The Sioux, for example, used geometrical patterns almost exclusively, although these were often worked into conventionalized but recognizable figures of men, women, birds, various beasts, mountains, trees, and other natural objects. The Blackfeet, Cheyennes, and most of the other plains tribes were also partial to geometrical forms of beadwork, but often combined these with curves, scrolls, or semifloral designs; the Utes were fond of broad bands of beadwork, the Sans Arcs combined floral patterns with squares, straight lines, and geometrical figures—star-shaped designs and rosettes of curved lines and semicircles. The Arikaras were partial to long lines and elongated rectangles of solid colors. Many of the Assiniboin beadwork designs were composed of circles. The Pottawattomies, Menominees, Chippewas and neighboring tribes employed unmistakable elaborate designs of involved geometrical figures totally unlike those of the plains tribes. Most of the tribes of the midwest—the Osages, Kansas, Sauks, and Foxes, Shawnees, and Winnebagos—preferred floral designs sometimes combined with a few geometrical figures, while practically all of the eastern tribes used floral designs exclusively. Which tribe made the best and most beautiful beadwork is perhaps a matter of personal taste and opinion. However, much depended upon the women who did the beadwork. Some were far more skillful than others, some had a better artistic taste for color combinations and designs, but taken all in all I should say that the most beautiful and elaborate beadwork was that of the Shoshones. Very often among the Shoshones a man's or woman's costume would be so completely covered with elaborate beadwork that it weighed as much as a heavy winter overcoat, and not infrequently a Shoshone's pony would be covered from head to tail (the head literally included) with fringed buckskin, every square inch of which was decorated with magnificent beadwork. In former times all beads were sewn on with sinew, and in the finest work each bead was sewn on separately. As a rule, however, several beads were threaded and sewn on at a time. Even in their loom beadwork the women or men (for many of the men did some of the best loomwork) used sinews or horsehair. But today what beadwork is done—mainly to sell to tourists—is usually made on thread. Very often it is carelessly made with the "lazy squaw" stitch, and is a very poor imitation of the beautiful work with which the Indians decorated their garments in the past.

XII

INDIANS OF NEW ENGLAND

WHEN THE EUROPEANS first reached what is now New England, they found that portion of the country inhabited by a great number of tribes and subtribes. All or very nearly all were of Algonquin stock; and while in their physical characteristics, in many of their habits, in their houses, their costumes, and their dialects they differed greatly, nevertheless their weapons, utensils, arts and crafts were all very similar. Also, all were primarily agriculturists, with well-tilled and cultivated kitchen gardens and fields in which they raised maize, squashes, pumpkins, beans of various kinds, melons, etc. But the white potato was unknown until introduced by the white men, after having been carried from South and Central America to Europe by the Spaniards and back to Virginia by the British colonists.

When the Europeans first arrived on the scene the Indians were all friendly. Not only did they welcome the white men, but they supplied the settlers with food during the first winter and taught them how to raise and cultivate the many food plants new to the Englishmen. But, as usual, the whites soon began to reciprocate by treating the Indians like inferior beings, cheating and robbing them, and killing them like wild beasts on the least provocation. As a result, the peaceful friendly tribes soon became transformed into savage implacable foes.

No one really knows how many tribes inhabited New England at that time or who they were. Very often the same tribe was known by different names in different localities, or by different dialects; frequently, too, the British settlers would mistake clan groups for tribes. Long before anyone began to take an ethnological interest in the Indians, a number of tribes or subtribes had been completely exterminated. We know that there were the

Massachusetts, the Gay Heads, the Narragansets, the Pequots, Mohicans, Wepawaugs, Naugatucks, Quinnipiacs, Shepaugs, Nipmuks, Peconics, and numerous other tribes or subtribes in Massachusetts, Rhode Island, and Connecticut. In all probability, however, many of these were members of one tribe, and were named by the white men after the localities they inhabited; or they may have been nothing more than clan groups.

Many of these tribes of southern New England have completely died out, and where there are remnants, such as the Narragansets and the Gay Head Indians, there are very few of pure Indian blood, the majority having more white and Negro blood than Indian. There are a few Pequots and Mohicans at the reservation near Norwich, Connecticut, and a few Mohicans in Litchfield. Until recently there were a half a dozen or so Wepawaugs still living in the Naugatuck Valley, and when I was a boy there were one or two families of Quinnipiacs near New Haven.

In the early colonial days there were several tribes dwelling along the Connecticut coast which were to be completely exterminated by the white men in a few years. Among these were the friendly Mianus Indians who sold the site of Greenwich for twenty-five coats in 1640. Maltreated, robbed, their women kidnapped by the British and Dutch, the Indians became hostile and attacked the settlement. In reprisal the whites surrounded the Indian village at dead of night, set fire to the Indians' homes, and shot down nearly one thousand men, women, and children, thus in a single night utterly destroying the entire tribe. It was an even worse massacre than that of the Pequots, for quite a number of the Pequots managed to escape and to survive. Although the Pequots were implacable foes of the white men, having suffered greatly at their hands, the Mohicans, on the other hand, were lauded as firm friends of the settlers and fought the Pequots as the white men's allies. Yet the Pequots and Mohicans were one and the same tribe until civil war broke out, and the two factions had separated less than fifty years before the arrival of the Europeans.

It may seem strange that a mere handful of white colonists could have wiped out dozens of Indian tribes within a comparatively short time, but we must remember that they took advantage of such intertribal hostilities as the one just mentioned, and enlisted the services of Indian allies, who, as a matter of fact, played a far greater part than the white man in the extermination of their fellow Indians. Cortez would have found the conquest of Mexico a far greater task had he not allied himself with the Tlascalans and other tribes who were deadly enemies of the Aztecs; Pizarro might never have conquered Peru had he not arrived there when a civil war threatened, and the history of New England would have been entirely different had it not been for the enmities and lack of cohesion among the Indian tribes.

In northern New England, in Maine, there were numerous tribes and subtribes of the Wabenaki nation. The largest of these tribes was the Tarratine (now known as the Penobscots), who inhabited the Penobscot Valley from the coast to above the present site of Old Town. Along the upper reaches of the Kennebec were the Norridgewocks. The rich intervales and valleys about the Little Androscoggin were the home of the Passaconnoways, while farther west, in the vicinity of present-day Fryeburg and extending over into what is now New Hampshire, were the Sokokis. From the very first the Wabenaki were friendly to the whites. It was a Maine Wabenaki, Chief Samoset, who welcomed the Pilgrims, and the provisions that enabled the settlers to survive the first New England winter were provided by the Wabenakis of Maine. But never in the history of our Indians have the white men shown their gratitude for the favors and friendship of the Indians.

When the British colonists commenced to settle in Maine they soon began to follow the same tactics they had employed in Massachusetts, not realizing what they were up against. Instead of numerous small tribes with their intertribal enmities, there was one great nation with all its tribes and subtribes in perfect accord and unity. There were no malcontents, no renegade Indians that the whites could enlist as allies. For many years the Wabenakis had been firm friends of the French in Canada; French priests had established numerous missions in Maine (that on Panawamske Island near Old Town is the oldest church north of Florida). The French had always treated them fairly and honestly, and a French nobleman, the Baron de St. Castine, had joined the tribe and had married the daughter of Madokawando, the Tarratine chief. As a result, when the French and Indian Wars broke out, the Wabenaki allied themselves with the French and played havoc with the British, whose only Indian friends were the Micmacs of Nova Scotia. Not until 1694 did hostilities cease; then Sir William Phipps signed a treaty of peace with Chief Madokawando—a treaty that never has been broken by the Indians.

But the British had no such compunctions. In August 1723 a force of two hundred men, bound on a scalp-hunting foray, ascended the Kennebec, took the mission by surprise, and massacred every man, woman, and child—including Father Rasle, whose scalp, together with those of the murdered Indians, was taken to Boston, where the bounties were duly paid. The Sokokis were also massacred for their scalps when raiders from Massachusetts attacked the peaceful Indians at Lovewell's Pond, but in this case the British were the losers and more white men's than Indians' scalps were taken. The surviving Sokokis joined other Wabenaki tribes and lost their identity. The last Passaconnoway died seventy years ago, and the only Wabenakis in Maine today are the Tarratines who dwell on Panawamske Island near Old Town and the Passamoquoddies who occupy a reservation at Pleasant Point near Eastport, also there are a few members of the Malecite, a Canadian tribe, living in Aroostook County.

Although the Wabenaki were forest-dwelling Indians and relied upon game and fish for much of their food, yet they were also agriculturists and had well-cultivated fields and gardens on the rich bottom lands along the streams. Their houses were well built of logs, usually with an arched roof of saplings covered with sod, although houses of bark slabs lashed or sewed to a pole framework were also used. Many of the houses were very large, accommodating a number of families; for temporary use or special purposes they also erected conical wigwams of birch bark on poles. For hunting the Wabenaki used rather slender bows four to five feet in length, with the inner side slightly convex, as well as peculiar double bows consisting of a shorter bow lashed to the outer surface of a regular bow with the string so adjusted that when the larger bow was drawn to a certain distance the auxiliary bow was bent, thus doubling the power without increasing the actual size of the bow. Their arrows were about two feet in length with three feathers, and were fitted with various types of heads, each adapted to the specific game being hunted. For fishing they used nets, tridentlike spears, hooks and lines, and cleverly designed fish traps. In addition to their bows and arrows they used war clubs of hard wood with globular heads, often fitted with a stone blade. By the time the British settlers arrived, however, steel hatchets or tomahawks obtained from the French were the rule, iron or steel arrow points had supplanted those of stone or bone, and steel-bladed hunting knives were universal.

These Indians had developed snowshoes to a high state of perfection, and used toboggans for transporting loads over the snow. But their most outstanding achievement was the birch-bark canoe. Practically all the tribes of the northern states and Canada used birch canoes, but none compared with those of the Wabenaki in grace, speed, and stability. It was the Maine Wabenaki canoe that served as the model for the famous Old Town canvas canoes, as well as for the New England whaleboats, the most seaworthy craft for their size in the entire world. The Wabenakis made, and still make, beautiful baskets, but the little pottery they had was very poor and crude, and wooden or bark utensils were used for cooking until iron pots and kettles were obtained from the whites. Although they obtained tobacco by trade, this was reserved for use during ceremonies or for special purposes, the usual material smoked being the shredded bark of the red willow, or "Killikinick," used in soapstone or talc pipes with short wooden stems. Baby carriers or cradle-boards were used, and these usually were elaborately and beautifully decorated with porcupine quill and moose-hair embroidery and painted designs, although beads obtained from the whites were also extensively employed. In their painting, beadwork, quillwork, and hairwork the Wabenaki showed a highly artistic skill, using curved lines to form more or less conventionalized floral designs.

Before the arrival of the white man and for many years afterward, the Wabenaki dressed in tanned deerskins, the man's costume consisting of long-skirted fringed coats or "hunting shirts," trouserlike leggings, and soft buckskin or moosehide moccasins.

In winter, fur garments and robes were worn. The women wore knee-length buckskin skirts, short leggings, moccasins, and a light buckskin cape over the shoulders. The hair was worn long and either tied loosely or braided, but the head was never shaved to leave a scalp lock or roach. The headdress commonly worn was a skin cap or band decorated with quill- and beadwork, and sometimes with one or two feathers at the back. But for ceremonial and special occasions the cap worn was completely covered with feathers from the heads of wood ducks, the scarlet feathers of the woodpecker's crest, or white snowy owl feathers, and with an upstanding central pompom of eagle, hawk, owl, wild goose, and other feathers, plus a pendant "tail" of feathers and quillwork in the rear.

XIII

LAST OF THE PASSACONNOWAYS

THE FIRST INDIANS I ever met were the Passaconnoways or Pascatawayas, a branch of the Wabenakis, who had a small village on the banks of the Little Androscoggin near Norway, Maine. I was a small boy at the time, visiting my grandparents, but even at that distant date the Passaconnoways were a vanishing race. Measles, chicken pox, whooping cough, and other maladies of little consequence to the whites had decimated the Indians, many had migrated eastward to join their kinsmen, the Tarratines, on the Penobscot, and barely half a dozen families still dwelt in their wooden shacks built of slabs and scrap lumber from the local saw mill.

During the summer they cultivated their crops of corn and vegetables in the rich bottom land by the river and peddled berries and medicinal roots in the village. In winter the men hunted and trapped and the women sold beadwork, sweet-grass baskets, birch-bark boxes, and other products of their handiwork. There was little of the Indian about their appearance. All spoke English of a sort, and aside from the universal moccasins they wore the same sort of clothing as their white neighbors, although some of the women wore fillets of beads or porcupine-quill-decorated buckskin about their heads.

Although they eked out a somewhat precarious existence, they did not suffer for lack of food or shelter, and were a happy, contented lot, honest and trustworthy and rarely intoxicated, for Maine was a strict prohibition state and hard cider was the strongest liquor obtainable. They were born traders, and as keen on a swap as the proverbial Yankee. Nothing pleased them more than to get the best of a white man on a deal. Sometimes their methods were a trifle unethical—as, for example, the Indian who "did" my uncle on one occasion.

It was customary for the store to let the Indians have goods and supplies on credit against their catch of furs and the fresh meat they brought in, and they invariably made good. One autumn day an Indian known as Jim came into the store carrying his musket and having apparently just returned from a hunt. Leaning his gun by the door, he enumerated the various articles he wanted on credit. There were flour and pork, cotton cloth and sugar, powder and shot, and numerous other things.

"That's a mighty big order, Jim," my uncle, who was tending store told him. "How you aimin' to pay for it?"

"Me got one moose," the Indian told him.

"Where's he at?" my uncle wanted to know. "Why didn't you fetch him in?"

"No can bring 'em," Jim replied. "Plenty big moose, plenty far. You know big cedar swamp Crooked River side?"

The other nodded.

"Know big hakmatak tree this side swamp? 'Longside tree one big rock," said the Indian. "Longside rock find 'em moose."

"Reckon he'll cover what you got," agreed my uncle, as Jim shouldered his pack, picked up his gun, and left.

Hitching up his team and with a friend to help him, my uncle drove to the cedar swamp, but search as they might they could find no trace of a dead moose.

"That Injun just naturally lied," declared Uncle Byron. "Thought Jim was an honest Injun, but I'll know better next time."

Not until spring did Jim show up at the store carrying a heavy pack.

"Dern ye, Jim," my uncle greeted him as he entered. "What the heck you mean by lyin' an' cheatin' like you did?"

"You find 'em big hakmatak tree?" the Indian asked.

Byron nodded.

"Find big rock 'longside tree?"

"Sure, but there wasn't any moose there."

The Indian grinned. "Pretty good Injun tell two truths to one lie," he declared. Then, opening his pack, he spread his winter's catch of furs on the counter. "Mebbe more better'n moose," he said.

The chief of the little band was a tall, lean, very old Indian known to everyone as Indian John, although his real name was Paukonoxin. He was a fine-looking Indian, keen-faced, with aquiline nose, who might almost have stepped from the pages of one of J. Fenimore Cooper's tales.

Neither he nor anyone else knew how old he was, but he must have been over the century mark, for he had been a pal of my great-grandfather in his youth, and told fascinating stories of the early days when most of Maine was an unbroken, unexplored wilderness: tales of hunting and trapping, how my ancestor built the first sawmill and grist mill in the interior of Maine—and Indian John would chuckle as he told of his terror when he first saw horses and cattle. His first wife had borne him a son who had been killed at Gettysburg, and a daughter by his second wife had married a white man and lived in Bangor. John had visited them, and on one of his visits had met and talked with the governor regarding the status of the Passaconnoways in the old treaty payments. His Excellency had become greatly interested, and asked John a number of questions in regard to important historical events of which he had personal knowledge. As a result of the conference, the Passaconnoways thereafter received a share of the money paid by the state each year as provided by treaty with the Wabenakis.

John's second wife, Mary, was much younger than he, and was a jolly roly-poly woman who was considered the most skillful basket-maker and bead- and porcupine-quill-worker of the Indians. She found a ready sale for her handiwork; there was scarcely a man in Norway who did not have carpet slippers ornamented with Mary's beadwork, while in every house there were wall pockets, pincushions, and other objects beautifully decorated with her floral designs in dyed porcupine quills and colored beads.

Old as he was, Paukonoxin still hunted and trapped, traveling immense distances on snowshoes and sleeping in flimsy lean-tos during the bitterly cold winters. I doubt if the tall old Indian weighed over 150 pounds, but he was all "whipcord and sinew," as my grandfather expressed it, and never seemed to tire. Once, when someone asked him how a man of his age could be so strong and active, he replied: "Me all same like dog. Eat plenty. When finish eat, sleep plenty. When tired, sleep more plenty."

Sometimes, as the village menfolk gathered about the huge stove in the store or in the village tavern, John and grandfather would get to swapping yarns of their younger days. It was great fun to listen to the two old-timers, each trying to outdo the other in the tales of their youthful adventures. There was no need for them to exaggerate or to resort to fiction, for both had had plenty of thrilling adventures, and narrow escapes from death. As a general rule neither of the two ordinarily mentioned these, but when they were together surrounded by neighbors and friends with a keg of cider on tap and pipes aglow, some chance remark would start them off. To my mind, the best of my grandfather's stories was that of his battle with a wolverine. I had heard it many times, and the "varmint's" hide still hung on the wall over the huge fireplace in the old homestead.

It had happened when grandfather was a youth and lived with his young wife in a log cabin on a farm hewn from the wilderness by my great-grandfather. When following his trap line one morning he had fired at and wounded a huge wolverine that instantly had attacked him. Partly protected by a fallen tree, he had battled the maddened creature with hands and a hunting knife until it was killed. Terribly scratched, clawed, and bitten as he was, he had stopped to skin the creature before returning to his home. I always liked the end of the story best.

"Sakes alive, George!" cried Grandmother as he entered the cabin covered with blood and with one leg wrapped in a crimsoned strip torn from his shirt. "What happened to ye?"

"Just a argument with a pesky wolverine," he told her as he limped across the room and hung his rifle and powder horn on the antlers over the fireplace.

"Laws, that varmint must have fit somethin' awful," declared his wife, as she hurried about getting bandages and salves.

"He done so," grandfather replied. "But I got his derned hide."

"Looks like to me he got a deal of yours, first," she said.

"Calc'late he did," he admitted, "but I got plenty left."

"Ye'd no business tacklin' a wolverine," Grandmother reminded him.

"Didn't have a choice," he told her. "'Twant so much me tacklin' him as he tacklin' me—and 'twas a derned good fight while it lasted."

John's most exciting story, to my youthful mind, was that of his wild ride on a wounded moose. He had shot a huge bull moose that had fallen in its tracks, and, feeling sure it was dead, he had not stopped to recharge his muzzle-loading musket but had stepped forward to cut the animal's throat. Suddenly the moose had leaped to its feet and charged. Hampered by his snowshoes, the Indian had no chance to dodge or spring aside, but threw himself full length in the snow. Then as the moose with lowered head reached him he seized the forward spikes of the horns, hoping to save himself from being trampled, and that his weight might bring the moose to his knees. Instead, the creature threw up its head and John was swung around into the basinlike hollow of the broad-spreading antlers. Clinging to the tines for dear life as the wounded animal dashed through the woods, Paukonoxin expected at any instant to be torn from his perch by a low-hanging branch or crushed against some tree.

Badly wounded as it was, the moose was gradually weakening, but still raced on. At last, drawing his hunting knife and taking a firm hold on the animal's horns, the Indian bent forward and plunged the blade into the creature's throat. As its knees gave way and it lurched forward Paukonoxin leaped clear, unharmed but shaken, and, as he freely admitted, "Me plenty scared that time you bet 'em."

His most recent exploit had taken place only the preceding winter. When traveling on snowshoes through the big cedar swamp one night he had been trailed by a huge Canada lynx that, leaping from tree to tree, drew closer and closer. John had no gun and he didn't feel there was much danger of the big cat's actually attacking him, yet he had known of men being attacked by a lynx and even by bobcats, and he kept a wary eye upon the great cedar trees whose swaying branches betrayed the animal's presence. Finally, when the Indian had about decided that the lynx had no intention of attacking but was merely following him out of curiosity, the creature suddenly sprang.

Fortunately it overshot its mark and landed in the deep snow, where it sank to its belly. Turning swiftly, John seized the struggling animal by the hind legs and swung it with all his strength against a tree trunk. Then, shouldering the lynx, he continued on his way.

I do not think there was anyone in the county who was more popular and more highly regarded than Indian John. Despite his name, no one ever seemed to think of him as an Indian. He was welcome everywhere, in every home, and the children fairly adored him. He was always ready with a story or a joke and, very often these were at the expense of members of his own race. Although not strictly a teetotaler, he never had been known to drink to excess; but he was thoroughly aware of the Indians' fondness for rum and the dire consequences that often resulted. One of his favorite stories was of an Indian who came into a store where some white men were discussing what they would ask for if they could have three wishes granted.

"Let's ask the Injun what he'd want," suggested one. Then, to the Indian, "Hi, Tom—'spose you have three wishes, what things you wish for?"

For a space the Indian was silent, thinking it over. Then: "Give me all tobacco in world. Give me all rum in world."

"Well, what else?" demanded the white man. "Ye got another wish comin' to ye."

The Indian pondered for a moment. Then: "Gimme a little more rum."

Although Paukonoxin always dressed like his white neighbors aside from his moosehide moccasins, yet it was known that he possessed a complete tribal costume of buckskin and feathers, together with bow and arrows, a tomahawk pipe and—so rumor had it—a belt fringed with scalps. There was no secret about the costume, for he had repeatedly expressed the wish that when he died he might be buried attired in his full tribal regalia, and Grandfather and others had promised him that if they survived him they would see that his wishes were carried out.

When, several years after I last saw him, the old chief passed away, he had one of the largest funerals the village ever had seen. People came from far and near to attend the ceremonies; from Portland and Bangor, from Bethel and Pemmaquid, from Fryeburg and North Conway. Even the governor was there. As a special honor, Paukonoxin was to be buried in the village cemetery.

Dressed in beaded buckskin, with a cap of wood ducks' feathers on his head, wrapped in his robe of beaver skins and surrounded by his Indian weapons and cherished possessions, the body of Paukonoxin was laid to rest among those of his white friends.

XIV

PEOPLE OF THE DAWN

THE WABENAKI, or People of the Dawn, they call themselves—for, according to their traditions, their ancestors came over seas from the East, "from the Land of the Sunrise." Once a large and powerful nation, the Wabenaki, with their numerous subtribes, occupied most of Maine and parts of New Hampshire and southern Canada. Naturally they were a peaceful agricultural people living in villages, where they had good-sized garden clearings in the forests. But they were unexcelled hunters and trappers as well as fishermen. And when necessity arose they became brave and valiant warriors.

Although all of the various tribes and subtribes of the Wabenaki spoke the same tongue and could converse with one another, yet their dialects varied somewhat. And despite the fact that all were members of the same race, each tribe or subtribe had its own territory, its own chiefs, even its own types of houses, canoes, weapons, and costumes, and were often enemies of one another.

Although there are still a large number of the Wabenaki in Canada, the only members of the race dwelling in the United States are the Passamaquoddies and the so-called Penobscots of Maine.

Taken as a whole, the Dawn People were a very superior lot of Indians. They were normally peaceful; they never were the aggressors when trouble broke out with the white men; they were industrious, moral, honest, and, until debauched by Europeans, clean, healthy, and temperate. And a very large portion of the Maine Indians had become devout Catholics years before the *Mayflower* arrived.

The nine hundred and more Indians now living in Maine are

about equally divided between the two tribes, but whereas a goodly number of the Passamaquoddy are of mixed Indian, white, and even Negro blood, only one or two families of their Penobscot kinsmen are not pure Indian. Although the Indians are always referred to as Penobscots and have taken to calling themselves by that name, yet in reality they are the Tarratines, with their village on Panawamske Island in the Penobscot River near Old Town.

Although nominally "wards of the state," the Wabenaki are far from being objects of charity or dependent upon the funds paid them annually for the sales of their ancestral lands in accordance with the old treaties. On the contrary, they are a most self-respecting, proud, and independent people: quiet, law-abiding, industrious, and largely self-supporting. During the summer they do a thriving business in baskets, rustic furniture, Indian curios, and handicrafts, and in the autumn the men are in demand as guides to hunters in search of moose, deer, and other game. A large number are also employed in the Old Town canoe factory, where the canvas-covered replicas of their famous birch canoes are made.

Each spring a number of the Indians leave their homes for the seashore and mountain resorts, where they set up camps and sell their handiwork. With the coming of autumn most of these wanderers return to harvest their crops and to pass the winter at lumbering, trapping, hunting, or working in factories. Some never do go back, but settle down to live and die far from the little island in the Penobscot; there are members of the tribe even in Miami, St. Petersburg, and elsewhere in Florida. But the average white man would never recognize these people as Indians, for they live, dress, talk, behave, and look like dark-skinned white folk.

They are perhaps the least Indian-looking of Indians, and there is as much difference between a Sioux or a Seminole and a Tarratine as between a German and an Andalusian. Their eyes are full rather than beady; they seldom have aquiline features: their hair is often fine and brown, and many have gray eyes. All are well-educated. On their island they have a school conducted by the Sisters of Mercy, where the children reach the eighth grade.

They are taught to speak both French and English, although among themselves they use their tribal tongue, and through the efforts of the Indian Island Women's Club the public schools and high school of Old Town are open to the Indian children. Many have graduated with high honors, the first girl graduate having been Mrs. Florence Nicola Shay, whose great-grandfather was one of the few survivors of the Massacre of Father Rasle and his Indian converts at Norridgewock in 1723.

Unlike most Indians, the Penobscots do not have a tribal chief but are governed like a real state with a governor, lieutenant-governor, and other officials elected by the people, and with a single policeman. Moreover, these Indians also elect a representative to the state legislature of Maine—the first Indians in the United States to have had a senator. Although so thoroughly up to date and progressive, they are yet keenly aware of the necessity and value of perpetuating their tribal customs and traditions. With the passing of the years, as the older people died off, the ancient lore—the dances and ceremonies, the customs and costumes, even the folklore and traditions—were passing into oblivion. But within recent years there has been an awakening interest in the tribe's past, and annually the Indians hold a fete in which, dressed in Indian costumes, they re-enact scenes from their past, dance the old-time dances, retell the tribal traditions, and for a space are transformed into Indians such as white persons imagine they should be.

At first some of the tribe, especially the younger generation, did not take too kindly to being transformed temporarily into "wild Indians." Shortly after their first fete when I visited the island I asked Little Smoky, then a boy of eight, if he had taken part in the spectacle. "Yeah," he told me, "and I didn't like it either. Wearing moccasins and feathers was all right, but they had to go and put diapers on me." The fact that the "diapers" were a breechclout did not in the least assuage his injured self-respect.

Those who imagine the Indian to be a silent, distant being, aloof and dignified, would have the surprise of their lives could they visit a Tarratine home as friends of the family. They would find the Indians the most hospitable of hosts; friends, relatives and neighbors would drop in, and the strangers would find themselves the center of a happy, laughing, chattering group full of fun and jollity.

I cannot recall any more pleasant and enjoyable times than those I have spent with my Penobscot friends. Just outside the door the children are frolicking with pet bear cubs, and the huge kitchen is filled with odors of broiling venison, steaming corn on the cob, luscious succotash, and pumpkin pies, as the plump, smiling hostess bustles about preparing the feast for the visitor and the Indians who have dropped in.

Nearly all of my friends were there. White-haired Great-grandmother Ronco, who had passed the century mark, still active, as keen-sighted, and as alert-minded as any of the girls, but who never learned English and preferred the Wabenaki or the familiar French. There also was the middle-aged, thin-faced president, who looked more like a bank president than an Indian; Mrs. Shay and her famous daughter, the songstress; hawk-faced John Saukolexis, together with their wives and daughters, sons and kinfolk, and old and young all laughing, chattering, telling jokes, munching popcorn and maple sugar, and drinking home-brewed birch beer or sweet cider.

Fondly I cherish the memories of those gatherings, for I fear that never again will I visit my Indian friends and relatives on the Penobscot. However, if by some remote chance I should reach Panawamske I would find new faces and strangers to greet me, for most of my old-time friends have passed into the Great Beyond. Mrs. Shay, Old Lady Ronco, Saukolexis, President Mitchell, all have gone forever. Little Smoky is a veteran of two wars. A number of the Indian boys whom I knew have given their lives on the battlefields of Europe and Korea, yet now and then by chance I meet a member of the tribe even here in Florida.

Of all the many Indians I have known, the Wabenaki are my favorites. Perhaps I am prejudiced in their favor, because blood of the Dawn People flows in my own veins. Thin as it is, it makes me kin to many of the Tarratines, and for all I know I may be a very, very distant relative of the Baron de St. Castine. Moreover, my wife is one-fourth Wabenaki and over one-fourth Tuscarora.

XV

WHITE WAR CHIEF

No account of the Indians of Maine would be complete without the story of the white war chief of the Wabenaki, the amazing French nobleman Vincent Baron de St. Castine, the most romantic, most spectacular, and most picturesque figure in the entire history of New England.

The Basque nobleman, who had immense estates near Oléron in the Pyrenees, an income of five million livres a year, and a fortune of over half a million gold crowns, was a born soldier. At the age of fifteen he was credited with being one of the best swordsmen in all France. Preferring a life of adventure to the humdrum existence of the landed nobility, he offered his services and his sword to the Carignan Salières as ensign before he was sixteen. At the close of the campaign in France he and his regiment were sent to Canada, where the Salières were disbanded and each officer was given three to four leagues of "good land." Since Castine neither required nor wanted land—of which he already had enough and to spare—he made over his allotment to his orderly.

During the time he had been in Canada he had become deeply interested in the Indians. He had acquired a knowledge of their dialects and had won the firm and enduring friendship of many of the tribesmen, among them Chief Madokawando of the Tarratines of Maine, who often visited Canada to trade. So when Castine's regiment was disbanded and the youthful Baron was free to do as he pleased, instead of returning to France he joined Chief Madokawando and journeyed with him down the Penobscot to Panawamske Island, the site of the present-day Penobscot Indian reservation near Old Town. Meeting the chief's daughter, he fell madly in love with her. Very soon after his arrival the two were married with all the imposing Indian ceremonies, and also by the Jesuit Father in the little church that still stands upon the island, the first mission to be established among the Indians of the eastern United States north of Florida.

Castine first appeared upon the stage of American history when, in 1670, he offered his services, together with those of two hundred Tarratine warriors, to the Chevalier de Grande Fontaine. The latter placed Castine in charge of Fort Pentagonet, which had been restored to the French. For four years the little colony, in later years to be named after the white war chief of the Tarratines, led a peaceful existence. Under the protective shadows of the fort the French settlers built their cabins, and near by Castine's warriors erected their lodges. Then one day Dutch warships appeared in the bay and attacked the fort. Aided by their heavier cannon and outnumbering the defenders, they captured the fort; but it was an empty victory, for Castine had removed all supplies and had spiked his guns before evacuating the fort and taking to the near-by woods with his Indians. Constantly harassed by the hidden braves of Castine, the Dutch finally withdrew. During the Dutch occupancy of the fort a number of the French settlers had allied themselves with the invaders. Once the Dutch had left, these were promptly expelled by Castine and their homes burned. Having thus disposed of the disloyal Frenchmen and the Dutch, Castine built a stronger fortress, which he held against all comers, including a British party with over three hundred Mohawk allies, although a number of the Tarratines were killed and others were carried off as prisoners.

But even Castine and his valorous Indian allies had to bow to the assault of the British fleet under Sir Edmund Andros in 1688, whereupon the white war chief with his braves withdrew to Panawamske Island. But not to a peaceful existence by any means. The French and Indian Wars were flaming over Maine. Castine's own home had been burned by Sir Edmund Andros' orders, and the Baron, who was idolized, revered, and regarded almost as a deity by the Wabenakis, once again took to the warpath at the head of his seasoned warriors. Swiftly, silently, they struck, suddenly appearing where least expected, vanishing the instant their mission was accomplished, and moving so rapidly from spot to spot that the British believed and declared that over one thousand Indians were under Castine. The British settlements were devastated all the way from Eastport to York and beyond, and the mere mention of Castine's name brought terror to the hearts of the colonists. The settlements along the Sheepscot River were utterly destroyed, Newcastle was burned to the ground, and even Portland (then known as Falmouth) was attacked and the garrison driven off. The victorious Castine vanished with more than a hundred prisoners, after firing the town, having himself lost less than a dozen men.

In 1690 a truce was signed at Sagadahoc, but the British, regarding a treaty with Indians of no consequence, soon violated its terms, paid bounties on Wabenaki scalps, and raided their villages, and once again Castine and his Indians swept down on the British settlements. He attacked York and for the first time was repulsed, yet left the town in ashes, with over half of its inhabitants killed. Unable to withstand his destructive raids, the British arranged another treaty, but, just as our government, in later years, regarded Indian treaties as mere scraps of paper, so once again the English colonists violated their promises, attacked Indian villages, and collected bounties on scalps. Castine and his braves retaliated by capturing the new fort at Pemmaquid and by utterly destroying Scarborough, Sourwink, Casco, and Purpooduk in rapid succession.

Within the dank and tiny dungeon of the fort at Pemmaquid, Castine found a mutilated, dying Indian who had been inhumanly and horribly tortured by the British, and in his blazing fury he ordered every prisoner put to death, the first and only time in his career that he resorted to savagery. For over twenty years the wars continued. Admired, respected, and honored by the French, regarded as almost a semideity by the Indians, the white war chief was hated, feared, and vilified by the British. He was credited with being even more ruthless and cruel than his Wabenaki warriors, a monster in human form without a redeeming feature other than his reckless bravery, yet the only case of savagery that could be proved was his massacre of the prisoners at Pemmaquid, for which, under the circumstances, some justification might be found. Even the British had to admit that the white captives he carried to Panawamske were well-treated, that during the intervals of peace they were permitted to return to their homes, and that many preferred to remain among the Indians. And neither Castine nor the French ever promulgated the doctrine that the British, being heretics, did not possess souls or were spiritually unworthy of consideration, as did the British in regard to the Indians and the French respectively.

But even Castine could not fight time, and he was getting old. He was weary of battles and fighting, and desired only a life of peace surrounded by his friends and family on Panawamske. So he urged his only son, who had inherited all of the Baron's fighting spirit together with the woodcraft, the cunning, and the courage of his mother's race, to lay aside the tomahawk and, as hereditary chief of the Tarratines, to use all his influence toward a lasting peace between the white men and the Indians. And when Lovewell's infamous scalp-hunting raid aroused the tribesmen throughout the land and another outbreak of war appeared imminent, young Castine moved from village to village, from tribe to tribe, attending the Indians' councils, and eloquently urging them to refrain from further hostilities. Falsely accused by the British of fomenting trouble, he was taken prisoner and sent in chains to Boston, where he was confined for seven months, despite his declaration that, as a tribal chief, he had every right to attend the councils of his mother's people, and that he was urging peace and not war. But it was not until the British learned that the Indians, aroused to frenzy by the treatment of the son of their white war chief, planned to rise en masse and destroy every white settler in Maine, that he was freed. Only young Castine's eloquence, and the deep veneration the Indians held for his father, dissuaded the Wabenakis. Finally the smoke of the peace pipes rose everywhere above the lodges of the People of the Dawn, and what would have been the bloodiest war in the history of the colonies was averted.

By this time the old Baron, the great white war chief of the Tarratines, has passed away. His beloved wife had already been laid to rest in the churchyard of her island home. The several daughters she had borne him had been educated in France and had married French noblemen, never to return to the land of their birth. And young Castine, with his father's last wishes carried out, his mission fulfilled, and peace firmly established, bade farewell to Maine and also sailed for France. The Baron de St. Castine had left his chateâu in the Pyrenees to become an Indian chief. His son, who was half Indian and a chief, left *his* home in Maine to become a nobleman of France. And the colonists in Maine, having won their freedom, perpetuated the white war chief's memory by changing the name of Pentagonet to Castine.

XVI

SPEARERS OF POLLOCK

In their own language they are the Pestumokadyk or "The People Who Spear Pollock," but to the white men they are the Passamaquoddies, a tribe of the Wabenaki who dwell on a small reservation at Pleasant Point near Eastport, Maine.

I first met these Indians when, as a boy, I accompanied my father on a collecting trip to the Bay of Fundy. We drove to the shore in a horse-drawn buggy and left the horse hitched to a tree not far from the Passamaquoddy village. When, laden with specimens, we returned several hours later, we found the horse and carriage standing where we had left them. But what an amazing sight the animal presented!

The Indians never before had been able to examine closely a harnessed horse. Curious to learn the whys and the wherefores of the harness, they had taken it completely apart during our absence, and had then attempted to reharness the horse.

Not a single buckle or strap was where it belonged. The surcingle was about the horse's neck, the reins took the place of traces, the headstall was upside down with the blinders under the animal's throat, and the breaching and breast-band had been transposed. But the Indians were immensely proud of their success in having mastered the mysteries of the horse's "clothes," even to "tying" him to the carriage properly!

My father was a very patient and good-natured man, and despite the bother the Indians had caused he saw the humor in the episode and chuckled as we busied ourselves reassembling the harness while the Indians stood about watching every move. Then, as he adjusted the bridle, he addressed the horse: "Well, old boy, what did *you* think about it?"

At the time of this memorable introduction to the Passamaquoddies they were a bit primitive in some ways. To be sure, they wore white men's clothes, but they all wore moccasins; most of the men had shoulder-length hair and wore hoop earrings, and a few even had feathers in their homemade straw hats. They lived in log cabins or houses of pole and wattle construction, and in summer had birch-bark wigwams. They made and used their own unexcelled birch canoes, the women made beautiful baskets and objects ornamented with beads and porcupine quills, and the majority were pure-bloods.

But during the seventy years that have passed since I first met the Passamaquoddies great changes have taken place. Today shoes and rubber boots have taken the place of moccasins. The Indians dwell in well-built frame houses. Sport shirts, blue jeans, and wrist watches are popular, quite a number have automobiles, there is scarcely an Indian home without its radio, and wooden boats and outboard motors have taken the place of birch canoes, while pure-blooded members of the tribe are in the minority.

Formerly the Passamaquoddies were the most skilled of all Indians when it came to handling a birch canoe in the open sea. To see two Indians hunting porpoises in the choppy tide-rips of the Bay of Fundy was a sight never to be forgotten, and to accompany them, as I have on more than one occasion, gives one a thrill that verges on a nervous panic.

Crouching in the stern of the frail craft, one Indian wielded his paddle while the other stood in the bow with a loaded musket, and by some amazing acrobatic feat maintained perfect balance as the canoe lurched and rolled, bobbed and bucked, in the rough sloppy seas. But the real excitement was when the hunter shot a porpoise on the jump. Dropping his paddle, the Indian in the stern leaped to his feet, and together the two men reached over the side of the canoe and dragged the heavy cetacean over the rail. No one who never has witnessed the feat would believe it possible to lift a two-hundred-pound porpoise into a birch canoe without capsizing it, even in the smoothest water; yet I have seen it done many a time when an ordinary human being would feel that merely to paddle a canoe through the angry waves would be far too hazardous to attempt. Often, too, the Passamaquoddies would paddle far out to sea, their frail craft filled with men, women, and children and a few dogs, to spend the day fishing. Then, with their canoes laden to the gunwale at the close of day, they would come scudding home with an old blanket or a scrap of torn canvas for a sail, when the white man's schooners were making heavy weather of it under double-reefed sails.

Even long ocean voyages were sometimes made by these Indians in their birch canoes. On one occasion, when I answered the doorbell at our home in New Haven, Connecticut, I found a tall Indian outside. "Mebbe Professor, he home?" he inquired. As he entered the library my father glanced up, then sprang to his feet.

"Why, hello, Peter!" he exclaimed. "What are you doing so far from home?"

"Come make visit you," the Indian replied. "Come visit cousin live Bridgeport."

"How did you come—by train or steamer?" my father asked him.

"Come canoe," he declared, as casually as though paddling a birch canoe from Eastport, Maine, to New Haven, Connecticut, were a matter of no importance. And he had undertaken the long voyage merely to call on my father, for whom he had worked on a scientific expedition, and to visit a relative in Bridgeport.

There is also the story told by a captain of a steamer bound for Halifax from Boston. Having sighted a canoe out of sight of land with its Indian occupant wildly signaling the ship, and thinking the fellow adrift and helpless, the skipper shifted his course and stopped his vessel within hailing distance of the canoe. Paddling alongside, the Passamaquoddy scrambled to the steamer's deck and calmly asked for a match to light his pipe! For a space the captain was too flabbergasted at the Indian's nerve to find words to express his feelings. Then he saw the humorous side of it and roared with laughter. To the Indian, stopping a steamship seemed of no more importance and no more trouble than stopping a canoe. With a box of matches in his pocket he climbed down to his canoe, waved farewell to the departing steamer, and paddled on his way, contentedly puffing at his pipe.

XVII

INDIANS OF THE EASTERN WOODLANDS

SOUTH OF New England there were a number of tribes inhabiting what are now the eastern states. They lived in good-sized villages and cultivated the soil, although also depending largely upon hunting and fishing. In southern New York, parts of Pennsylvania, New Jersey, Delaware, and Maryland, were the Delawares. In Virginia were the so-called Powhatans. In the Carolinas were the Suchi and Catawbas, as well as the Cherokees, and in Georgia and Florida there were the Creeks and Seminoles.

Because of the romantic episode of Pocahontas and Captain John Smith, the name of the Powhatan confederacy is familiar to nearly everyone. But fully as interesting as the Pocahontas affair is the fact that one of the principal chiefs of the Powhatans, and an implacable enemy of the whites, was the adopted son of a Spanish viceroy. An Indian of Axacan, Virginia, the son of a chief, he was captured by the Spanish under Mendez and was taken to Mexico, where he was bought as a slave by the viceroy. Finding the boy very intelligent and taking a great fancy to him, the viceroy adopted him as his son and sent him to Spain to be educated. Being a devout Christian and having become thoroughly Spanishized, it was thought that he would be able to convert his tribe and induce the Indians to be friendly toward the Spaniards, who had established a mission and small settlement at Axacan. He was returned to Virginia for this purpose. But upon reaching his boyhood home, and learning of the ill treatment his tribesmen had suffered at the hands of the Spaniards, he cast aside all his civilized ways and led his warriors in an attack on the settlement. Had it not been for the timely arrival of a Spanish ship with re-enforcements, every Spaniard would have been killed and the settlement totally destroyed. As it was, only a few Spaniards were left alive, and only ruins of the mission remained. Opposed by overwhelming numbers of Spanish troops, and having lost the greater portion of his Indians, the son of the viceroy fled with his few remaining tribesmen and joined Powhatan. But he had accomplished his purpose. The Spaniards abandoned their settlement at Axacan, where a monument and tablet now mark the site. Of all the Virginia Indians who once formed the powerful Powhatan confederacy, the only survivors are a few Pamunkeys and Chickahominies, most of whom are mixed with white and Negro blood.

Among all the tribes of the eastern woodlands, the largest and most important were the Delawares or Leni-Lenape, who were regarded as "Grandfathers" by more than forty different tribes. Although originally occupying southeastern New York, and parts of Pennsylvania, Delaware and New Jersey, they were born wanderers and by the middle of the nineteenth century were almost everywhere throughout the United States. By 1850 they reached the great plains and had become true horse Indians and like various plains tribes, depended upon the buffalos for their living. Many had penetrated to the far Northwest to what is now Oregon and Washington, and as far into the Southwest as the Mexican border. Their language became the lingua franca of the central and midwestern states.

Either by coincidence or design, many of their most famous chiefs bore names most appropriate to travelers, such as "Always Walking," "Walking Turtle," "Walks Everywhere," "Walking Bear," and similar appellations. Born traders—the real "Yankees" among the Indians—they were welcomed by tribes that were hostile to all other strangers, and were as much at home among the Apaches, Kiowas, and Comanches as among the Sioux and the Cheyennes. Thoroughly familiar with the trails and passes of mountains and deserts, speaking many Indian languages of the far west, and perfectly welcome among so many tribes, the Delawares, who were friendly toward the whites, made the best of scouts and guides for our troops and explorers. Black Beaver, a Delaware of Illinois, was a famous guide and interpreter. He was the first to arrange a conference between the Kiowas, Comanche, and Wichita tribes, and General Dodge, which was held in 1834. From that time until his death in 1880 he was constantly employed by the government, and was the most efficient and trusted scout on nearly all of the early transcontinental explorations.

At the present time, of all the remaining Delawares that are scattered far and wide over our country, the most interesting and in some ways remarkable members of the tribe are the Sand Hill Indians of Monmouth County, New Jersey. Now numbering only about thirty individuals, and dwelling in one of the most densely populated areas, only a comparatively short distance from New York City, these Indians have yet retained their old tribal customs, councils, ceremonials, arts and crafts, and their clan system, as well as their chieftainships, although surrounded by the whites and civilization for over two hundred years. Many are members of the true Leni-Lenape or Turtle Clan, among these being Lone Bear Revey who maintains a trading post and factory where the Indians make authentic Indian costumes, artifacts, etc., for sale in various stores and for use in the movies, pageants, stage, etc. They have some Cherokee blood from members of the latter tribe who passed New Jersey on a northward migration in 1713. Outwardly thoroughly civilized and indistinguishable from their white neighbors, and following numerous trades, yet at their green corn dance and their council meetings they don the old tribal costumes and behave like Indians. Their present chief is Ryers Crummel, who, in accordance with the clan system rule, became chief because his mother was the oldest daughter of Chief Isaac Richardson, who died in 1904.

From the time of the earliest colonists until the War of 1812, the Delawares were an important factor in our history. They were signers of the treaty with William Penn, and were made famous by J. Fenimore Cooper in his *Leatherstocking Tales*. Friendly toward the whites, they became allies of the colonists in the French and Indian Wars. But the white men maltreated the Delawares, broke promises and treaties, robbed them of their land, and even massacred them wholesale (See Chapter V), with the result that many of the tribe became hostile, even joining their hereditary enemies, the Iroquois and the Shawnees, but never violating their treaty with the Quaker colonists of Pennsylvania.

In central and northern New York, the Iroquois reigned supreme. Probably the first of all Leagues of Nations, they were a confederation of six tribes, founded about 1570 by Haion-Hwe-Tha (Hiawatha to the whites)[1] an Onondaga who had joined the Mohawks. Aided by Dekanawide, a Huron, he endeavored to induce the five Iroquois tribes to unite with the purpose of abolishing war, murder, and hostilities and to maintain order and peace. The reformers started their campaign among the Onondagas, but were strenuously opposed. They then turned to the Mohawks, but made no headway until they approached the Oneidas, who were quick to take up the ideas. Once started, the league grew rapidly. The Mohawks and Cayugas joined the Oneidas, and were followed by the Onondagas and Senecas.

More than a century later, in 1712, the Tuscaroras of the Carolinas joined the Iroquois, thus making it the Six Nations, and the most powerful group of Indians in the country. It was in many ways a most remarkable and unique organization. Penalties were provided for breaking the law; ten strings of wampum, each a yard in length, was the fine for taking a human life. It was further decreed that the murderer had forfeited his life to the family of his victim, and that only by the payment of twenty strings of wampum could his life be spared. There were various punishments decreed, covering practically every offence against peace, well-being, and order, and a most remarkable and admirable Constitution was adopted. In fact this was so perfect that when Thomas Jefferson was called upon to draft our own Constitution he used that of the Iroquois as the basis of his draft, even copying portions of it word for word.

Idealistic as was the purpose of the Six Nations confederation, the members soon found, as have modern confederations of nations, that in order to maintain peace it was necessary to go to war. Although still adhering to their laws and constitution among

[1] Not to be confused with Hiawatha, a mythical titular divinity of the Iroquois who was believed to be the humanized form of the son of the Creator or his visual manifestation.

themselves, the Six Nations were soon fighting both other Indian tribes and the white settlers. Their original friendliness to the white men was outraged when a small party of Mohawks met a French expedition near Lake Champlain and several of the Indians were killed without reason. As a result, in this case the French became their Public Enemies Number One, and as the English colonists were at war with the French, the Iroquois joined the British and became their firm and most useful allies. Their war parties became a scourge to the French and their Indian allies, raiding as far eastward as the Penobscot River and the coast of Maine, as far south as the Virginias, and as far west as the settlements about the Great Lakes and the Mississippi River.

But with the termination of the French and Indian Wars, and the beginning of the American Revolution, the Iroquois were in a quandary. If they allied themselves with the British they would be fighting the colonists who had been their friends; on the other hand, if they took the part of the Americans they would be fighting those who had aided them in their war with the French. For the first time there was dissension among the members of the League. The majority were for neutrality, but they soon realized this would be impossible. Eventually some fought on one side and some on the other. Most notable of those who allied themselves with the Continentals were the Oneidas. Never, during the war, did they take scalps, nor did they molest women, children, or elderly persons. They were regarded as the best scouts and most useful allies of the Continental Army, and won the praise and respect of General Washington.

A fine race and of the highest intelligence, the Six Nations have occupied a conspicuous spot in American history, and many of them have risen to fame and prominence in nearly every profession and trade. Although among the most highly civilized Indians, yet the Iroquois still maintain their original organization, their tribal laws and traditions, and many of their old customs. They still have their long house, with its pepetual fire, where councils are held, and their leaders encourage the preservation of the old ceremonies and dances, and an intimate and exhaustive knowledge of woodcraft. This is particularly true of the Mohawks of the St. Regis Reservation, whose Akwesasne

Mohawk Councillor Organization, under the leadership of Aren Akweks (Ray Fadden) is somewhat similar to the Boy Scouts, although far more exacting in its requirements.

Ordinarily the Iroquois wear conventional clothing, but for ceremonials and dances many don the old tribal costumes. These consist of buckskin tunics and leggings, breechclout and low, soft moccasins, all decorated with quill and beadwork in artistic semifloral designs. In addition there were belts and shoulder bands of dyed fibers woven in beautiful patterns and often trimmed with feathers and scalp locks, and pouches of heavily beaded buckskin. The typical Iroquois headdress was a close-fitting buckskin cap, overlaid with feathers and with a feather plume at the top and a "bob" or "tail" trimmed with feathers. An Iroquois costume that was given to one of my ancestors by a friendly Mohawk chief was of snow-white buckskin, almost completely covered with dyed porcupine quill and bead decorations. The belt and shoulder bands were woven in a red-and-white design; the buckskin cap was completely covered with feathers of the snowy owl, and had a plume of eagle feathers and a "bob" covered with the iridescent scalps of wood ducks.

In nearly all of the pictures of the Iroquois and other eastern Indians they are shown naked to the waist and with their heads shaved with the exception of a stiff upright roach of hair extending from the forehead to the nape of the neck. Although these Indians stripped to breechclout, leggings and moccasins when hunting or fighting, and while many of the warriors, as well as couriers and runners, had shaved heads with the roach, yet it was by no means universal. It was a custom common to almost all the eastern tribes and was more popular with the Hurons, Wyandottes, Shawnees and some others than with the Indians of the eastern woodlands.

XVIII

TRIBES OF THE MIDDLE WEST

BETWEEN THE Allegheny Mountains and the Mississippi River, and from the region of the Great Lakes to the Gulf of Mexico, there were a great many tribes who were mainly sedentary agriculturalists with permanent villages.

Largest and most powerful of the midwestern tribes was the Chippewa, or more properly Ojibway, who occupied both shores of lakes Huron and Superior and across Minnesota into Dakota. Although a sedentary tribe, the Chippewas were a militant lot, and were constantly at war with the Sauk and Fox and the Central Sioux tribes, finally driving the latter across the Mississippi into Dakota. They even outfought the Iroquois and forced them to withdraw from the Great Lakes area. Until 1812 they were hostile to the whites, but in 1815 signed a treaty that never has been broken. There are about thirty thousand of the tribe living today, about half the number being in the United States and half in Canada. Although thoroughly civilized, and prosperous farmers or following various other occupations, the Chippewas, like the Iroquois and many other tribes, still retain many of their old customs and ceremonials, and at such times many of them wear their tribal costume of buckskin decorated with beadwork in bold, handsome floral designs, and their feather-bedecked caps and handsomely woven shoulder belts. Not far from the Chippewa territory were the Hurons or Wyandottes, a confederacy of tribes related to the Iroquois, although they warred with the latter. Originally dwelling mainly in Canada, they gradually spread southward, and at one time controlled the entire Ohio Valley.

Other tribes that occupied portions of the Great Lakes area were the peaceful Menominees of Wisconsin and Michigan, and the Miamis, who lived about Green Bay, Wisconsin, and the site where Chicago now stands. Later they moved to Ohio and Indiana, eventually selling their lands and moving to Kansas and Oklahoma, although some still remain near Wabash, Indiana. At one time they were famous for their elaborate tattooing, which often covered the entire body. A hard-working farming tribe, they also hunted the buffalo, although they were never horse Indians. From the hair of the animals they spun very fine thread which they wove into cloth. Always peaceful, mild, and good-natured, they dwelled in small villages in houses built of rush mats.

The most interesting and puzzling of all of these midwestern tribes are the Pottawattomies. Occupying the area about Green Bay, Wisconsin, when first known to the white men, they spread westward across the Mississippi in 1846, and at one time were in possession of the greater part of Michigan, Illinois, Wisconsin, and Indiana. They allied themselves with the Chippewas, Miamis, and Menominees, and became so thoroughly affiliated with these tribes that their own language was completely lost, except when used for ceremonial purposes. And for general use they adopted the dialects of their neighbors, the Na 'Nosi or forest group adopting the Chippewa, and the Mascoutens or prairie group using a mixture of Miami, Shawnee, and other words. At one time allies of the French, they allied themselves with the British during the Revolutionary War and also during the War of 1812. Noted for their temperate habits, their hospitality, and as being a humane and kindly people, they were quick to become Christians and to adopt civilization.

According to their traditions, they came originally from northern Mexico, and migrated up the Mississippi Valley to the area about the Great Lakes. In many of their religious beliefs and customs they more closely resemble the Indians of the Gulf coast and Mexico than those of the middle west. Moreover, on some of the old maps of Mexico an area in Coahuila is marked *"Indios Quinquejas,"* which might well be the Spanish spelling of *Kindewas* or Eagles, the name of the most important and largest of the Pottawattomie clans. Also, in burials and mounds along the route which they naturally would have followed on a northward migration, numerous sculptured or incised tablets and other artifacts have been found with figures identical with those on engraved seashells from the Spiro Mound in Oklahoma, some even depicting Quetzalcoatl, the Plumed Serpent god of the Aztecs. Many of the tribe are still in the vicinity of the Great Lakes, others are in Kansas and elsewhere west of the Mississippi, and some are in Canada, with others in Oklahoma. Although thoroughly civilized, they still retain their ancient clans and chieftainships, their medicine lodge and sacred bundle. At the present time their chief and keeper of the records and traditions—in other words the tribal historian—is Mr. Howard L. La Hurreau (Chief Shup She Waupaca), who is the great-great-grandson of Chief Metea of the Kindwah or Eagle Clan. In addition to being a peace chief and medicine man of his tribe, he is also the leader of the Lodge of Kee-Way-Din ("From Blue Hill snakes of the Burning Sky, sing of conquest"), an organization to promote the welfare of the tribe, to teach scientific methods of agriculture and stock-raising, and to preserve the old traditions, religion, folklore, and tribal customs.

Another Midwestern tribe that has held an important place in our history is the Sauk or, as more commonly known, the Sauk and Fox. Forest-dwelling nomads, although to some extent agricultural, the Sauks originally occupied eastern Michigan. More warlike than their neighbors, they moved westward and fought with the Sioux; later on, the two tribes became allies. Joining the Fox tribe, they spread southward into Missouri, where they became friends of the Spaniards. They were also friendly toward the English settlers until, finding they had been cheated and tricked into losing their lands, they became hostile, and the Black Hawk War followed. Although the Indians were defeated, they succeeded in driving the Sioux from Iowa and spread into Kansas.

The Kickapoos were another tribe that originally lived in the vicinity of what is now Columbia County, Wisconsin. They moved to Illinois about 1765 and spread south and west, abandoning their sedentary, agricultural life and becoming nomadic horse Indians. Related to the Sauk and Fox, they aided Tecumseh in his campaign and were allies of Black Hawk. In

1837 the United States employed about one hundred Kickapoos to fight the Florida Seminoles. In 1809 they ceded most of their territory to the government, and moved to Kansas and Missouri. About 1852, together with some of the Pottawattomies, they went to Texas and thence into Mexico, where they became raiders and terrorized the country. In 1873 many of them returned to the United States and settled in Oklahoma; here most of them remain. Over one-half of the tribe remained in Mexico, where they live on a reservation allotted them by the Mexican government.

The most important, powerful, and troublesome Indians of the central part of the Middle West were the Shawnees. Originally occupying much of Tennessee, Ohio, Pennsylvania, and the Carolinas, these warlike wanderers fought the Cherokees, Catawbas, and practically every tribe with whom they came in contact. One group, known as the Savannas, gave the name to the town of Savannah, Georgia. Friends and good neighbors of the whites until the outbreak of the Revolutionary War, they became allies of the Americans and boasted that they killed more British than any other tribe. To the Iroquois they were "brothers" or "grandfathers." After the Revolution they became deadly enemies of the whites because of the massacre of a number of their people by the settlers. For over forty years they waged an unceasing, relentless war with the colonists, and were regarded as the most hostile and dangerous of all the midwestern tribes. Eventually the majority moved to Kansas, Texas, and Oklahoma, where they joined their former enemies, the Cherokees.

Inhabiting the western Carolinas and portions of Georgia were the Croatans and Catawbas, the most easterly of all Siouan tribes, now numbering about fifteen thousand. The majority of them are of mixed Indian, white, and Negro blood, although intermarriage with whites or Negroes is forbidden by law. They still retain some of their tribal customs, make excellent baskets and pottery, and elect a chief every four years.

Originally occupying all of the mountainous area of western Virginia, North and South Carolina, Georgia, Tennessee, and Alabama, were the Cherokees, a large and powerful tribe of Iroquois stock. Noted far and wide for their warlike character, they maintained well-fortified towns and were more or less continually at war with other tribes and the white men, even besting the war parties of the Iroquois on several occasions. Although some of the tribe still remain in the Great Smoky Mountains, the majority are on the Cherokee Strip in Oklahoma, where they form one of the so-called "Five Civilized Tribes," the others being the Choctaws, Chickasaws, Creeks, and Seminoles, with their independent "states" or communities, with legislatures, governing officials, courts, public school systems, newspapers, etc. Those of the tribe still dwelling in the Carolinas, although outwardly thoroughly civilized and farmers, still retain their tribal legends, folklore, magic, dances, games, and ceremonials, and elect a chief every four years.

The Chickasaws, another of the "Five Civilized Tribes," occupied northern Mississippi and part of Tennessee. Famed for their bravery and fighting ability, they were constantly at war with other tribes. They defeated the Iroquois but sided with the British against the French, and, joining the Cherokees, drove the Shawnees from the Cumberlands. Later they turned on their former allies and drove off the Cherokees. In 1882 they migrated to Oklahoma, only a few remaining in their original homeland.

The Choctaws, still another of the "Five Civilized Tribes," occupied portions of Mississippi and Georgia. They were allies of the French but later divided, some fighting with the French and others with the British, but otherwise they were always friendly toward the whites. At one time they artificially flattened the heads of the children and became so-called "flat heads." They skeletonized their dead and preserved the bones in boxes and baskets in their "bone houses." Practically all of the tribe moved to Oklahoma, where they number between seventeen thousand and eighteen thousand, although some still live in Mississippi and Louisiana.

In Georgia and portions of Florida were the Creeks, still another of the "Five Civilized Tribes," with the Seminoles in central and southern Florida. In the Creek language Seminole (pronounced Sem-e-no-lay) means outlaw or renegade, and was applied to the Florida Indians because the tribe was composed of

Indians who, for one reason or another, had left their tribes and had settled in the Everglades. Today a great many of them are of mixed Indian, white, and Negro blood. The Seminoles had never given any trouble and had been friendly toward the whites until the government attempted to transport them forcibly to Oklahoma, and treacherously made prisoners of Osceola and other chiefs when under a flag of truce. The result was the Seminole War, the longest, costliest, bloodiest war, in proportion to the numbers involved, that ever was waged by the United States. It was also the only war we have not won, and it accomplished nothing, since the Indians were the victors and remained in possession of their homes and freedom. Although a number have made peace with the United States, there are many living in the Great Cypress Swamp who never have signed a treaty and are still technically at war with the United States.

While the Seminoles still wear their Indian costumes, the men have discarded the multicolored skirts and wear trousers, and have replaced moccasins with brogans, while the women wear gypsylike skirts, loose blouses, and multiple strings of beads as of old. This is not so much for their own satisfaction and tribal pride as to attract the attention of tourists, who purchase curios and handiwork of the Indians, or pay to see the young men wrestle alligators. In former times the Seminoles wove magnificent belts, shoulder bands, and other articles of dyed fibers, were experts at tanning hides, and made splendid moccasins of the unique Seminole type. Woven fiber articles are now things of the past, the Indians have discarded buckskin in favor of cloth, and I doubt if there are any of them, aside from some of the older members of the tribe, who can make moccasins or tan a hide. Although the Seminoles of Florida still live in their open thatch-roofed houses elevated a few feet above the ground, and in many ways are still far from being civilized, those who migrated to Oklahoma have lost practically all of their Indian ways and now are one of the "Five Civilized Tribes."

XIX

THE OSAGE, QUAPAW, PAWNEE, CADDO, UTE, AND PAIUTE

On the farther side of the Mississippi were a number of tribes of Indians. Many of these were Indians whose original homes had been in the Middle West, but who had spread westward across the Father of Waters, while others had dwelt west of the river from time immemorial. Among these were the Osages and the Pawnees.

The Osages were the most important of the southern Siouan tribes, but unlike their Sioux relatives farther north and west they were only seminomads; they had permanent villages, and cultivated some crops. Friendly toward the whites, they were usually at war with other tribes, including the Pawnees who were their next-door neighbors. In 1808 they ceded their lands, including most of Arkansas and Missouri, to the United States, but retained Oklahoma. The boundaries of the latter land were established in 1870, and in 1906 their present reservation contained 1,470,000 acres. With the discovery of vast deposits of oil on their lands the Osages became the richest Indians in the United States, and, in proportion to their numbers, the wealthiest group of persons in the world. During World War I, an Army officer who commanded a company of Osage Indians was prone to boast that his soldiers were the richest in the entire Allied forces, for "every one was a millionaire."

Near relatives of the Osages, and also of Siouan stock, were the Quapaws, who originally inhabited the area on the western banks of the Arkansas River in what now is Arkansas. They were a sedentary, agricultural tribe with large well-tilled fields, and lived in villages surrounded by stockades, with towers for the defenders, the whole surrounded by a moat. They also built mounds of a peculiar type in which they buried their dead. Unlike the Osages and most of the other Siouan tribes, the Quapaws were not pugnacious but were a quiet, peaceful lot, gay, fun-loving, honest, and friendly with most of the other tribes as well as with the whites. With the increase of white settlers in their area the Quapaws migrated, some going to Texas, others to Louisiana, and in 1877 they were placed on a reservation in Oklahoma, where they joined the Osages. At the present time they number between four and five thousand, although many of them are of mixed tribal blood, having intermarried with the Osages, Caddos, and other tribes.

Of Caddoan stock and totally different from the Osages were the Pawnees, a confederation of four tribes known as the Skidi, Pitahauerat, Chauti, and Kitkehahki. Their popular name of Pawnee was a corruption of *Peeriki,* meaning a horn, owing to their custom of wearing a scalp-lock of hair stiffened with grease standing upright over the head. Unlike the Osages, who were tall and splendidly proportioned, often standing well over six feet, the Pawnees were inclined to be rather stocky. Unlike the other plains tribes, they had permanent villages of log huts, and cultivated many crops, although typically horse Indians who hunted the buffalos. Although brave and terrific fighters when occasion arose, they were famed mainly for their boldness, skill, and mania for stealing horses, even raiding as far south as New Mexico for that purpose, and were known to the Sioux as the "Horse Stealers."

Always friendly toward the whites, they never molested them except in self-defense, although at times they even stole horses from Army posts under the very noses of the guards. Many members of the tribe were employed as scouts for the Army, and were considered the very best in the service. A highly intelligent tribe, the Pawnees were very quick to learn anything new, as is well illustrated by an anecdote in a book telling of experiences with Indians that was published in 1844:

> On the 4th of July, the usual commemoration took place, of firing twenty-four guns; after which ceremonies we adjourned to an excellent dinner when a hundred and fifty Pawnees arrived,

> under guidance of Mr. Dougherty, the principal Indian Agent. Upon being invited by the officers, fourteen of their chief warriors joined us in the mess-room. They entered with ease and dignity, shook hands with us all and sat down comfortably to cigars and madeira. I was astonished at the tact and self-possession of these Indians who had never been among white men before, nor had they ever seen a fork, table or chair in their lives; yet without asking questions, or appearing to observe what was passing, they caught the idea with intuitive readiness, and during the whole dinner were not guilty of a single absurdity or breach of decorum.

Belonging to the same racial stock as the Pawnees, and speaking an almost identical language, were the Caddos. Originally inhabiting the area of the Red River in Louisiana, they spread north and west. A peaceful, agricultural tribe, they were friendly to the whites and were our allies during our warfare with the Comanches. Despite this, their lands were seized and a wholesale massacre of the tribe was planned by the whites. Fortunately the plot was discovered in time, and the Caddos were safely transferred to Oklahoma. During the Civil War the tribe was loyal to the Union, thus incurring the enmity of the Confederates, who were in the majority in the Caddo country.

Near relatives of the Caddos and also related to the Pawnees were the Wichitas, a confederacy or group of tribes among which were the true Wichitas, the Tayovaya or Tawehathe Waco, Yacani, Ajwesh, Aisidahetsh, Kishkat, and Korishkitsu. All of them have disappeared with the exception of the true Wichitas, the Wacos, and Tawakonis. Originally ranging through Kansas and Arkansas to the Brazos River in Texas, those remaining are now mainly in Caddo County, Oklahoma. To the Sioux they were known as the Black Pawnees, the early French called them the Tattooed Pawnees, and to the Kiowas and Comanches they were known as the Tattooed Faces because of their elaborate tattooing that often covered them from head to foot. Originally friendly toward the whites, they were allies of the French against the Spanish. Having been greatly reduced in numbers by smallpox, they allied themselves with the Wacos and Tawakonis. In 1833 they made a peace treaty with the United States in which they agreed to dwell peacefully with the Osages and the whites, and settled down north of Lawton, Oklahoma. The Texans were so hostile to the tribe that the government removed the Wichitas to the Washita River district in Oklahoma. Like the Caddos, they were our allies against the Comanches. In 1902 they were given allotments of land in severalty, and became citizens and prosperous farmers.

Naturally a sedentary tribe with small areas of cultivated crops, they lived in permanent villages consisting of conical houses made of poles covered with grass thatch, but when traveling or hunting or at war they used the typical skin tipis.

Farther west, originally occupying central and western Colorado, Utah, and Nevada, as well as portions of California, and northern New Mexico, were the Utes, a tribe of Shoshonean stock. Although naturally warlike they never were at war with our government, although at times they raided, burned, and killed mainly as reprisals for hostile acts by white men. Although on more than one occasion many of the Utes were anxious to wage war on their white neighbors, they were largely restrained by Chief Ouray, who was always an advocate of peace and a friend of the whites. However, they were inveterate raiders of other tribes, mainly to seize women and children to be ransomed or held as slaves. During our war with the Navajos a number of Utes were employed as irregular troopers by the Army. In 1861 a treaty was signed giving them the Uinta Valley, where, like others of the tribe elsewhere, they took lands in severalty, became citizens of the state, and settled down as farmers and ranchers.

This led to a rather amusing situation when in 1906 four hundred of the tribe, afflicted with the wanderlust and anxious to see more of the country, left their lands and trekked northward. Although perfectly peaceful, they created a near panic among the whites, who demanded that the Indians should be forced back to their lands and reservations. Then a problem arose. Although the Utes were citizens of the state, yet they also were "wards" of the government, and the civil authorities questioned their legal right to take any action in the matter. Moreover, there was no law that forbade a citizen to leave home and go where he pleased, so they got in touch with the federal authorities, who, after due consideration, replied that as the Utes were citizens of the state and were not on government reservations, it was up to the state officials to take such steps as were necessary. In their turn, the civic officials informed the federal authorities that as the Utes had crossed from one state into another they became a government problem. Meanwhile, as state and federal bigwigs passed the buck back and forth, the Utes were thoroughly enjoying themselves, wandering about sightseeing and laughing at the fears of the white skins and the lurid headlines in the "yellow journals" stating that there was another Indian uprising. Finally, when the federal government agreed to take over and sent word to the nearest Army post to corral the Indians and escort them to their homes, the Utes had tired of wandering, and, having abandoned their original plan of visiting their Shoshone relatives in Wyoming, had headed back to their homes and farms. (Today, with the discovery of oil on Ute lands in Nevada, the tribe bids fair to become wealthy.)

Related to the Utes are several tribes known as the Paiutes, although the name, meaning Water Utes, is that of the Corn Creek tribe of Utah. They are also called Digger Indians, a term used to designate any tribe that dug roots for food. Originally the Paiutes occupied parts of Utah, Idaho, Arizona, Nevada, California, and Oregon. As a rule they were friendly and peaceful, but in the 'sixties they were attacked by whites and several Indians were killed. In reprisal, the Paiutes raided and killed for a time, but there was no real warfare and the troubles were amicably settled. Since they are contemptuously referred to as Digger Injuns, one might assume that they are a poor, primitive lot with no culture. On the contrary, they have long been famed for their splendid buckskin and magnificent beadwork that often completely covered their garments and even the buckskin coverings of their horses. They also made very fine baskets and many other artifacts. They are an extremely industrious lot, with great mechanical ability, and are remarkably free from all vices. They are noted as top cowhands, and are a necessity to the ranchers and farmers, but despite their prosperity and civilization many prefer their wickiups to houses.

XX

I JOINED THE SIOUX

TO BOYS OF TODAY our Indian wars are almost legendary, but when I was a boy they were current events. The Apaches under Geronimo and Cochise were raiding and fighting in the southwest, and I vividly recall the excitement aroused when word of the Battle of the Little Big Horn was received.

It was only a few years after the so-called Custer Massacre that I met my first Sioux. This was the famous Oglala chief, Red Cloud, who had taken a prominent part in the epochal battle. He had come east to see the Great White Father in Washington, and came to New Haven to visit some of the professors whom he had known when they were on a scientific expedition to the Dakotas.

Much to my disappointment the tall, heavily built, broad-faced war-chief was not arrayed in beaded buckskin, paint, and feathers, but wore a dark blue suit of clothes and a black felt, broad-brimmed hat. But he did wear moccasins, and his hair fell in two heavy braids to his waist. As he neither spoke nor understood English worth mentioning, he was accompanied by an interpreter, a young Sioux who was named Many Bears and spoke English fluently, and from him I learned a great deal about his people.

Red Cloud himself was a very taciturn and dignified Indian who never showed any surprise at anything he saw. But there was one thing that interested him greatly. This was a hairdressing establishment, and he gazed fascinated at the ladies' switches, the transformations, and the toupees displayed in the window. Here, he thought, was the pale faces' display of scalps, but he must have wondered why the hair was obviously that of white persons instead of Indians. Although Many Bears explained that the objects on display were not scalps but were used by the whites to improve upon nature, Red Cloud purchased several dozens of the "scalps." Sensing a good story, Many Bears told the reporters and others that the chief intended to exhibit them to his tribe as scalps he had taken, and the yarn was accepted as truth. As a matter of fact no Indian could have been hoodwinked by them, and Red Cloud intended them only to be used as ornaments and trimmings to garments and weapons in place of real scalps. Until quite recently—perhaps even today—there are Sioux garments and weapons trimmed with blond, brown, titian, gray, and black hair still attached to the woven foundations.

It was a number of years after Red Cloud's visit that Colonel Cody and Dr. William Carver toured the east with their Wild West Show. Dr. Carver had been taken prisoner by the Oglala Sioux when a small child, and had been reared by the Indians like one of their own children. With the signing of the final peace treaty he had been taken over by an Army doctor. As William Carver (his benefactor's name) he had been educated, and had become a dentist and married a New Haven woman. Their home was only a block from our house, and their son Billy and I were great pals. His father would entertain us by the hour with true tales of his life and experiences among the Sioux. He was a most picturesque and striking figure, over six feet tall and heavily built, with yellow hair falling to his shoulders and with a sweeping blond mustache. He invariably wore a broad-brimmed, low-crowned sombrero and a heavily beaded buckskin vest, and whenever the show was in town or near by he donned a costume of fringed buckskin. He always rode a handsome bay-and-white pinto pony with ornate silver-mounted, hand-carved saddle and jaguar-skin saddlebag covers, and dashed at full gallop through the city streets between his home and his business. He was probably the most expert rifle shot who ever lived, many of his feats of marksmanship being really phenomenal, and it was his skill as a marksman that finally aroused so much jealousy on the part of Colonel Cody that the two broke off their partnership in the show.

However, long before they separated, Billy and I had spent a lot of time with the Indians, scouts, cowboys, and other members of the "Wild West," for of course we had free access to the show whenever it came to town. At that time many famous Indian chiefs were with the show, among them Shot in the Eye, Gray Wolf, Wounded Knee, Gall, Yellow Elk, Striking Bear, Tall Man, Iron Tail, Lame Man, and others, all wearing their tribal costumes and living with their families in their tipis pitched in a field on the outskirts of the city. Billy and I, however, were not so much interested in the grim-visaged warriors as in the Indian boys of our own age. Few of them spoke any English, and we of course did not speak Sioux, although we had learned a few words and common sentences from Bill's father. But lack of a common language did not hinder our having a grand time, and the Indian boys very quickly acquired a smattering of English, while we learned enough Sioux to get along. We found them a most likable, good-natured, jolly lot, full of fun and fond of games. We taught them how to play "one old cat," hopscotch, marbles, snap-the-whip, prisoner's base, and other games, and they in turn taught us the hoop-and-spear game, archery, Indian softball with racquets in place of bats, whip-top spinning, and other games. Obviously both the boys and their elders must have taken quite a liking to us, for we were welcomed in their tipis and were officially adopted as members of the Oglala Sioux. In fact, I was even given the name of Wambdi or The Eagle, because I had a photograph of Old Abe, the famous bald-eagle mascot of our troops during the Civil War, and who had been exhibited at the Centennial Exhibition where I had obtained the photograph. Little did I dream at that time that, not so many years later, I would take part in the show myself and would join the Sioux.

My father was a professor at Yale University, and among his students was an Oglala Sioux youth. He was a plump, round-faced Indian with an ochreous skin and a perpetual grin. His English name was John Rogers, but he was always known by his nickname of Johnny Punkin Face. Although ordinarily a thoroughly civilized Indian wearing conventional clothes, yet whenever Buffalo Bill's Wild West came to town Johnny would temporarily go native, and for the duration of the show would don buckskin, paint, and feathers, and join his fellow tribesmen.

I had told him about my boyhood association with the Indians, and he insisted that when the show again came to town I should go with him and "play Indian." Naturally I accepted his invitation, and had a most enjoyable time. Johnny introduced me to his Sioux friends and relatives, among them an enormously fat, jolly-looking squaw who constantly was surrounded by a bevy of children ranging from tiny papooses strapped to cradle-boards to boys and girls six or eight years old. They were not all hers by any means, but she loved children and attracted them like a magnet, and had been appropriately named Too Many Toes.

Also I was delighted to find among the Indians one of my old boyhood friends, a young Sioux named White Eagle who had been adopted by Buffalo Bill and whose English name was George Cody. He was an exceedingly smart and intelligent youth, spoke fourteen Indian dialects in addition to English, Spanish, French, and some German, and was the official interpreter. He was as pleased as I at renewing our old friendship, and we soon became such pals that Johnny and the other Indians called us the Eagle Twins. He and Johnny managed to find a complete Sioux costume that was a good fit, and with Annie Oakley helping with my make-up and Johnny Baker offering advice, I became transformed into a very realistic-looking Sioux. In fact, I was such a genuine-appearing brave that I completely fooled the scouts, cowboys, and others, and passed unnoticed among the Indians, who, after White Eagle had told them of our boyhood associations, accepted me as one of the tribe. For several years, until the Wild West went on its European tour, I temporarily became a Sioux whenever the show came to town. When it finally went to Europe, White Eagle passed out of my life, so I thought —and then, nearly forty years later, I experienced one of those amazing coincidences that occur in real life but would be ridiculed in fiction.

We were driving north from Florida and took a route we never had followed on previous trips. Passing through a small town in North Carolina we noticed a house decorated with paintings of Indians and western scenes, and with a sign INDIAN MUSEUM over the door. The place contained a fairly good collection of Indian artifacts, relics, and specimens of handicraft, and numerous framed newspaper clippings and pictures of Buffalo Bill Cody and his famous show.

"Who owns this?" I asked the white woman in charge.

"White Eagle," she replied.

"Do you mean White Eagle the Sioux who was with Buffalo Bill?" I exclaimed. "Where is he?"

"He has the filling station and barbecue stand down the street," she told me.

Scarcely able to believe that by such a remarkable coincidence I had run across my old friend of the Wild West Show days, I entered the little lunchroom. Never would I have recognized the tall, gray-haired Indian wearing glasses and a chef's hat, who was serving some customers. But he recognized me instantly, even greeting me by my Sioux name Wambdi, although since we had last met I had been renamed Tchanku-Tanka or Big (Long) Road because of my many travels among the Indians.

He was fully as surprised and delighted to see me as I was to run across him, and we had a wonderful time talking over the old days. In her will Annie Oakley had left him several thousand dollars, and he had also inherited Johnny Baker's pearl-handled revolvers. After Cody's death he had toured most of the southern states with a small show of his own until, while exhibiting in Ashboro at the county fair, he had met and married a white woman and had settled down. With his museum, his barbecue stand, and his filling station he was doing well, and kept open house for any and all Indians who happened to pass that way.

"You'd have met another of your old-time friends if you'd been a day earlier," he told me. "Walks With the Wind, the Winnebago, was here for a few days."

Later on, Walks With the Wind, who heard of my visit, sent me, in White Eagle's care, a beautiful hatband of beadwork on horsehair bearing my Sioux name sign and symbols reading: "Tchanku-Tanka will always be welcome within the tipis of the four tribes of the Sioux during peace or war."

If ever there was a "live wire," White Eagle was one. Never have I known a more active man. Although nearly seventy, he was constantly on the go, moving as if actuated by steel springs and with amazing speed, and he talked as rapidly as he moved. He had a monomania for neatness and order. His home was spotless, and so was the tiny farm and its denizens. His pigs were scrubbed daily until they were as pink as babies, and their pen was deep in wood-shavings fresh each day. It was the same with his cow and other livestock, and the growing crops were in beds and rows as geometrically perfect as if laid out by a surveyor's transit. Aside from his museum he had two hobbies, woodworking and animal freaks.

There were jars of alcohol containing two-headed pigs, a three-eyed calf, five- and six-legged cats and dogs, a double-headed turtle, and other monstrosities, and his poultry yard was an ornithological nightmare. He had started out with such bizarre varieties as frizzled fowl, silkies, almost legless Japanese bantams, and Houdins. Then, somewhere, he had obtained a tailless rooster, a four-legged hen, and a wingless bantam, and had added these to his flock. The result was most amazing. There were fowl half-frizzled and half silky, some wingless, others tailless, a rooster happily scratching about the pen with three legs instead of two; squat bantams with extra long, naked necks and heads, and every imaginable combination of all, with scarcely a dozen normal birds in the lot.

Like all Indians, he was very fond of animals and pets of all kinds, cardinals, mockingbirds, and jays would eat from his hand or perch on his shoulder. He had pet snakes, a tame mountain goat, a giant land tortoise, a tame talking crow, and several dogs, but he drew the line at cats. In fact, I do not recall ever having known or seen an Indian who did not detest the felines.

I visited White Eagle a number of times as we motored north or south between Springfield and Florida, but he eventually moved farther north into North Carolina and I settled down in Florida. Although we correspond, I have not seen White Eagle for several years.

Big Elk, another Oglala Sioux, came of distinguished Indian lineage, for one of his grandfathers was Red Cloud and the other was Crazy Horse. His wife was a Passamaquoddy named Pretty Woman who had won a number of prizes in beauty shows. I met him at a sportsman's show in Springfield, Massachusetts, where they had a booth and tipi and sold Indian curios and autographed photographs. They also appeared upon the stage and sang Indian songs accompanied by tom-tom and rattles.

He was broad-faced, heavily built man, easy-going, good-natured, and inordinately lazy, a typical show Indian, yet his brother was a well-known and distinguished surgeon. Both boys had had the same opportunities and education. Sponsored by a wealthy Englishman who took a fancy to them while visiting Standing Rock Reservation, they had been graduated from Staunton Military Academy, gone to Carlisle and the University of Oklahoma, and had entered Johns Hopkins Medical School. But the education was entirely wasted on Big Elk—which goes to prove that Indians, even if brothers, vary as much as white men.

An excellent musician and fine trombonist, Big Elk organized an all-Indian band and toured the country for a time, then for a while he was with the Ringling Brothers circus. Noted as the most expert maker of war bonnets among the Sioux, he made all of the headdresses used in Eddie Cantor's *Whoopee,* and for a space he settled down and had a job in the post office at Boston. But once a show Indian always a show Indian, and, moreover, he had been a very heavy drinker—although when I met him he had joined the Peyote Ceremonial cult and in accordance with the rules had become a strict teetotaler. One of his greatest delights was to get another Indian drunk, then, when the fellow was suffering from a bad hangover, lecture him on the evils of liquor and try to induce him to become a fellow member of the cult (which, as described earlier, is a strange mixture of Christianity and Indian religion).

He was a likable fellow despite his shortcomings, and, despite his education and the fact that the greater part of his life had been spent among white people, he was thoroughly Indian. He was a member of the Bear Clan medicine cult, he was steeped in Sioux rituals, legends, and folklore; he was a highly skilled craftsman when it came to beadwork, feather headdresses, or other Indian handicraft and arts, and his family line and famous ancestry gave him quite a standing in his tribe. However, he was a confirmed believer in the Indian law of reciprocal hospitality.

Uninvited, he and his wife came bag and baggage to our apartment. It never occurred to him that it might inconvenience us and add greatly to our living expenses, for we would have been quite welcome to have lived in *his* house on the reservation for as long as we pleased. In true Indian fashion and in accordance with Indian custom he and Pretty Woman helped themselves to almost anything that took their fancy, and would give us some present in return. The comparative value of the gifts meant nothing, but I must admit that, as a rule, the many Indian objects they gave us more than equaled what they had acquired. But when it came to food it was a very different matter, for never have I known a human being who could equal Big Elk when it came to eating. Two loaves of bread and from three to five pounds of meat, in addition to vegetables and other edibles, were just an ordinary meal to him. Then there were the lobsters. He had expressed the greatest disgust for the "red bugs" he had seen in the fish market, despite the fact that he was fond of grasshopper bread. Then one day we had lobsters, for Pretty Woman, being from Maine, was fond of the crustaceans. For a space Big Elk watched her eating. At last he tentatively helped himself to a claw and tasted it. A broad grin spread over his face. The "bugs" were mighty good, and in short order his wife's plate held only empty shells and Big Elk was looking for more. From then on he always wanted lobster, but I drew the line. I could visualize him getting away with a couple of dozen at a sitting, with lobsters at a dollar a pound, so as far as his edible "bugs" were concerned there was nothing doing.

Eventually Big Elk and Pretty Woman went on their way, leaving me with a fine collection of Sioux handiwork and weapons. There was a magnificent horseback war bonnet with double tails, an initiation bonnet with beaded band telling in Sioux picture-writing of my membership in the tribe and my name; a Bear Clan medicine man's bonnet with buffalo horns and the painted story of the clan; beaded gauntlets, moccasins, pistol holster, knife sheath, and other objects; stone-headed "skull crackers" trimmed with scalp locks; a minkskin-wrapped coup stick with four coup feathers used by Crazy Horse; a war club with blades made of sabers taken at the Battle of the Little Big Horn; a fine drum; rattles of many kinds, and other things—not to mention a notebook full of Sioux folklore, stories, songs, and traditions. Taken all in all, our Indian guests had more than repaid their debt.

XXI

NOBLEMEN OF THE PLAINS

IN THE MINDS of most persons the name Sioux is synonymous with Indians of the great plains. Rarely is there a "Western" that does not feature the Sioux, yet nearly every instance displays a dearth of knowledge of these Indians.

To begin with, there is not, nor ever was, any one tribe properly named Sioux, despite the fact that many plains Indians use the name when referring to themselves. However, the word is a French term meaning "a tribe of enemies," and originally was applied to many tribes, although most frequently to those of the confederation known as the Dakotas, Lakotas, or Nakotas, the variation in the name depending upon which of the four tribal dialects is used, but all meaning "allies." Although all of the tribes forming the confederation readily converse, yet the dialects differ considerably. Thus, the Tetons never pronounce "d" or "n," but use the sound of "l" instead of "d." For *dina* of the Oglalas, the Tetons say *lila.* Others pronounce the same word *nina,* and *wambdi* or eagle becomes *wambli.* For *mita kola* (my friend) of the Oglalas, other tribes say *mita koda* or *nila koda.* The Dakota confederation or league is made up of the Oglala, Teton, Brûlé, Wahpeton, Yankton, Cuthead, Hunkpapa, Minneconjou, and Oohenonpa tribes, while usually included as "Sioux" are the Sans Arcs and Assiniboin tribes, who are of Siouan stock but are not included among the true Dakotas.

The names of some of these tribes have most interesting origins, although the original meanings of the names of others have been lost. During an intertribal quarrel when a Yankton band separated from the tribe, the rebel leader was wounded in the head, and henceforth the band were known as "Cutheads" and are now a subtribe. In their language the word "Oglala" means "a thrower of dirt," which in the sign language is denoted by flicking one's fingers toward another person, a gesture denoting the utmost contempt. At the time when the Oglala and Brûlé tribes separated, the leader of the former showed his contempt of the Brûlé by the dirt-throwing sign. The Minni-akiya-oju, known to us as the Minneconjou, received their name meaning "Planting near the water" because they cultivated a few crops in the bottom lands of streams. The "People of the leaf camp," or Wahpeton, were so called on account of their habit of camping in the shade of trees rather than in the open, while the Hunkpapa had the recognized privilege of putting their tipis at the entrance to a village, the name meaning "At the border."

Although most persons think that the so-called Sioux were confined to the far western plains, there were southern Sioux, such tribes as the Osage, Oto, Iowa, Ponca, Omaha, Quapaw, Kansas, Missouri, and Winnebago. Although they all are of Siouan stock and speak dialects of the Sioux language, yet they differ greatly from the plains Dakotas. Instead of being nomadic they were sedentary agricultural Indians with permanent villages, but they were as much horse Indians as their more westerly relatives, and hunted the buffalo. In many ways they formed a connecting link between the nomadic tribes of the far west and the woodland Indians of the eastern states. While their permanent homes were rectangular sod houses or were built of poles and mats, they used the plains type of tipi for temporary camps, while many of their artifacts, weapons, and customs were more like those of the Algonquin tribes than those of their Dakota cousins. The majority of these tribes occupied the Mississippi valley on both sides of the river, while the Winnebagos dwelt in the vicinity of the Great Lakes. Most of them were hostile to the Dakotas and were almost constantly at war with them.

Probably no other group—with the possible exception of the Apaches—has ever been so widely publicized or so falsely represented as the so-called Sioux. Invariably they are pictured as savage, warlike, hostile, cruel, and fiendish savages who inflicted diabolical tortures upon their captives and killed for the sheer blood lust. In reality, their greatest desire was to maintain peace. To live and let live, and to be on friendly terms with their neighbors, was their greatest aim in life, and almost from infancy this attitude was instilled in the boys.

No one, either Indian or white man, ever questioned the bravery or the fighting abilities of the Sioux. Never were they known to war with another tribe for mere conquest or tribal enmity, but when it came to a question of losing homes, lands, or freedom, or when attacked by other Indians or white men, they fought with a bravery and ferocity never excelled by any other tribe. Magnificent horsemen, next to the Comanches their mounted warriors were considered by our Army officers as the finest, most efficient of Indian cavalry, and time after time they outfought, outgeneraled, and outmaneuvered our veteran troopers and our most outstanding generals. They were probably the most independent, most freedom-loving, and bravest of all our Indians, and were referred to by General Nelson Miles as "noblemen of the plains."

Even their worst enemies, whether white men or other Indians, respected and admired the Dakotas for their honesty, their truthfulness, and their fairness. Never were they known to be the first to break or violate a treaty or to break a promise, and instead of torturing their captives they treated them almost like guests. Even members of the Crow and Pawnee tribes, their greatest enemies, when taken prisoners were well treated. Spotted Calf, a Sioux friend of mine, told me of a number of Pawnee captives taken in battle and brought to his father's village. They were treated like friends rather than foes, were well fed and housed, and in the end were sent back to their tribe unharmed. Among these prisoners was a boy about the age of Spotted Calf, and the two became fast friends and played together with the other Sioux boys. When the adult prisoners were to be returned to their tribe, the boy refused to go and remained with the Sioux, eventually being adopted into the tribe. Many white prisoners captured by the Sioux during their long warfare with our government refused to rejoin their fellows when peace was made and they were at liberty to leave, but remained with the Indians for life.

In their home life the Dakotas set an example we might do well to emulate. The children from their earliest infancy were given the utmost care and every attention, for, like most Indians, the Sioux were passionately fond of children. But they were never spoiled. They were taught to respect their elders, to obey without question, to be honest and truthful, and to regard as almost sacred the property of another. Although a tipi might house several family groups and there were no partitions separating the areas allotted to the several occupants, yet never would a child of one family overstep the invisible boundary of another or touch any object that did not belong to him or to her. In order that the parents should have enough time to train their children properly, it was an unwritten but strictly obeyed law that at least six years must elapse between the births of children to one mother. Both the fathers and mothers attended to rearing their offspring, and although no Sioux child was ever known to say "I won't" or to refuse to obey an order they were never whipped, struck, or subjected to corporal punishment. Merely to be chided and disgraced was sufficient punishment to them. They were always taught that to give is one of the greatest of virtues, and that the highest reward in life is achievement in hunting, warfare, peace, religion, or wisdom.

Like many Indians, the Dakotas believed that all living creatures possessed souls or spirits and were watched over by Wakan Tanka, the "Great-Grandfather" or "Great One in the Sky," and that to destroy life without cause or necessity was a sin.

Among the Sioux, before they acquired the vices of the white men, cleanliness was most rigidly enforced. The tipis were the property of the women, and it was a serious breach of etiquette, and showed lack of respect for the housewife, to leave anything in disorder or scattered about. Indians had a mania for order, which was essential in the limited space of the tipi, and everything was in its place, while the earth forming the floor of the tipi was swept daily. In their personal habits also the Indians were scrupulously clean. They devoted a great deal of time to bathing and swimming in the streams, and used soap made from the roots of the Yucca. In addition they had steam baths similar to our own Turkish baths, and custom decreed that before any food was eaten or a drink of water swallowed, all men, women, and children must rinse the mouth with water and wash face, neck, and hands. As for the "stench" of the Indians so often mentioned in western tales, the only noticeable odors within a tipi were the pungent smell of a buffalo chips fire, the smoky scent of tanned hides and, if the man had been painting body and face in preparation for warfare or ceremonials, the smell of bear or buffalo tallow that might be rancid.

Another term we often hear is "Indian giver," used to denote some one who gives a present and later wants it returned. But that is far from being the way of the true Indian giver, for gifts were an important part of every ceremonial or important event. When a child was born, custom decreed that the father must give away a pony. When the child reached the age of nine months and the ear-piercing ceremony took place, the father presented the ear-piercer with two ponies. When a boy reached the age of nine, all his garments were destroyed and he was given elaborate new ones. Also, at this time a "confirmation badge," consisting of a tuft of eagle's feathers, was attached to the hair on the left side of the head. This was a highly important ceremony, and in connection with it the child's godfather was given all of the father's ponies with the exception of a few that were essential to his own needs. Quite frequently a man would give away everything he owned, thus acquiring great merit, and knowing the other members of the tribe would in their turn provide food, shelter and all other necessities. Ordinarily when an Indian gives a present to some friend, he expects a gift in return—although the relative values do not matter—and if an Indian receives a present he feels in honor bound to return the favor with a gift.

The Dakotas, as well as other plains tribes, did not abuse and maltreat their horses, as is often stated. The boys were taught that as the lives of the Indians depended upon their mounts, the ponies must be cared for and kept in the best of condition. A warrior returning from battle or a hunter in from a hunt always watered and fed his mount before he rested or dined himself. To be sure, the Indians often rode their horses to death, but this happened only when it was a question of the pony's life or his own, and many white men did the same. A great deal of time was devoted to washing, currying, and cleaning the horses, and when in rough or rocky country their feet were covered with thick buffalo-hide coverings for protection. It has been claimed by some that this was only to prevent wearing away the ponies' feet and to thus enable the Indians to get the last ounce of service from their mounts. Whatever the basic purpose, the result was the same. When a white man shoes his horse with steel, it is just as much to insure longer and better service as to benefit the animal.

Another fallacy regarding the Sioux is the prevalent idea that the youths were forced to undergo tortures as tests of courage before they were considered "braves." The only tests were those of marksmanship, skill with various weapons, bareback riding, obedience, and self-control. There is nothing the Indian dreads more than failure or ridicule, and if derided he "loses face."

In their social life the Dakotas were to a certain extent socialistic but in no way communistic, for every family and member of the tribe owned personal property, and there was neither rule nor custom to prevent a man from becoming rich in ponies, clothing, blankets, robes, weapons—or wives. On the other hand, no member of the tribe hesitated to sacrifice and divide what he owned for the mutual benefit of his tribe. Although they were ruled by a chief, the latter rarely made an important decision until it had been approved by the council, and in many cases the head medicine man had even greater influence than the chief himself, while in some instances the chief might also be a medicine man. Although the word of a chief and his council was law, he was always willing to listen to the opinions of his warriors, and quite often some important decision was reached by vote. However, when a definite course had been decided upon, the chief was in supreme command. Because of the widespread publicity given the Sioux, owing to their long war with the United States, the names of many of their famous chiefs are familiar to nearly everyone, and such names as Spotted Tail, Crazy Horse, Rain-in-the-Face, Red Cloud, and Sitting Bull have become traditional. Yet Sitting Bull was a Hunkpapa medicine man and not a chief; he has been confused with the Oglala chief of the same name who was never hostile and died several months before the famous Custer battle. He was not, however, the only Sioux chief who desired peace instead of war. Red Cloud, Spotted Tail, and others all strove to find some means of averting war that would be mutually satisfactory to both sides, but without success, and Spotted Tail sacrificed his life by his efforts: he was shot by Crow Dog, a militant leader of the "all for war" faction. For that matter, the entire Dakota or so-called Sioux nation did not join in the war. The Wahpeton, Oohenonpe, Yankton, and some other tribes took no part in the hostilities, and remained neutral.

The Sioux War itself, costing the United States hundreds of lives, immense losses in property, and vast sums of money, was entirely the fault of our own government, which broke the promise made in its treaty with the Dakotas that "as long as the grass shall grow and the waters flow" the land should belong to the Indians. In addition, our government promised the Sioux that the Black Hills should belong to the Dakotas and no white should be allowed to cross the Indians' lands, yet with the discovery of gold in the mountains the government sent engineers and surveyors to build a road through the Indians' land to the Black Hills.

Quite naturally, the Sioux protested. In every possible way they tried to induce the government to abide by the treaties and to avoid hostilities, but without success, and only as a last resort turned to war. To be sure, they lost—as the Indians always did in the end—but they gave the Army a good run for its money, won lasting fame, and maintained their independence.

Today the Dakotas live on various reservations or on their own lands, where most of them are farmers and ranchers. Many, however, are cowhands, mechanics, or follow other pursuits, and numbers of the tribe live unnoticed in our great eastern cities. On the plains, frame houses have taken the place of conical tipis, the Sioux wear conventional garments, they have their own papers printed in the Sioux language, and are thoroughly civilized. Yet, like the other outstanding Indian tribes discussed earlier, the majority still own the costumes and feather headdresses of their tribe and retain many of their old customs, legends, dances, and ceremonials.

XXII

THE INDOMITABLE CHEYENNES

In all the history of our dealings with the Indians there is no blacker, more shameful page than our treatment of the Cheyennes. It is bad enough to betray, double-cross, and shoot one's foes in the back, but to do so to one's friends is an unpardonable crime. Yet our government did all this and more to the friendly Cheyennes, with the result that we were plunged into a bloody war that culminated in the Battle of the Little Big Horn and the annihilation of Custer and his entire command—for it was the Cheyennes rather than the Sioux who turned the tables. Instead of being massacred without mercy, as Custer had planned, the Indians utterly destroyed the troops. Yet neither the Cheyennes nor the Sioux, encamped by the Little Big Horn, had any hostile intentions. They had not prepared a "trap" for Custer, as he assumed, and did not even know that he and his men were in the vicinity. Moreover, not until the battle was over did they realize whom they were fighting.

When Custer dismounted his men in preparation for battle, his sole opponents were three Cheyennes who were fishing in the river, while the horsemen who had been seen near Crow Creek were not a war party but that of Little Wolf, the Cheyenne chief, who, with a number of women and old men, was on his way to visit the Sioux camp.

One of the greatest, bravest, proudest and at the same time peace-loving of all our tribes, the Cheyennes had always been friendly with the white men. But finally, after fifty years of treachery, mistreatment, and broken vows and treaties on the part of our government, they took to the warpath, and, joining the Dakotas, carried on a war that lasted for twenty-five years and cost countless lives—the greatest Indian war our country has ever fought.

The Cheyennes were of totally different racial stock from their Sioux allies, for they were of Algonquin ancestry, related to the prairie tribes of the Middle West. They came originally from the area around Lake Superior, where they cultivated their farms and lived in permanent villages of earth and sod lodges. For some unknown reason, during the early part of the nineteenth century they migrated westward. Their own name for the tribe was Tisi-tsi-ista or "The Real People," but when they eventually came in contact with the Dakotas the Sioux referred to them as Sha-Hi-Ena, or "Those Who Talk Red," a term they applied to anyone whom they could not understand. This term was corrupted by the whites to Cheyenne, by which name they have been known ever since. In fact, they practically forgot their original tribal name and referred to themselves, as they do today, as Cheyennes. Moreover, finding themselves among Indians of the Siouan group, they were obliged to learn and use a new tongue, although still retaining many of their own words, so that their dialect, in many ways similar to that of the Sioux tribes, is quite distinct, although the Cheyennes and the Dakotas have no difficulty in conversing. They changed their name, their language, their manner of living, to suit conditions and environment, adopting the conical tipi, becoming horse Indians, hunting the buffalo and other game instead of cultivating crops. Yet they did not alter their natures, their inherently peaceful disposition, and their desire to remain on friendly terms with their fellow men, including the whites.

Before 1831 and until 1880, the Cheyennes were affiliated with the Suhtai tribe, who spoke a variation of their original language. Living and traveling together and intermarrying, they eventually became one tribe, with no traces remaining of the Suhtai customs or dialect. Later on, the Masikota Sioux joined the Cheyennes, and still later they were joined by the peaceful Arapaho, with whom they formed a more or less unified confederation. Still later the tribe divided into two main groups, the Northern and the Southern Cheyennes, the former living about the headwaters of the North Platte and Yellowstone

Rivers, while the Southern group occupied the valley of the Arkansas. Here they were almost constantly at war with the Kiowas, Comanches, and Kiowa-Apaches until 1840, when an intertribal council arranged peace and the Cheyennes became allies of their former enemies. Although together with their allies the Southern Cheyennes raided other tribes as far south as Mexico, they did not molest the white settlers. Even among the other tribes the Cheyennes were noted for their fighting ability when necessity arose, their bravery, their pride, their horsemanship, and their kindly treatment of prisoners. At one time captives belonging to twenty-eight different tribes were among them, and the majority of these became members of the Cheyenne. In addition, many whites joined the tribe and married the Cheyenne women. The moral code of the tribe was very strict, and they had a very high esteem for women.

The political organization of the Cheyennes was unusual. There was no one head chief with dictatorial powers, the governing body consisting of a council of forty chiefs who were elected by the several bands every ten years. This council selected four elderly men or "old man chiefs" to act in an advisory capacity, while, in addition, each warrior clan or group had its own war chief as well as nine other chiefs, all of whom acted as representatives at the general council. In addition to all this, each of the warrior clans had three attendants, whose duties were to prepare the food as well as to care for the horses and act as guards when the braves fought on foot. They were not regarded as menials but as individuals of high standing, who were always consulted when important decisions were to be made. In other words, the Cheyenne form of government was a true democracy, with many of the features of the Six Nations or Iroquois of New York.

Throughout their long wanderings from their original home in Minnesota to their final home among the Black Hills of Dakota, the Cheyennes had literally to fight their way through numerous hostile tribes, most of whom possessed firearms, although the Cheyennes had only their bows and arrows and their war clubs. But in every battle they were the victors, and became famous for their magnanimous treatment of captives and their strict code of honor, for even when they were fighting the Crows, who were their worst enemies, the prisoners were well treated.

When Lewis and Clark penetrated the Cheyenne territory, they found the tribe peaceful and friendly, and later trappers and settlers had no trouble with them. Even when forts were being built and settlements established, the Cheyennes remained friendly and there was no friction. In fact, several white men married Cheyenne women. Among them was George Bent, one of the two brothers who built Fort Bent, whose wife was a daughter of Coyote Ear and who held an important place in the tribe and took part in their councils.

The first wagon train to cross Cheyenne territory passed through in 1841 without molestation, nor did the Cheyennes trouble the emigrants and settlers who followed, yet the whites included them among the "hostile tribes." When, in 1849, Forts Kearney and Laramie were established, the commandant reported that there was nothing to fear from the Cheyennes, who were all anxious to avoid any friction with the white men. Unfortunately, as it turned out, they were firm allies of the Sioux, and it was this association with a hostile tribe that got them into trouble.

It all started when a Minneconjou Sioux, having been refused passage across the river in a soldier's boat, accidentally discharged his gun. The soldier, terrified, rushed to the fort, while the Indian, frightened also, hurried to the Indians' camp. At that time there were nearly ten thousand Indians camped about the fort, which was garrisoned by about a dozen soldiers. Having heard the frightened trooper's story that he had been fired upon by the Indian, Lieutenant Fleming with five men charged into the Indians' camp. Only women and children were there, for the men were all away on a hunt. Having fired a volley which killed five of the Sioux women, the soldiers returned to the fort.

On the following day the Indian leaders visited the fort, and, assuring the commandant that it was all a mistake and they were not hostile, protested the murder of the five innocent women. However, nothing was done about the matter, and despite the fact that the incident had nothing to do with the Cheyennes, Second Lieutenant J. L. Grattan, a hot-headed Indian hater, boasted that with ten men he'd wipe out the entire Cheyenne tribe. It was then that the incident occurred that brought about the bloodiest war in the history of the west, and again it was a Minneconjou and not a Cheyenne who caused the trouble. He had found a sick, half-starved cow that had been abandoned by a wagon train, killed and skinned it, and reported what he had done to his chief. The Brûlé chief, Bear Who Scatters His Foes, at once reported the matter to the officers at the fort and offered to pay ten dollars for the old cow. However, the former owner demanded twenty-five dollars, and the matter was referred to Grattan, the Indian agent. With a posse of over twenty men he set out to arrest the Minneconjou who had killed the animal, despite the fact that the treaty in force provided that disputes between Indians and whites were to be settled by the chiefs. Accompanied by twenty-nine armed men with two howitzers, Grattan headed for the Indians' camp. Fully realizing the dire results that might follow, Man Afraid of His Horse and Bear Who Scatters His Foes begged the soldiers to wait, but to no purpose. Upon arriving at the camp the cavalry halted about fifty yards away, and without warning fired into the camp. At the first volley Bear Who Scatters His Foes was killed, together with a number of other Indians. Then howitzers opened up and shells tore through the tipis, wounding women and children, and killing many. It was not until then that the Indians opened fire, with the result that every member of the attacking whites was killed.

Even after this, the Indians did not go on the warpath but merely broke camp and separated. So far, all the trouble had been with the Sioux, and the Cheyennes had taken no part in it, having returned to their own villages. In Washington, however, demands were made to exterminate the "red devils," and Grattan was pictured as a martyr. As was almost always the case, the whites failed to discriminate when it came to Indian tribes or bands, and in 1855, when Colonel Harney led his troopers up the Platte Valley and found a camp of peaceful Brûlés under Little Thunder, he at once surrounded the Indians and demanded the surrender of those who had wiped out Grattan's force. Naturally this was not possible, for Little Thunder's band had not even been in the vicinity at the time of the Grattan affair. Flying into a rage, Colonel Harney ordered his men to attack, and the soldiers opened fire, killing eighty-six Indians, most of whom were women and children, and wounding many more. Later, seventy women and children were captured. No resistance had been made by the Sioux, who had not fired a shot.

Harney's next act was to order all Indians in the area, both Sioux and Cheyennes, to meet him at Fort Pierre. At this conference the Sioux agreed to obey the white man's orders, but the Cheyennes, who so far had taken no part in any of the troubles, refused to appear, and Harney swore that in the spring he would lead an overwhelming force against them. By this time the Cheyennes had begun to realize that their association with the Sioux was certain to lead to hostilities with the whites. Their chiefs, Crazy Head, Dull Knife, Lame Man, Old Bear, Little Wolf, and others all foresaw that war was almost inevitable, but determined to use every endeavor to avoid hostilities short of breaking their pledged word of allegiance with the Dakotas. Several clashes between the Army and the Cheyennes followed, although none were very serious, and Indian Agent Twiss wrote to Washington stating that if some one would control the U. S. Army he could control the Indians.

It was about this time that the Sioux outbreak in Minnesota took place, and for two years the government had its hands too full with this and the Civil War to bother with the Cheyennes. Then, later, another crazy-headed Indian-hating Army officer committed a bloody, inexcusable massacre that was denounced by many white men, including Kit Carson, the famous scout, and struck the spark that flamed into open war.

About twenty head of stampeded steers had been found by a party of the Cheyennes, who brought the cattle in to be delivered to the owners, but were accused of having stolen them. Without waiting to hear the Indians' story, Lieutenant George Layre, with a troop of cavalry equipped with howitzers, set out to "kill every damned Cheyenne I can find." The first Indians he met were a party of buffalo hunters with chief Lean Bear, who, a few years previously, had visited Washington and had met the President. As the soldiers approached, the chief reassured his braves, telling them there would be no trouble when he showed the Lieutenant the medal and papers given him by the President. Accompanied by his attendants, the chief rode toward the cavalry making the peace sign. When Lean Bear had approached within twenty paces, Layre ordered his men to fire, and Lean Bear and his men were torn to pieces by the bullets. Then, charging over the bodies and riddling them with shots, the soldiers brought the cannon into action and killed twenty-six of the fleeing Indians and wounded many more.

In the meantime, another troop, under Lieutenant Dunn, came upon a small band of Cheyennes and killed and wounded a number of the Indians. Several other attacks were made on camps of the Cheyennes, most of whom never had heard that hostilities had broken out. In every instance these unprovoked and inexcusable murders of the peaceful Cheyennes were reported as "glorious victories" by the Army, and Governor Evans of Colorado declared publicly that it was the duty of every white man to kill every Indian he met, irrespective of the tribe. The open season on Indians resulted in hundreds of white men killing and scalping to collect the scalp bounties, and the war was on. The whites even resorted to torture; when Major Downing captured a Cheyenne scout he roasted the Indian's feet in a fire until the man revealed the position of the Cheyenne camp. Attacking the camp the next morning at daybreak, when the men were absent hunting buffalo, Downing ordered his men to butcher every woman and child without mercy. Nearly thirty were killed and as many more wounded before the soldiers' ammunition was exhausted. Then, after sabering the wounded, they seized the Indians' ponies and left.

There is no need to enumerate in detail all of the murders, massacres, and unwarranted attacks that followed, for whenever the blood-crazed whites came into contact with Indians, no matter of what tribe, they shot them down. When, at Fort Larned, the friendly Arapaho chief, Left Hand, came in under a flag of truce, he was fired upon, and as a result this friendly tribe for once became hostile. Cheyenne, Sioux, and Arapaho united in an all-out war. In a short time they had killed hundreds of whites, had burned farms and settlements, and had cost the government over thirty millions of dollars. When possible, the settlers everywhere fled eastward, stage and freight lines ceased operating, and Denver, surrounded by Indians, was threatened with starvation.

At last, finding that the Indians had the upper hand, Governor Evans, who had boasted he would wipe out every Indian to be found, appealed for peace. There were other white men who had never approved of the treatment of the Indians and recognized the justice of their reprisals, while, on the Indians' part, Black Kettle, Yellow Wolf, and others also wanted hostilities to cease. Others, especially the younger warriors, insisted upon war, and the Indians divided, the more hot-headed younger men heading northwest while the others made all efforts to arrange an honorable peace. Honor, however, was unknown to Army officers when it came to dealing with Indians. Major Walter Scott invited Black Kettle and his band to come to Fort Lyon to arrange peace terms, and then sent word to Colonel Chivington, an ex-minister who was in charge of the Colorado military district, that he had lured the Cheyennes within reach, and asked for additional troopers to attack them. With the utmost secrecy Chivington and Anthony with their seven hundred men moved on the Cheyenne camp, where the Indians, feeling assured that peace was near, were waiting quietly for the promised conference to begin. Their camp, consisting of about one hundred tipis, housed more than two hundred Cheyenne men and about five hundred women and children, under chiefs Black Kettle, White Antelope, Yellow Wolf, Lone Bear, and War Bonnet, with a few Arapahos under Chief Left Hand.

The first to sight the approaching soldiers were some women who had gone to a near-by stream for water just as day was breaking. In the dim light the women at first mistook the dark mass of troopers for a herd of buffalo, and aroused the camp. When the men came hurrying from the tipis and realized that soldiers and not buffalo were approaching they were in a panic until Black Kettle, declaring the soldiers were coming on a peaceful mission, ordered his warriors to remain unarmed. At the signing of the treaty of 1860 the chief had been given an American flag, which he now hoisted on a pole above his tipi, while the Indians stood about him, feeling confident of safety beneath the Stars and Stripes. The next moment the troops, who now were within pistol shot, opened fire, killing scores of the Cheyennes. As those still alive or unharmed tried to escape they were shot down by the troopers, who then drew knives and bayonets and commenced a wholesale slaughter of men, women, and children, while Chivington urged them on, shouting: "Obey orders! No prisoners to be taken!"

Beneath the flag Black Kettle and his wife, with elderly White Antelope, stood motionless, dazed and horrified by the butchery, until they were the only Indians remaining alive. Then a volley from the soldiers literally tore White Antelope to pieces. Black Kettle's wife was shot down, and as the cavalrymen rode over her body they fired shot after shot into her back. By some seeming miracle Black Kettle survived and, believing his wife dead, concealed himself until the soldiers left. He then returned and, finding his wife still lived, gathered her in his arms and started for the nearest Cheyenne camp. During the massacre a few of the Indians had managed to reach their ponies and had ridden to the Smoky Hill camp. When these Cheyennes heard the story told by the refugees they started at once for the scene of carnage, with led horses laden with robes, blankets, and food, to rescue possible survivors. On their way they met Black Kettle struggling along carrying his wife—who, remarkable as it may appear, eventually recovered, although there were more than eight bullet holes in her body.

For once the public had its fill of the Army's treatment of the Indians. As true accounts of the butchery reached the east, citizens everywhere demanded a court-martial for Chivington, who, realizing how the wind blew, resigned from the Army before a court could be convened. Although a Congressional investigation bared the entire matter, the public denunciation of the massacre came too late for justice to be meted out. As the Sioux chief, Big Mouth, declared: "You white men have set the prairies on fire."

Despite all they had suffered, the Cheyennes under Black Kettle still argued for peace, until, finding the others refused to listen to his pleas, he moved his band out of the hostile area and south of the Arkansas River.

The first and one of the most disastrous victories of the Indians was in December 1866, when Colonel Fetterman and his men were trapped near Fort Kearney and the entire force was wiped out by Sioux and Cheyenne warriors. Had Fetterman heeded the warnings of the peacefully inclined Cheyennes he would not have fallen into the trap, but, like the other Army men, he regarded all Indians as enemies to be shot down without mercy.

Adding fuel to the fire it had started, the government violated its treaties with the Dakota nation, opening up lands it had sworn to leave inviolate to the Indians and, as a result, the Oglala, Teton, Brûlé, Hunkpapa, and other Sioux tribes under Red Cloud, Crazy Horse, and other famous chiefs joined in open warfare with the United States.

In the meantime, a new Indian leader was making history. Although he was known to the whites as "Sitting Bull," the real name of this Hunkpapa Sioux was "Buffalo Bull Who Waits." An immense amount of misinformation, lies, and utter nonsense has been written and told of him. He has been accused of having planned the Custer "massacre," and has been pictured as a mighty chief and warrior. As we have seen, in reality he was neither a famous warrior nor a chief, having been confused with the Oglala chief of the same name, who was never hostile, and who died several months before the Battle of the Little Big Horn. He was merely a medicine man who always argued for peace, and at the time of the Custer battle he was in the hills ten miles away, "making medicine." As Sitting Bull the medicine man was regarded as a very great shaman and a man of wisdom, as well as a prophet, the Indians held a very high opinion of him. Among his followers had been the Cheyenne chief Black Kettle, who, in spite of his never-failing desire for peace, had been killed during Custer's disgraceful slaughter of the Cheyennes at Washita. With the death of Black Kettle the only surviving great chief of the Cheyennes was Little Wolf, and with his band he joined the Sioux followers of Sitting Bull.

The next event of importance was the battle of Tongue River, when General Crook met a small party of Northern Cheyennes under Little Hawk. Although the troops were compelled to retreat, leaving a number of dead on the field, Crook reported it as "a smashing victory over the Sioux under Crazy Horse!" A week after this skirmish the Cheyennes in daring charges worsted the soldiers at the Rosebud, although once again it was falsely reported as a victory by the Army.

Having lost everything they owned in a desperate battle with General Reynolds, a band of Cheyennes, together with a few Sioux, reached Sitting Bull's camp on the Little Big Horn. There were some ten or twelve thousand Indians assembled, mainly Hunkpapa, Brûlé, Minneconjou, Oglala, and other Sioux tribes, with about fifteen hundred Cheyennes, all having gathered for a general conference. Not even suspecting that soldiers were near, they held dances and ceremonials, and went to sleep, to be aroused by the women shouting that soldiers were coming.

There is no need to retell the story of the Battle of the Little Big Horn. It resulted in bringing the long Indian war to an end when honorable and sensible officers, such as General Nelson Miles and others, were placed in command. But before final peace had been established, the Cheyennes were doomed to suffer another terrible fate at the hands of their captors. About one thousand of the tribe, with chiefs Little Wolf and Dull Knife, were herded onto reservations at Fort Reno and Darlington in Oklahoma. Here, in a barren desert land, torrid in summer and bitterly cold in the winter, with no game and no adequate shelter, the Indians starved and suffered tortures. Rations promised by the government failed to arrive, and what little meat the Indians received was mostly bone and gristle unfit for human consumption. There was only one doctor to attend to more than five thousand Indians, and for over six months he was unable to obtain needed medical supplies. Within two months after the Cheyennes reached the reservations more than one-half of them were ill, and during the first winter forty-one died of the cold and malnutrition, while the survivors were living skeletons.

Little Wolf and Dull Knife sent pitiful pleas to Washington, but nothing was done, and when they appealed to the Indian agent for permission to go to Washington and report conditions, they were refused. It was then that Little Wolf delivered his ultimatum, telling the agent that he and his people were leaving to return to their own country. The following day the two chiefs and about three hundred Indians started north. On the second day they were overtaken by troops, and although Little Wolf ordered his men not to fire on the soldiers, the latter fired at the chief, although he was under a flag of truce. Instantly the Cheyennes charged the troopers. The skirmish lasted until the next day, when the soldiers withdrew, leaving a number of dead. None of the Indians had been killed, although several were wounded, the lack of casualties being due to the fact that, for the first time, the Cheyennes had entrenched themselves.

Resuming their northward march, avoiding the settlements and ranches and committing no depredations, the Cheyennes plodded on. Then, once more, they were overtaken and surrounded by the cavalry. Many of the Indians' ponies had been killed and eaten, many of the band were riding double and all —men, women and children—had been marching for days across an arid waste, emaciated and weak from hunger at the start. But the indomitable spirit of the Cheyennes could not be weakened by hunger or hardships. Taking refuge behind rocks on a hillside, they beat back the charges of the troops until they were forced to withdraw. Then, charging, the Indians drove the white men from their wagons and secured ammunition and much-needed food. At dawn the next day, when the soldiers returned to renew their attack, there was not an Indian to be seen, for all had slipped away during the night.

Soon after they had crossed the Arkansaw River, the Cheyennes came upon some buffalo-hide hunters. Surrounding the men without harming them, the Indians permitted the hunters to go, leaving the animals they had killed in addition to their guns and ammunition. Having gorged themselves on the buffalo meat, and taking a supply to be dried, the Cheyennes resumed their march. A number of times they sighted troops, but managed to avoid them, and although the papers everywhere printed screaming headlines about the "marauding Indians" ravaging Kansas and Nebraska, the Cheyennes molested no one and committed no depredations whatever.

It was then that General Crook, with twelve thousand troops, set a trap for the homeward-bound Indians. Columns of soldiers closed in on the east, south, and west, and two troops were loaded into trains that shuttled back and forth across the route of the approaching Cheyennes, while, in addition, two companies of cavalry were stationed at Oglala. Within two and one-half miles of this spot the Indians reached the railway, but Crook's trap was never sprung. Having muffled the feet of their horses, the Cheyennes slipped at night beneath the two troops of cavalry. When daylight came the only trace of the Cheyennes to be found were the tracks of their ponies.

Once they were beyond the Platte River, the Cheyennes were in the sand hills with no water, almost no vegetation, and no game. Even the soldiers on their trail suffered terribly, and marveled at the endurance and courage of the Indians, who had separated into two bands, one under Little Wolf continuing toward the Black Hills, the other under Dull Knife turning to the west. Reaching the Running Water, Little Wolf and his people settled down for the winter. They were not located by the troops, and in the spring continued on to the Powder River, where they were seen by two government spies. The spies reported the Indians' whereabouts to Lieutenant Clark, who a few days later came up with the Cheyennes. "Thank the Lord I have found you!" he exclaimed, as, riding forward, he grasped Little Wolf's hand. Then he added, "I come as your friend, not as your enemy. I want you to surrender your arms and go with me to Fort Keogh." For several days the Indians and the troops camped together while the Cheyennes held a council. Finally all agreed, and Little Wolf told Clark that they would go to the fort peacefully. As they neared the fort General Miles rode up and shook hands with Little Wolf, saying, "Today we meet and shake hands. We will always be friends from now on."

The story of Dull Knife and his band was very different. Not knowing that the Red Cloud Agency had been abandoned, he headed for it, intending to surrender and to request permission to remain on tribal land. By mere chance he and his band almost ran into a troop of the Third Cavalry, who had no idea there were Indians in the vicinity. Ordering his men not to shoot but to ride forward with hands in air, Dull Knife shook hands with

Captain Johnson, telling him that he and his followers were on their way to the Agency. The soldiers appeared to be friendly and, as they turned back, they left hardtack and other food for the starving Cheyennes. When the Indians had eaten they followed the troopers, but when they discovered they were being led toward Fort Robinson and away from the Agency they protested. Although the officers declared that they were merely being taken to the Fort to surrender, and that they would be housed and fed, the Cheyennes feared it was a trap. Despite the zero weather and a blizzard they refused to go farther, and dug foxholes in the frozen earth. All of their arms with the exception of five carbines had been taken by the soldiers, but with these five guns they held their own against the Army for ten days, when a cannon shell burst among the women and children, killing several of them. The Cheyennes then surrendered, but were so weak from exposure and hunger that they could not walk but had to be loaded into wagons and hauled to the fort, where they were fed and well treated. Then they were informed that Indian Agent Carl Schurtz (not to be confused with Carl Schurz the great German-American), in Washington had ordered them sent back to the Oklahoma reservation.

When they protested at this treatment they were locked in an abandoned barracks, one hundred and fifty Indians being herded into the tumbledown building. It was subzero weather, there were chinks between the logs of the walls, there was no food, no blankets, and only a broken-down small stove. The chiefs begged the commandant to give them food, blankets, and fuel, but instead Commandant Wessels had Dull Knife and two lesser chiefs dragged to his office. One of the Indians was barefooted, having eaten his moccasins, and Dull Knife's only garment was an old ragged blanket. When the latter asked if the Great White Father had sentenced them to die there, Wessels flew into a rage and, banging his fist on the table ordered: "Lock the damned rascals up! Give them nothing. No food, no fuel, nothing. They'll give in right enough. God damn them all!"

Three days later, with the temperature six below zero, without food, heat, or clothing, and with no water after they had scraped the snow from the window sills, the Indians began chanting their death songs. Wessels was furious, for he realized at last that the Indians never would give in; to all his threats their only reply was: "We will die here." He then ordered them dragged out and put in irons, but as the soldiers attempted to obey, Wild Hog, weak as he was, drew a knife, and the others joined in the hopeless fight. Two Indians were killed, and a third regained the barracks through a broken window.

Eight more terrible days passed. Then the Cheyennes, aware that their end was near, bade one another farewell, and armed themselves with a carbine and some pistols that somehow they had managed to retain. Resolved to die fighting, Little Shield smashed a window and shot down the sentry. Instantly all of the Indians crawled and stumbled through the window and headed for the river while the few armed men kept the soldiers at bay, killing one and wounding five. Then, crazed by thirst, they threw themselves down beside the stream and drank until unable to move. Charging on the helpless Cheyennes, the troopers trampled them under their horses' feet, cut them down with sabers, and pistoled them, whether men, women, or babes in arms. The bodies of sixty-four Indians who had escaped from their prison were piled in the snow, but the others of the eighty-five were never accounted for. By some seeming miracle Dull Knife, together with his wife and son and the latter's wife and child, had escaped the carnage. Weak and emaciated as they were, they struggled onward, subsisting on snow and their moccasins, until, more dead than alive, they crawled into the Pine Ridge Agency and told of what had taken place.

When the story of these pitiful survivors appeared in the press a tidal wave of revulsion swept the country. It might be all right to fight hostile Indians in open warfare, but to torture and starve them when prisoners was a different matter. The public was shocked at the inhuman outrages committed by Captain Wessels, while the courageous actions of the starved and dying Cheyennes was applauded. In Washington, Carl Schurtz, who was responsible for the whole disgraceful affair, trembled in his shoes and sent frantic telegrams to Pine Ridge and Fort Keogh, granting the Cheyennes their freedom and their ancestral lands.

It had taken them many years and had cost them hundreds

of lives, with sufferings beyond description, but the Cheyennes had won. All they had desired, all they had fought for, was theirs at last. They had peace and their homeland, although fewer than five hundred of the tribe were left. Safe and free from warfare, these brave, proud, hard-fighting but peacefully inclined Indians prospered and increased. Today there are about fifteen thousand of the tribe living, but it is doubtful if there is a single pure-blooded Tisi-tsi-ista among them. They first absorbed the Suhtais; then for many years they were affiliated with the Dakotas, the Blackfeet, and the Arapahos, and intermarried with them. Many of their prisoners, both Indian and white, joined the Cheyennes and married the women. But despite their mixture of blood, the Cheyennes' character, their tribal pride, their desire for peace, their love of freedom, and their indomitable spirit have never changed. As a Cheyenne youth said, when he and some companions volunteered for service in the War: "Since when have the Cheyennes failed to fight for freedom?"

XXIII

FRIENDS AND NEIGHBORS OF THE SIOUX

NEXT-DOOR NEIGHBORS of the Dakotas, as well as their friends and allies, were the Siksika or Blackfeet, a confederation of the Siksika, Blood, and Piegan tribes; closely related and allies were the Sarsis and Atsines. They occupied a vast territory extending from the Missouri River in Montana to the Saskatchewan in Canada and westward to the Rocky Mountains. Although plains nomads, they often lived for long periods in permanent camps and even cultivated some crops. They were noted for their bravery and fighting prowess, but were friendly toward the whites, and never caused trouble except when some of them joined the Cheyennes in the latter's war with our government.

Of a totally different racial stock from the Sioux, being Algonquins like the Cheyennes and speaking an Athabascan dialect, yet, like the Cheyennes, they had so modified their language by adopting Sioux words that the two conversed readily. They were a very superior lot, famous for their good nature, their love of revelry, laughter, and merrymaking, and for the beauty of their women. Many white men married into the tribe, while others lived among them for years, and all were loud in their praise of the tribe. Mr. George Bird Grinnell, the author-naturalist, lived with them for a long time and wrote *My Life with the Blackfeet.* Mr. Willard Schultz, who married a Blackfoot girl and lived for thirty years with the tribe, wrote a fascinating book, *My Life As an Indian.* The Blackfeet also were the favorite tribe of the late Charles M. Russell, the famous painter of Indians, who lived so long among them that he actually came to look like an Indian, and when in native costume was indistinguishable from a member of the tribe.

The Blackfeet's religion was a form of sun-god worship, and

they had a great number of fetishes, lesser deities, and sacred objects. To them the most sacred of all was a white (albino) buffalo, and the man who killed one was regarded as being especially favored by the sun-god and was greatly honored. It was considered a sacrilege to eat any portion of the creature, the meat and heart being carefully dried and placed in the medicine lodge or shrine dedicated to the sun-god. The hide, carefully tanned, was also suspended on the central pole of the lodge, where it remained until it disintegrated and fell to pieces. No passing Indian or war party dared molest it for fear of bringing down the vengeance of the sun-god. The medicine men, however, were allowed to use trimmings of the hide for wrapping their medicine bundles, or for a band about the head that was worn only at sacred and highly important ceremonies.

In their social organization and home life the Blackfeet did not differ greatly from other plains tribes, although, as a general thing, their tipis contained more comforts and luxuries than those of their neighbors. As a rule the men wore their hair long in two braids. The costumes of fringed tunic or shirt, leggings, and moccasins were often covered with beautiful beadwork in geometrical designs, and while some of the men at times wore the typical plains bonnet, the Blackfeet had a great number of elaborate and often beautiful headdresses and were partial to bonnets of badger or weasel skin bearing antelope or buffalo horns. When about to attack an enemy, they dressed themselves up in their finest garments, so that in case they were killed they would appear properly dressed before the sun-god. Like the Sioux, the Cheyennes, and other tribes, the Blackfeet were constantly at war with the Crows until 1885, when the government induced the two tribes to sign a treaty of peace. They also fought the Crees, the Assiniboins, and some of the other tribes, the battles usually consisting of brief skirmishes between small war parties.

Today all these old enmities have been forgotten, Blackfeet, Crows, and other tribes intermarrying freely. The majority of the tribe are on reservations or are well-to-do farmers and ranchers. However, a number camp in their tipis in national parks, where, arrayed in their tribal dress, they form a drawing card for the tourists.

Other near neighbors of the Sioux were the Aditsas, Arikaras, and Mandans. When white explorers first penetrated to their district the Mandans were dwelling in villages of log and earth houses, many partly underground, and were surrounded by palisades. They were a peaceful agricultural tribe, and always have remained friendly with the whites. Owing to the fact that they were lighter-skinned than some of the neighboring tribes and that a number of them were blonds (although whether their hair was bleached or they were partial albinos is not known), the explorers jumped to the conclusion that they were "lost" members of some European expedition. Also, there was a rumor that the Mandans could converse in Welsh with Welshmen who were members of the English Army, although this was never verified. As a result, the Mandans were supposed to be descendents of survivors of an expedition under Prince Madoc, who is thought to have reached the Atlantic coast in 1170 and, heading westward, to have disappeared. Much has been written on the matter, but there is no real basis for the theory. The Mandan language is Siouan; many other tribes dwelt in the same type of houses and built stockades; there are various tribes lighter in color than the Mandans, and, as partial albinos with light-colored hair are not uncommon among many tribes, such matters are no evidences of European blood. No trustworthy person has ever been found who could converse with the Indians in Welsh, and if, as alleged, there are words and syntax common to both languages, they are probably purely coincidental. Considering that the Norsemen, far better equipped and in larger numbers than the Welsh explorers, were completely wiped out before they reached the Mandan area, it would seem incredible that enough Welshmen to have left any linguistic or other impressions on the Indians could ever have reached the remote Upper Missouri River region. Moreover, the Mandan dialect is very similar to that of the Winnebagos, and is distinctly Siouan.

Following the arrival of the white men, a smallpox epidemic swept through the tribe, killing the Indians by thousands, until only about one hundred survived. These joined the Hidatsas and were absorbed by them, and later the two tribes joined the Arikaras, all three becoming affiliated with the Sioux.

The Hidatsas of Siouan stock were known to the Dakotas, the Arapahos, and the Cheyennes as Hewaktokto or "Tipis in a row," while the Crows knew them as the Amashi or "Earth People," so called because their lodges were partly underground. To the whites they were Gros Ventres or "Big bellies," being confused with the Atsinas, one of the Arapaho bands. This was because in the sign language their gestures of identification were almost identical, and consisted of sweeping the hands before the body. In reality it had nothing to do with the abdomen but meant "many lodges" or "spreading tipis." Decimated by diseases introduced by the whites, the Hidatsas merged with the Arikaras and Mandans. They now number about a thousand and are mainly on a reservation on the site of their original village on the northeastern side of the Mississippi.

Still another tribe closely associated with the Mandans and Hidatsas were the Arikara, a name derived from *ariki,* meaning a horn, derived from the tribal custom of wearing the hair twisted in the form of horns on either side of the head. Unlike the Mandan and Aditsas tribes, the Arikaras were of Caddoan stock, with a dialect almost identical with that of the Pawnees. Originally they inhabited the Missouri Valley as far south as Omaha, but migrated north and became associated with the Sioux. They have always been friendly toward the whites except on one occasion when there was a skirmish over their ill treatment by some white traders. Today they number about two thousand, but very few if any are of pure Arikara blood. It is the same with the Mandans and Aditsas, for the three tribes have been mixing and intermarrying for years, and there has been a considerable mixture with the Sioux, Winnebago, and other tribes. My good friend Walks His Horses claims he is over ninety per cent Arikara, as he probably is, for he can trace his lineage back for many generations. His wife, however, is a Winnebago, so his children would be considered Winnebagos. Red Bear, another of my friends, considers himself a Mandan, but one of his grandmothers was a Cree and one of his grandfathers was an Hidatsa. His father was a Mandan, but his mother was one-half Cree, while his wife is mainly of Hidatsa and Arikaka blood. He was an enormously fat Indian, and when, on one occasion, I asked him why he considered himself Mandan rather than Hidatsa or Arikara, he chuckled. Sweeping his hands in front of his paunch and pointing to his wife, he replied, "One big belly in the family is enough, even if it is not that of the Gros Ventre but of the Mandan."

Other friends and neighbors of the Sioux, and also allies of the Cheyennes and Blackfeet, were the Arapahos—or, as the Cheyennes and Sioux called them, "The People of the Blue Sky." Like the Blackfeet and the Cheyennes, they were of Algonquin stock, and were originally a sedentary agricultural tribe living in the upper Red River Valley of Minnesota. But like so many of these sedentary midwestern tribes, they migrated to the great plains about the same time as the Cheyennes went west. Although they became seminomads and hunted the buffalo, yet they still cultivated small fields or gardens and had more or less permanent villages. The tribe consisted of five dialectical groups, probably representing five original tribes who became merged into one. They are affable, good-natured, admirable people, and not naturally warlike. They were friendly toward the whites, and were one of the few tribes who were friends of the Kiowas and Comanches as well as the Sioux and Cheyennes. Aside from one time when a few of the tribe joined the Cheyennes in their battles with the Army, they have never given trouble and have never been regarded as hostile. They were bitter enemies of the Pawnees, Utes, and Shoshones and, like the Sioux, Blackfeet, and Cheyennes, they were almost constantly at war with the Crows.

Just why the Crows, whose real name is Absaroke, meaning "The Hawk People," should have won the enmity of so many of their neighbors is something of a mystery, but the other Indians regarded them as a worthless lot, notorious thieves, liars, and troublemakers, and many of the white trappers and frontiersmen declared the Crows did not possess a single redeeming feature. However, today the Crows are regarded as honest, industrious, reliable, and fully the equals of their former enemies. Many are employed as cowhands and as Indian police on reservations, as well as in other capacities, although the majority are farmers. Surrounded as they were by their enemies and constantly fighting some of the most warlike and powerful of the plains tribes, it seems little short of a miracle that they were not completely wiped out. But they not only survived but held their own, often being the victors in battles where they were greatly outnumbered. Whatever their faults may have been, cowardice was not one of them. That they rarely troubled the whites was due to the fact that they regarded the white men as inferiors, looked upon them with contempt, and considered it beneath their dignity to kill them.

The Winnebagos were still another of the Sioux's neighbors. They are of Siouan stock, and originally inhabited western Minnesota, where they were peaceful agricultural Indians until 1862. Although they were friendly toward the whites, the settlers wanted the Winnebagos' land, and demanded that they should be deported. They were taken to the Crow Creek reservation in Dakota, where they were so badly treated that they sought refuge among the Omahas. During the Revolutionary War and the War of 1812 they allied themselves with the British.

XXIV

TRIBES OF THE FAR NORTHWEST

IN WASHINGTON, Alaska, Oregon, and northern California there were a great number of tribes, many of which were, in reality, merely groups or bands who were known by the names of the localities they inhabited, while, on the other hand, a locality was often named for the Indians. For example, the Rogue River in Oregon was named from the Tututni Indians, a quarrelsome and warlike tribe known to the settlers as "Rogue Indians"—then an appropriate name, although today they are respected business-men and farmers on an equality with their white neighbors. In the old days it was their custom to bury widows alive with the bodies of their dead husbands.

To describe all the Indian tribes of the far northwest would require far more space than can be devoted to them. Among the better known were the Walla Walla or "Little River" Indians in Oregon and Washington; the Klamaths and Modocs of southern Oregon, who are mainly noted for their so-called "Modoc Wars" (for full details see the *Biographies of Famous Indians),* the Bannocks, the Cayuses, the Shoshones, and the Nez Percés. Originally inhabiting northern Idaho and Wyoming, the Bannocks were related to the Shoshones and were friendly to the whites until driven to desperation by being half-starved on their reservation (only two and one-half cents per capita per day was allowed for feeding them), they revolted and killed a number of the whites. Conditions having been improved, peace was made a few months later. The Cayuse tribe, formerly inhabiting Oregon and Washington, were famed for their courage, their fighting abilities, and the superiority of their horses, which became known by the name of the tribe. Almost exterminated by small-pox in 1847, the survivors joined the Nez Percés. Inhabiting both sides of the Columbia and Yakima Rivers in Washington were the Yakima Indians, a quiet, peaceful tribe who were employed by the settlers as lumbermen, boatmen, and in similar capacities. They were honest, industrious, and trustworthy, but were cheated by the whites and debauched by the vile liquor of the white men, who robbed them when drunk and kept them in a form of peonage. In addition to the tribes mentioned, there were a number who ordinarily were referred to by the whites as "Chinooks" or "Siwash." The former inhabited the area north of the Columbia River in Washington. Although they were the best known of the Chinookan family group, they were a small tribe and became fused with the Chehalis, whose dialect they adopted, the original Chinook language becoming extinct. However, it was the basis of the Chinook-English trade jargon that is in use today from Alaska to California. The majority of these far northwestern tribes, as well as those in Alaska, depended mainly upon game and fish for a living, and caught vast quantities of salmon, which they dried and smoked for future consumption.

"In Alaska, within the United States area, there were a great many tribes of various families and stocks. On the upper Pelly, Stewart, and MacMillan Rivers of the Yukon were the Abbatotines or "Mountain Sheep People," while in the Copper River Valley were the Ahtenas or "Ice People," known to the whites as the "Yellow Knives," who were formerly warlike and hostile. Inhabiting the Kenai Peninsula are the Knaiakptanas, the only Indians of Athabascan stock on the northern Pacific coast. In their customs and ways they are very similar to the neighboring Eskimos. Another group of Alaska Indians of the Yukon district are the Kutchins, who are famous for their hospitality, often entertaining visitors for months at a time, each head of a family taking his turn at feasting the entire band but compelled by etiquette to fast himself. In former days it was the frequent custom of these Indians to kill female children in order to prevent a surplus of women. Related to the Kutchins, but quite different in habits and many other respects, are the Kutchakutchins or "Giant People," who dwell on the banks of the Yukon River. Unlike the majority of Alaskan tribes, who are sedentary and live in wooden houses, these Indians are nomadic and subsist by hunting and trapping. Born traders, they had a monetary system based upon strings of beads seven feet in length and known as the "Nakieikor." Each of the strings had the value of a certain number of beaver skins, the number depending upon the color of the beads, but the total value of seven strings was fixed at twenty-four skins. Their houses were made of hides stretched over poles and dome-shaped. The few survivors of this tribe are now living at Fort Yukon.

On the coastal area of Alaska were the Yakutats, noted for their beautifully carved horn and wooden ware, their splendid seagoing canoes, and their priests' strikingly Oriental costumes. Today they are thoroughly civilized and dwell in well-built wooden houses. It was these and other coastal tribes who erected the well-known totem poles, relating the family history in carved symbolic figures. Most of the tribes inhabiting the coast of Alaska and Washington depended upon the sea for a living, and in their enormous oceangoing dugout canoes they ventured far out at sea in quest of whales. The Quileutes of the Washington coast are particularly noted for their canoes, their skill at whaling, and their warlike character, which has enabled them to hold their own against all enemy tribes.

In the vicinity of the Dalles, in Wasco County, Oregon, were the Wasco Indians, a sedentary tribe depending upon wild roots and berries, the salmon, and some game. They were noted for their skill in tanning hides; they were master carvers of wood and horn, and made very fine baskets. Their houses were of two types, those for summer use being made of poles covered with grass and reeds, while their winter homes were of cedar planks and were half underground. They were notorious slavers, and even buried living slaves with dead chiefs so that the chiefs might be served by them in the hereafter. Although not included among the "flathead" Indians, they artificially deformed the skulls of their children. The term "flatheads" was applied to a number of the northwestern tribes who artificially deformed the infants' heads, especially the Indians of the Chinook group. Strangely enough, the tribe officially called Flatheads are the true Salish, who never deformed the heads but had normal skulls that were flat on top and hence rendered them conspicuous among their neighbors with deformed skulls. The early French traders, however, seeing slaves of the Salish with deformed heads, called them *Têtes Plates.*

Inhabiting the more mountainous areas of the Northwest, from northern Utah, Nevada, Wyoming, and Idaho to Oregon and southern Washington, were the Shoshones, or "Snake People," a name given them by the Cheyennes because they inhabited the Snake River area of northern Idaho. There were two general groups of the tribe. Those inhabiting the more easterly and northerly areas were nomadic horse Indians and buffalo hunters, and were famous as valiant warriors. On the other hand, the Shoshones in the westerly group were sedentary, and eked out a rather precarious living by gathering wild berries and roots and by salmon fishing. They were included among the so-called "Digger Indians." Their lodges were miserable brush shelters, while the homes of the easterly group were the conical skin tipis. Friendly toward the whites, the Shoshones were not troublesome, and as early as 1909 large numbers of the children were attending the reservation schools. Never having suffered greatly from epidemics that wiped out so many of the western Indians, the Shoshones are still a large tribe.

Another tribe that inhabited the northwest were the Nez Percés or "Pierced Noses"—a misnomer, as the tribe never practiced nose-piercing. The name was applied to several other neighboring tribes by the French, and was transferred to the Nez Percés through error and ignorance on the part of the whites. A fine tribe, inhabiting portions of Idaho, Oregon, and Washington, the Nez Percés were friends of the whites until forced to become hostile by the outrageous treatment accorded them by the settlers and our government. The culmination was Chief Joseph's amazing flight toward Canada. (For details see the Glossary.)

In northern California there were a number of tribes differing greatly from the other northwestern Indians, some being sedentary and agricultural, others nomadic, and others fishing Indians, and with arts, habits, and costumes peculiar to each. Among these were the Yuroks, Hupas, Tolowas, Karoks, Kawias, Shastas, and others.

The Yuroks, who lived on the lower Klamath River, remained unknown to the whites until as recently as 1850. They were a friendly tribe and never had trouble with the whites other than a few frays with miners in some areas. Physically they were superior to the majority of Californian Indians. They were unique in having no chiefs; the standing of a member depended upon his wealth of Dentalium or "tusk" shells which were their medium of exchange, highly prized "coins" of obsidian or volcanic glass often weighing several pounds, and the bright-colored scalps of woodpeckers. Their large spoons or ladles and other utensils made of horn and inlaid with Haliotis (abalone) shell were very beautiful, while their costumes of buckskin almost completely hidden by feather, bead, quill, and shell decorations, and their headdresses of woodpecker scalps, and bright-colored feathers, were magnificent. Although a sedentary race, dwelling in villages of houses built of split and dressed planks, with cellars and gable roofs, and often twenty-five to thirty feet square, yet they were wanderers in the sense that they were expert boatmen. Their canoes, made of redwood, were unique, being scowlike and square at both ends.

The Tolowas, who inhabited the extreme northwestern portion of California along the coast, were a rather primitive people, who have become debauched and demoralized by contact with the whites and are rapidly diminishing in numbers. The Karoks of the Klamath River area of northern California were a very primitive tribe, depending upon hunting and fishing in addition to agriculture. They were noteworthy for their exceedingly broad, powerful bows with narrow handholds. Although the majority of these tribes used boats or canoes, either made of planks or hollowed from logs, the Miwoks used rafts made from bundles of reeds lashed together that were almost identical with the *balsas* of the Peruvian and Bolivian Indians about Lake Titicaca.

Inhabiting the valley of the Trinity River, from the south fork to the Klamath River, were the Hupas. Strictly agricultural, the Hupas made magnificent baskets, often of immense size and so tightly woven that they served as water containers. Many of these, as well as those of other California tribes, have bright-colored beads or the iridescent throat-feathers of humming birds woven into the basketry. At times both beads and feathers are used, and the basket is so thickly covered that it appears to be made entirely of feathers and beads, while small baskets may be completely overlaid with the tiny hummingbirds' feathers. Although during the winter these Indians wore buckskin garments, in summer both men and women went almost nude. Today, they all wear conventional garments. Many of their former leather costumes were very beautifully decorated, while their head-dresses were most ornate. Among the Hupas the favorite and universal head covering was a bowl-like cap of basket work woven in attractive patterns of contrasting colors.

Through central and southern California the tribes were legion, and of a great number of racial and linguistic stocks. In no other portion of the world were there so many languages in use, over 150 dialects being spoken within an area of a few hundred square miles. In two respects all were much alike. None were nomadic, although moving about within their tribal limits, and none were warlike or hostile. Even when the white men arrived these Indians rarely resented it, and, making the best of the situation, found employment as farm hands, servants, herders, laborers, fishermen, or sailors. But their peaceful habits and natures, their dislike of trouble of any kind, and the fact that they regarded the white men as friends led to their own undoing. Thousands of these peaceful, industrious, and harmless Indians were slaughtered like vermin when Spanish rule in California came to an end and the United States took over. Here, almost alone of all the Spanish colonies in America, the Indians had always been well treated. Under Spanish rule there were countless missions, and practically all the Indians had been converted to Christianity. Many lived near the missions, others had their own lands; they were prosperous, contented and happy. But the transfer of California to the United States put an end to this. Our government refused to recognize the old Spanish grants, the Indians' lands were confiscated, the Indians were driven away from their homes, bounties were paid on their heads, and if they protested they were killed out of hand. Probably in no other section of the United States have the Indians suffered so greatly at the hands of the white men. With the discovery of gold in 1848, the country became overrun with lawless, tough characters to whom an Indian's life meant nothing, and in a comparatively short time entire tribes had been completely wiped out. However, a great many Indians still survive in California. Some still retain their tribal arts and crafts, some still follow tribal customs and life, but the majority live, dress, and act like their white neighbors, and many have little or no knowledge of their tribal tongue.

XXV

THE APACHES, KIOWAS, COMANCHES, AND OTHERS

OF ALL INDIANS in the United States the Apaches had the reputation of being the most savage, relentless, cruel, and bloodthirsty. Partly this is exaggeration and partly truth, but the fact remains that our Apache wars cost us millions of dollars and many hundreds of lives. But before condemning these Indians too severely, we must remember that they were fighting for their homes, their lands, and their freedom—exactly what every other race fights for and upholds. Moreover, nearly every episode was the direct result of hostile acts and mistreatment by the whites. The Mimbreños, for example, had always been friendly until a large number, invited to a feast by Santa Rita miners, were murdered for the sake of bounties offered by the Mexican officials.

The long and bloody war with Cochise was brought about when Army officers arrested him and two other chiefs on the "suspicion" that they had abducted a white child (who was found later), and tortured them in an effort to make them confess. Cochise escaped, but his two comrades were hanged, and quite understandably Cochise went on the warpath. Geronimo, who was a farmer, did not cause trouble until white men had stolen his cattle and devastated his crops. Moreover, there never was any one single Apache tribe, the term having been applied to a number of allied or related tribes, among them the Mimbreños, Akonyes, Mescaleros, Jicarillas, Faraones, Llaneros, Chiricahuas, Querechos, Pinaleños, Pinals, Arivaipas, Coyoteros, Megollones, Tontos, Gilas, Lipans, Kiowa-Apaches, Mohaves, Yumas, and others. Oddly enough, the term Apache is a corruption of the Zuñi word *Apachu* ("savage enemies") used by the Pueblo Indians to describe the Navajos, so the only true Apaches are Navajos!

The various so-called Apaches I have mentioned differed greatly in their lives, habits, characters, and many other respects, although nearly all were of Athabascan linguistic stock. Many were nomads; some subsisted by hunting, others dwelt in permanent villages, cultivated the soil, and depended mainly upon their crops. Some were exceedingly primitive, while others had reached a fairly high cultural state, and while some were warlike, others were peaceful, docile, and desired only to be left in peace. Moreover, it frequently happened that even in one tribe some bands under certain leaders would be hostile, savagely fighting our troops, while other chiefs with their bands would be peaceful, and might even serve as scouts for the Army.

It must be admitted that some of these tribes of the southwest were born bandits who gloried in raiding and killing other Indians or the whites with equal gusto, and reveled in bloodshed, and who were pastmasters at devising most painful methods of putting a man to a lingering death. Strangely enough, these so-called Apaches, as a general rule, treated their female captives rather well. While they took the places of slaves or servants in the Indian villages, they were not maltreated or abused, and rarely ever ravished.

Although, as I have said, some of the tribes were inherently raiders and killers, there were others who fought only in defense of their homes and freedom or to avenge some outrage committed by the whites. Moreover, even their worst enemies have always agreed that once they were a man's friends they remained steadfast friends, regardless of whether or not warfare was under way. Also, like the great majority of Indians, they never forgot a kindness or a favor, and on more than one occasion Cochise ordered his warriors to guard and protect the home and family of a white settler who at one time had saved his life.

Many so-called Apaches dwelt in well-constructed lodges in quite large villages, and produced beautifully designed textiles, beadwork, basketry, and other articles. Nearly all of the various "Apache" tribes made huge storage baskets for holding corn and other foodstuffs, graceful in form and decorated with harmonious colors in geometrical designs or with human and animal figures. Some of their baskets were among the finest of all made by American Indians. They were expert weavers, some of their blankets and other textiles almost equaling those of the Navajos. Their pottery, however, was crude and poor, and to hold liquids they used baskets coated with pitch or clay. They were experts at tanning skins, and decorated their buckskin garments with beadwork and painted designs in the form of narrow lines and intricate open patterns, often using the Greek key, ladderlike figures, stars, triangles, and sun figures, and preferring black and white or two shades of one color to the mixture of bright contrasting hues so popular with other plains tribes.

When on the warpath the braves stripped to breech-cloths and moccasins, seldom wearing feathers in their shoulder-length hair, but binding their heads with turbanlike strips of cloth or buckskin. Their moccasins were totally unlike those of any other tribe or group of tribes, being knee-high or nearly so, with hard, stiff soles sharply upturned at the toes and often with an ornamental toe-tab. The only exceptions to this type were the moccasins of the Jicarillos, who preferred fringed leggings and low moccasins made like those of the other tribes, with upturned toes. The dress-up costume of these Apache tribes featured fringed and beaded buckskin skirts and leather headpieces decorated with painted designs, varying from a skullcap to a high cap with a long tail of scalloped and decorated leather. As a rule there were ornaments such as feathers, scalp locks, or dyed hair forming a plume or tuft at the top of the cap or attached to the tail. Sometimes antelope, deer, buffalo or cow horns were fastened to the sides of the headdress, but the typical feather bonnet of the other plains tribes was never a part of the Apache costume —except when it had been captured from an enemy and was worn as a trophy on special occasions. Although the majority of these Apache Indians wore their hair shoulder length, the Jicarillos wore their hair long and in two braids after the fashion of the Sioux and other northern plains tribes. Also, their costumes were more showy than those of other "Apaches," with heavy fringe and elaborate beadwork on shirts and leggings. They also differed from other Apaches in many other respects, and were allies of the Utes and Taos Indians and deadly enemies of the Mescaleros, with whom they were constantly at war. They were also notoriously hostile to the whites.

All of these tribes had numerous ceremonials and dances, the "devil dances" being the most popular, and during these the participants wore enormous painted grotesque wooden headdresses and masks. Their medicine cults and secret societies were numerous and they were very fond of charms and amulets. Among these were seashells that were supposed to prevent sickness, and carved figures cut from trees that had been blasted by lightning, which were believed to be safeguards against lightning.

They were among the very first of the western Indians to obtain firearms, and among the last to abandon the use of bows and arrows. Their bows were rectangular in section, rather short and broad, backed by sinews glued to the wood, and were very powerful. Their arrows were of two types, one having a long shaft of cane with a false wooden foreshaft tipped with a stone or metal point, the other having a short, heavy wooden shaft. The arrows were sometimes feathered and sometimes not, and were so crooked that it seems little less than a miracle that they ever hit their mark, but accuracy did not count much, for most of the fighting was done at close quarters, and penetration and killing power was the important matter. In addition to bows and arrows, the Apaches used lances and war clubs of various designs. Some were of wood, but the favorite type was a stone-headed skull-cracker attached to the handle by a leather thong so that the head swung freely from the handle. For killing small game the Apaches, like several other tribes of the southwest, used boomerangs. They were not as sharply curved or bent as those of the Australians, and did not return to the thrower, but could be thrown with great force and remarkable accuracy by the Indians. Although horse Indians, the Apaches were not splendid riders such as the Sioux, Comanches, Cheyennes, and other plains tribes, and were notoriously cruel to—or perhaps I should say regardless of the welfare of—their ponies.

Perhaps the most unusual and rather remarkable fact about these savagely fighting Indians is that, once they were at peace, they took to farming as a duck takes to water, and today the once-feared and warlike Apaches are mainly well-to-do farmers and ranchers on an equal footing with their white neighbors and thoroughly respected by them. Many, however, took to railroad work, and today hundreds of Apaches are employed on railway construction jobs or as structural steelworkers on bridges and buildings in all parts of the world.

Although to the majority of persons the Apaches were the epitome of fiercely fighting Indians of the Southwest, the Kiowas and the Kiowa-Apaches (who were a distinct tribe, not a mixture of the two tribes as their name suggests), were more feared by the whites than the various so-called Apaches, and caused more trouble and depredations than the latter. Originally inclined to be peaceful and friendly toward the whites, the Kiowas soon realized that it was a question of wiping out the white men or being wiped out by them, and they did their level best to prevent the latter. To be sure, they failed to exterminate the whites, but the most reliable statistics prove that in proportion to their numbers they killed more white persons than any other tribe. A tribe of distinct linguistic stock, their original home was the area of the upper Yellowstone and Missouri rivers. Later they moved southward to the regions of the upper Canadian and Arkansas rivers in Kansas and Colorado. Until 1840 they were allies of the Crows and enemies of the Cheyennes and Arapahos, but made peace and became allies of their recent enemies. Having suffered greatly from the ruthless acts of the white immigrants and settlers, they carried on a relentless war along the whole frontier of Texas and Mexico, even extending their forays as far south as Durango, Mexico. Fearless, valiant fighters and splendid riders, they were famous among the other tribes for their ferocity, and as the most bloodthirsty of all the western Indians. Their first treaty with the government was signed in 1837, when they were placed on a reservation together with the Kiowa-Apaches and some of the Apache bands. Old enmities between the tribes, and the breaking of promises and ill treatment by the Indian agents, led to discontent and trouble, and in 1874 they again went on the warpath, joining the Comanches and Cheyennes. But as a tribe they were doomed. Never a large tribe, they had lost great numbers of their warriors in battle, and in 1852 about three hundred died from an epidemic of measles. The survivors are a peaceful, industrious lot, farming and ranching on the lands allotted them.

Unlike the Kiowas, with whom they often are confused, the Kiowa-Apaches are of Athabascan stock, and although from time immemorial allies of the Kiowas they retained their own distinct language and customs. Their own name for themselves was Na-i-shan-dina or "We, the people." The Pawnees knew them as the Kaskai or "Bad Hearts," while to the Kiowas they were the Semat or "Thieves." Despite the fact that the whites called them Kiowa-Apaches, they were not even distantly related to the Apache tribes, and never had heard of the latter before 1800. Although they later came to be on friendly terms with the Mescaleros, at one period the two tribes were constantly at war. Like the true Kiowas, they came originally from the northwestern plains and joined the Kiowas for mutual protection, but unlike the latter signed a peace treaty with the government, in 1874, and have remained friendly and at peace with the whites since then.

Last of the southwestern tribes that cost the whites vast sums in money and countless lives are the Comanches. As has been told in an earlier chapter, the trouble with the Comanches began when six Comanche hunters were murdered by four white men who shot down the Indians for their scalps while the unarmed Indians were roasting meat over a campfire. As was the case with the Apaches, the white men's term Comanche was applied to several subtribes or bands forming a group or confederacy similar to that of the Dakotas with its numerous Sioux bands or subtribes. Among the more important of the Comanche bands were the Yamparikas or Root-Eaters, the Kutsptekas or Buffalo-Eaters, the Kwahadies or Antelope-Eaters, the Penatekas or Honey-Eaters, and the Hokomies or Wanderers. All were of Shoshonean stock, and are considered offshoots of the true Shoshones of Wyoming. The same dialect is in use by both tribes, and until comparatively recently the Comanches and Shoshones were closely affiliated, while according to Comanche tradition their former home was in the far northwest. Later, in the early part of the nineteenth century, they roamed the plains of Kansas, Colorado,

Oklahoma, and Texas. As a rule they were friendly toward the white men, but were implacable foes of the Mexicans, with whom, for nearly two hundred years, they waged constant war, raiding, burning, and killing as far south as Durango. And when the Texans took possession of their best hunting grounds and drove them off, the Comanches included them in their hatred and for nearly forty years were at war with the Texans. Their first treaty with our government was signed in 1835, but it was not until forty years later, in 1874-75, that, together with the Kiowas and Kiowa-Apaches, they settled on a reservation in Oklahoma between the Washita and Red Rivers. Although in reality they were a small tribe by comparison with the Sioux, the Cheyennes, and other groups, the rapidity of their movements and the long distances between their raids gave the impression of far more warriors than were actually in the field. The finest of all Indian cavalry, and possessing great knowledge of military strategy, they struck suddenly, swiftly, when and where the least expected, and vanished before the settlers or the soldiers could saddle their mounts and start in pursuit. Moreover, unlike the majority of plains Indians, they did not maintain large fixed camps when at war but moved, bag and baggage, from place to place, and when too hard-pressed they slipped over the border into Mexico and played havoc with neighbors to the south.

Although the Comanches made their first treaty as early as 1835, it was not until 1874-75 that the long Comanche war came to an end and they settled down on a reservation in Oklahoma. Large numbers died from smallpox and cholera, and it is doubtful if there are more than one thousand pure-blooded Comanches now living. A proud and recklessly brave race, and famed as the finest horsemen of the plains, they were noted for their high sense of honor and their steadfast friendships and implacable hatreds. Their language, which is rich and sonorous and far less difficult to master than most Indian dialects, has become the trade jargon or lingua franca of the southwest.

Unlike the Kiowas, who were unusually tall and splendidly built, the Comanches had a tendency to be rather short and stocky. Both tribes were much lighter in color than the Apaches, and, as might be expected considering their origins and racial affinities, the customs, crafts, habits, and costumes of the two tribes more closely resembled those of the northern plains Indians than those of their neighbors in the southwest. Although they stripped, like most plains Indians, to breechclouts and moccasins when on the warpath, at home they wore fringed and beautifully beaded buckskin shirts and leggings, with moccasins of the regular hard-soled and soft-uppers type. At ceremonials and dances they wore the typical war bonnet of the plains Indians, but in addition they had numerous headdresses peculiar to the tribe. One type was a cap of otter or badger skin with a rosette of feathers over the forehead and a short leather tail trimmed with feathers; others had deer, antelope, or buffalo horns attached to a buckskin or fur bonnet with a tail of feathers, and a feather roach on the top. Today, when taking part in tribal dances or ceremonies, they usually wear the so-called war bonnets typical of the plains tribes. Before they acquired firearms, their weapons consisted of powerful double-curved bows and well-made but rather heavy arrows, lances often fourteen or fifteen feet in length, and war clubs and skull-crackers of several types. They were very fond of ceremonials and dances, the most attractive of which was the "eagle dance" in which the participants carried staffs edged with eagle feathers which the dancers waved and swung like wings. Even today, when the Comanches are thoroughly civilized, they still keep up the old tribal dances, partly for their own pleasure and satisfaction and also as a drawing card for tourists.

In addition to the foregoing tribes, there were several others who were frequently included in the term Apache, although not even related to the true Apache tribes. Among these were the Mohaves, often called Mohave-Apaches, although of Piman stock and not Athabascan, as were the majority of the Apaches. A very large tribe, the Mohaves were naturally warlike and inhabited both sides of the Rio Grande. They were a magnificent race physically, and were famed for their elaborate painting and tattooing, which often covered the entire body. Although primarily agriculturists, and dwelling in villages of well-built square houses with flat roofs of brush and earth, yet they were far from being a peaceful tribe, and again and again raided and devastated white settlements on both sides of the border.

Another tribe that caused a great deal of trouble for both the Americans and the Mexicans, and who often were included among the so-called Apaches, were the Lipans, or Naizan, as they called themselves. Purely nomads, they originally inhabited New Mexico and northern Mexico from the Rio Grande eastward through Texas to the Gulf Coast. They were dreaded and famed for their depredations in Texas as well as in Mexico, and from 1845 until 1856 they were constantly at war with the Texans until finally driven off with heavy losses. Taking refuge in Coahuila, Mexico, they joined the Kickapoos and raided, destroyed, and killed over a wide area. Eventually, between their losses in battle and the ravages of smallpox, they became reduced to a small remnant, and in 1905 the nineteen known survivors in Mexico were brought back to the United States and placed on the Mescalero Apache reservation, together with a few who had remained in the United States. They took readily to civilization and farming, but practically none of pure blood are alive today.

Another of these southwestern tribes were the Yumas or Kwichans, who inhabited both sides of the Colorado River. Physically a very superior lot, and valiant fighters when necessity arose, they were not warlike but dwelt in fixed villages and cultivated crops of fruit and vegetables. Although they never were troublesome to the whites, yet they too are often included among the so-called Apaches.

Finally, there were the Cahitas, Mayos, and Yaquis, who formed the Cahita group of Pima stock inhabiting northern Mexico and a portion of United States territory along the border from the Gulf of California to the Sierra Madre Mountains. All were sedentary people with permanent villages and small farms where they cultivated food-plants and cotton. But they differed greatly in temperament and other characteristics. The Mayos were peaceful and desired only to be left alone, whereas the Cahitas and Yaquis were warlike and carried on a desultory warfare with the Mexicans until subdued by President Diaz, who ordered hundreds of them transported to southern Mexico and Yucatan. As it turned out, the Indians benefited by their exile.

Although at first they were virtually slaves, with the passing of the Diaz regime they became freemen, and in the warm climate with its rich soil and abundant rains they prospered. Many of them in time voluntarily migrated to central and southern Mexico.

I have known a number of these transplanted tribesmen, and all agree that they are far better off than their fellows along the border. Many of them are miners, others are *vaqueros,* others truck or bus drivers, while still others are seamen, and they are generally considered outstanding in their jobs. Many who still remain in the north are employed as *vaqueros,* others as miners, while others have profitable farms. They do some silver work, weave baskets and cotton cloth, and find a ready sale for their products, the Yaqui serapes, blankets, and hammocks being considered the finest in northern Mexico.

Inclined to be short and heavily built, with unusually dark skins, they often have full bushy beards. All who have had first-hand dealings with the Yaquis speak highly of their capabilities, honesty, and good nature. Today all are thoroughly civilized, and are a quiet, peaceful, hard-working lot. They are the only tribe in North America who for several centuries have been surrounded by the whites, yet they were never subdued until 1906-1907.

Last of these border tribes are the Sandias, whose chief claim to fame is that the watermelon was named after them. The first watermelons the Spaniards saw were cultivated by the Sandia Indians, and for want of a better name the Spaniards called them *fruta de Sandia,* which became shortened to *sandia*—which is still the Spanish word for watermelon.

XXVI

TRIBES OF THE CAÑONS, MESAS, AND DESERTS

In the mountainous and desert areas of the southwest there are a number of Indian tribes, many of whom live in cañons or on mesas. The largest, most important, and best-known group of cañon-dwellers are the Navajos. Their name is not of Spanish origin, as most persons suppose, but is a corruption of *Navahu,* meaning a large area of cultivated land. Famed for their woolen rugs and blankets and for their beautiful handiwork in silver and turquoise, these Indians are today a peaceful, pastoral, friendly lot. Yet they are the true, original Apaches, for, as we have seen, the Zuñis' name for this tribe was Apachu, meaning a dangerous or savage enemy, which was corrupted to Apache by the white men.

In the past the Navajos were a warlike tribe, deadly enemies of the Utes and the Pueblo Indians, and hostile to the whites. It was their raids on Taos and other pueblos that led to the most disastrous and tragic, as well as uncalled-for, event in the history of the tribe. In 1846 a treaty of peace was signed, but, as usual, the government did not abide by it, and hostilities were renewed. Although few whites were killed, the Navajos raided the pueblos, killing a number of the inhabitants, and in 1863 the government ordered all Navajos rounded up and deported to Fort Sumner on the Bosque Redondo, New Mexico. This was much easier said than done. A small military force of between two and three hundred men, augmented by a number of Ute scouts, all under the direction of Kit Carson, failed to capture or destroy any considerable number of Navajos. Finally the Indians concentrated, several thousand strong, in their ancient home and stronghold, the almost inaccessible Cañon de Chelley, where they defied the Army.

Having slaughtered the Indians' sheep, goats, and other livestock, the soldiers and their Ute allies surrounded the cañon and entered at both ends. Although the Navajos undoubtedly could have wiped out the whites, their chiefs realized that they were faced with starvation by the loss of their livestock, and that a battle would mean the sacrifice of hundreds of Indians' lives. Some of the leaders were for fighting to the last man, while others thought it better to surrender; unable to agree, they left the matter to Manuelito. Under a flag of truce he met Kit Carson, whom the Indians trusted implicitly, and when the famous scout pledged his word that if the Navajos surrendered and went to Fort Sumner they would be returned to their cañon home in three years, the Indians surrendered. It was a long and terrible march across the desert to the distant fort. Many of the Indians had been wounded, many were half-starved, and numbers died on the way. At Fort Sumner still more succumbed, and only a pitiful few remained when, in 1867, the government repatriated the tribe as Carson had promised, and gave them several thousand sheep and goats.

History

Once back in their homeland, the Navajos prospered and increased until today they number between forty and forty-five thousand, the largest tribe in the United States and forming almost one-tenth of our entire Indian population. But it was not all smooth sailing for the Navajos; the government failed to fulfill its promises of adequate medical assistance and available schools, and opened up much of the Navajos' grazing land to the white cattlemen, as well as placing restrictions on the number of sheep the Indians could maintain. As a result the Navajos have suffered terribly, and even in recent times the majority have been forced to live in abject poverty. However, conditions have improved within the past few years, and the discovery of uranium on their lands may make them as wealthy as they were poor.

Although they are classed by ethnologists as of Athabascan stock, yet their language is a complex composite dialect made up of the languages of numerous tribes that long ago became fused with and absorbed by them. In their physical characteristics they are as composite as their language, and it would be impossible to describe a really typical Navajo. They vary from tall, stalwart men over six feet in height to near-dwarfs. Some have strong features, aquiline noses, and square chins, while others have the subdued features of the Pueblo tribes type. Usually they have pleasant, intelligent faces, with skins ranging from olive to quite dark. Many of the women, and especially the young girls, are strikingly handsome. By nature they are jovial and merry, love fun and banter, and even the proudest members of the tribe do not scorn to work. They are very industrious, progressive, and religious, and while many are professed Christians the majority still worship their ancient deities and follow the ancient rites, customs, and crafts of their ancestors. Among these are the making of their famous sand paintings. Although many now dwell in well-built wooden houses, the true Navajo home was the hogan, made of logs and covered with brush and earth, and partially underground.

Strangely enough, the Indians most closely resembling the Navajos are the Mapuches or so-called Araucanians of central Chile. Although separated by many thousands of miles, the two tribes are almost identical in many respects. The hogans of the Navajos and the rucas of the Mapuches are almost duplicates; many of the Navajo utensils are practically indistinguishable from those of the Mapuches, and their footwear is equally similar. Both tribes are famous for their silver work, and for their rugs and blankets. Like the Navajo men, the men of the Mapuches wear a turbanlike strip of cloth about the head. The deities of the two tribes are practically the same, as are their religious beliefs and ceremonials. Both are pastoral people with flocks of sheep and other livestock, both are agriculturalists, and, perhaps most remarkable of all, the baby-carrier or cradle-board of the Navajos is absolutely identical with that of the Mapuches—although there are no cradle-boards used by any of the tribes geographically located between the Mapuches and the Navajos. Moreover, although neither tribe uses canoes, yet the dead are interred in canoe-shaped coffins!

Another cañon-dwelling tribe are the Havasupai or "People of the Sky-Blue Water" who live in the Cataract Cañon of the Colorado River in western Arizona. At one time they were pueblo builders, with large villages of adobe houses, but because of raids by enemy tribes they changed their mode of life and took to the almost inaccessible mountain cañons. A very quiet and peaceful tribe, they cultivate many crops. In winter they dwell in caves, but in the summer time use wattled huts. They have no pottery, but make most excellent baskets, and are famous for the perfection of their tanned buckskin.

Very different are the Walapais, a Yuman tribe who inhabit the cañons of the Aquarius Mountains. They are an inferior race physically, and do not take to agriculture, but live by hunting and gathering wild roots, berries, etc. Unlike their neighbors, they are averse to civilization and schools.

Dwelling in the Arivaipa Cañon are the Arivaipa Indians, the name meaning "girls," which most certainly is a misnomer, for they were a very warlike and savage tribe often called Apaches by the whites. At the present time the majority of the tribe are on the San Carlos Reservation.

Inhabiting the valleys of the Gila and Sant rivers in Arizona, although not cañon-dwellers, are the Pimas. Today a pastoral and agricultural tribe with irrigated fields and living in pole houses covered with grass and sod, at one time they were pueblo Indians, the famous Casa Grande and other massive ruins having been built by their ancestors. As a rule, the adobe, fortresslike pueblos were built to serve as refuges from enemy attacks, but for some unknown reason the Pimas reversed this custom and abandoned their pueblos for the open. They were also unique in other ways. Believing that their enemies were possessed of evil spirits, they never scalped those they killed, fearing that if they touched the bodies the "devils" might be transferred to themselves. Although they never spared a man if wounded or captive, yet they treated women and children prisoners kindly, and adopted them into the tribe.

Of all Indians of the southwest, those best known to tourists are the Pueblos. Their villages are accessible, they are a friendly and colorful lot, and, being keen traders, they cater to the tourist trade, wearing their tribal dress, staging dances for the benefit of visitors, and offering for sale a bewildering array of their beautiful pottery, textiles, baskets, and other handiwork. Although thousands of white persons visit the Pueblos each year, yet they have only a superficial—and often erroneous—knowledge of these Indians. Many are under the impression that all belong to one tribe called "Pueblo," although in reality there is no tribe of that name, the word *pueblo* (Spanish for village or small town) being applied to all Indians dwelling in villages of adobe houses. Among them are a number of distinct tribes of several stocks, each with its own dialect, customs, dress, ceremonies, dances, costumes, and arts. Thus the people of Nambe, Tenuque, San Ildefonso, San Juan, Hano, Sandia, Taos, Picuris, Jemez, and Senecu are all of Tanoan stock. Those of San Felipe, Santa Ana, Sia, Cochiti, Santo Domingo, and Acoma are all of Keresan stock, while the Indians of Walpi, Sichomovi, Michongnovi, Shongopovi, and Oraibi (all commonly called Hopis or Moquis), are of Shoshonean stock. Some of these occupy several villages or pueblos, while others have only one—as for example the Sias, who are a small tribe with their single pueblo near Bernalilo, New Mexico—whereas the Hopis have six villages in northeastern Arizona.

Descendents of the cliff-dwellers who built their villages in caves and cañons of the mountains as a protection from enemies, these tribes took to the open and built their fortresslike villages on hilltops and mesas accessible only by means of ladders that could be drawn up when danger threatened. Now, with all fear of enemy raids over, a number of the pueblos are on level ground. Probably the best-known and most popular of the various pueblos are those of the Zuñis and the Hopis. The former occupy a large pueblo on the north bank of the Zuñi River in New Mexico. The name Zuñi is the Spanish corruption of the Keresan Sunyitsi, the Zuñis' own name for themselves being A-Shi-Wi or "People of the Flesh Country." Always friendly toward Americans, but suspicious of the Spanish, the Zuñis were quick to see the potential gold mine in the form of tourists, and opened the door to visitors, permitting them to witness the tribal dances —although the majority of their rites are held within the pueblo in secret and are never seen by outsiders, with the exception of a favored few who have been long associated with the Zuñis and are regarded almost as members of the tribe. A quiet, industrious people, the Zuñis adhere closely to their ancient religion with its innumerable complicated ceremonies, its secret societies and its dances.

Also visited by thousands of tourists are the Hopis, or, as they call themselves, the Hopiyu or "Peace People," who are usually but mistakenly called Moquis by the whites. Born traders, shrewd and always on the lookout for the tourist trade, they are a merry, joking, docile, and hospitable tribe, and are famed for their snake dance, during which the participants handle live rattlesnakes, often holding the reptiles in their mouths, and apparently being unaffected by their bites. How they manage this is a closely guarded secret, but for a long period preceding the dance they go through ceremonies and undergo treatment to render themselves immune to the venom, and, at the close of the dance, use powerful emetics. In the past, visitors were permitted to witness and even photograph the snake dance, but today this is prohibited.

Pre-eminently religious, and few of them Christians, the Zuñis are very strict in their moral codes. Murder is unknown among them. Theft is very rare, and lying is regarded as a sin. They are monogamists, and heavy penalties are exacted for immorality of any sort. Among them partial albinos are quite common, and these fair-skinned, blond or brown-haired individuals are greatly revered. In common with other pueblo tribes they hunt small game with a form of boomerang called rabbit sticks, which, in the hands of an expert, are remarkably accurate and highly effective.

The best-known pueblo of the Lagunas is the village of the same name on the San José River in New Mexico, about fifty miles from Albuquerque. Unlike the other groups, the Laguna tribe is composed of several linguistic stocks, including Shoshonean, Keresan, Tanoan, and Zuñian. The most easterly of the pueblos in Arizona is that of the Hanos, or, to use their own name, the Hopiyu or "Eastern People." In addition to all these, there are the well-known pueblos of Taos, San Ildefonso, Acoma, and a number of others, each with its distinctive forms of pottery and other handicrafts, and all welcoming with open arms the visitors who today are a source of revenue rather than despoilers.

XXVII

INDIAN LEGENDS, FOLKLORE, AND JOKES

WHY THE WOOD DUCKS HAVE RED EYES
An Oglala Sioux Legend

THE ARIKARA STORY OF CREATION

THE ORIGIN OF THE THUNDERBIRD CLAN
A Winnebago Legend

THE MANDAN STORY OF THE POLE STAR

THE FIRST FIRE
A Legend of the Cherokees

HOW CORN CAME TO THE INDIANS
A Legend of the Senecas

THE INVENTION OF THE BOW AND ARROW
A Mohawk Legend

THE MOHAWK LEGEND OF THE WAMPUM BIRD

THE MOHAWK LEGEND OF CREATION

HOW THE EARTH WAS CREATED
A Yuchi Indian Legend

YOU GREAT WHITE MAN
By Johnny Canoe

JOKES THE INDIANS LOVE

WHY THE WOOD DUCKS HAVE RED EYES

An Oglala Sioux Legend

DESPITE his shortcomings, which were mainly laziness and a mania for exploiting his friends' hospitality, Big Elk was a likable character. He had a keen sense of humor and was also an excellent artist; when he told the Oglala legends and folklore tales, he illustrated them with pencil sketches, usually of a more or less humorous character. A very good example of these was his story of "Why the Wood Ducks Have Red Eyes." When I asked Big Elk if he thought the story was true, he replied that it must be—because everyone knows that all wood ducks do have red eyes.

Many, many years ago, in the very old times before even the Indians were in this land, a huge spider set out on a long journey. He carried a bag filled with food on his back, but he was a big eater like all spiders, and after he had traveled for several days the bag was empty. He became very hungry, but he could find nothing to eat, and he puzzled his brains trying to think up some way of getting food.

After some time, when he was walking up a little hill, he saw a pond on which many kinds of ducks were swimming about. There were black ducks, redhead ducks, mallards, pintail ducks, and a little wood duck.

"Ah, ha!" thought the spider, "how nice a good fat duck would taste," and as he sat watching them he felt more and more hungry every minute. But try as he might, he could not think of any way he could catch a duck. Finally he had an idea. He knew that all ducks are very curious birds and always want to find out about anything new or strange that they see. So the spider gathered a great lot of dry grass and filled his bag with it. Then putting the bag on his back he walked toward the pond. As soon as the ducks saw the spider with his burden they all began to quack, all asking at the same time what he had in his bag.

"Don't bother me," said the spider. "Don't ask so many questions. Just stop your noise and I'll tell you. I've been sent to carry a bagful of new songs to a place far from here."

That made the ducks more curious than ever and they quacked louder than before, all asking him to sing one of the new songs. But the spider told them he could not do that because among them there were some medicine songs that held magic powers, and that if he opened the bag and took out a song it might be one of the medicine songs, which would be very bad for them all. One song, he told the ducks, always brought a tornado, and before it could be sung a strong tornado-proof lodge must be built. Perhaps, he said, this might be the song on top within the bag, so it would not be safe to try to take out a song.

As he talked, the spider kept walking about the pond as if in a great hurry to reach the spot where the songs were to be delivered. But the ducks were so curious to hear a new song that they did not notice that the spider was just going around and around, and they kept following him, begging him to sing. At last he stopped as if out of patience. "If you must have a song I'll take a look and see which one is on top," he told them. Then he opened his bag and pretended he was looking inside.

"Just as I thought," he told the ducks. "The first song is that tornado song." Then he told the ducks that if they wanted to hear it they must all help to build a strong lodge of willows and mud. "It must be very tight," he said, "with only one small door. Then we will be safe when the song brings the tornado."

When at last the lodge had been built, the spider told the ducks to go inside and to shut their eyes, for it was a very magical song and if any duck kept its eyes open they would turn bright red. After all the foolish ducks had gone into the dark lodge, the spider went in also and shut the door behind him. Then he began to sing, and as he sang he swung his war club and began knocking the ducks over their heads.

He had already killed several of them when the wood duck decided to take a peep, for he wanted to see what was happening.

"Quack! Quack!" he cried when he saw what was going on. "Run away, brothers," he shouted, "the spider is killing us! Run away before he knocks you all over your heads!"

The spider stopped singing and rushed at the wood duck, but the wood duck was small and very quick, and he slipped between the spider's legs and got away safely. While the spider was trying to catch the wood duck the other ducks ran from the lodge and flew off. None of their eyes changed color, but the wood duck had opened his eyes while the spider was singing, and ever since that time all the wood ducks have had red eyes.

THE ARIKARA STORY OF CREATION

My old Arikara friend, Joseph Walks His Horses, did not live in a tipi and did not wear fringed buckskin and feathers. Instead, he dwelt in a well-built frame house surrounded by well-tilled fields and bountiful crops, and he was clad in blue-denim overalls and a checked shirt, for he was a prosperous independent farmer on his own land. But he still wore his hair long in two braids and with a beadwork fillet about his head, and he preferred moccasins to boots or shoes. Although he had adopted so many of the white men's ways, yet stowed away in his parfleche trunks were garments of fringed and beaded buckskin, elaborate headdresses, bear-claw and bear-teeth necklaces, magnificently beaded tobacco pouches, bows and arrows, red pipestone pipes, and skull-crackers decorated with scalp locks; outfits to be used at tribal councils, ceremonials, and at rodeos. Joe had no idea of his exact age, but he had been a well-grown youth at the time of the killing of Sitting Bull, and he remembered having seen Red Cloud, so I surmised he was about my own age.

Having lived among the Sioux, the Cheyennes, the Blackfeet, the Arapahos, and other tribes, he was a living encyclopedia of Indian lore, and knew most of the folk tales and traditions of the Arikaras and other tribes.

On this particular evening we were seated on the porch of his home, together with Smiling Girl, his Winnebago wife, and corpulent old Red Bear, a Mandan neighbor. The conversation turned to the ancestry and origins of the various Indian tribes.

"According to my people, all races were alike at one time," said Walks His Horses as he filled and lit his brier pipe, and then he went on to tell the Arikara story of Creation.

Even the animals and birds were then of one kind. But they were all within the earth, where there was no light and they were much crowded. There were no fishes in the lakes and streams, no birds or insects in the air, no four-footed beasts, and no men or women on the earth. Within the earth the living things were struggling and working to break out and find light and freedom, but they met great obstacles. The mole managed to bore a hole to the surface, but as he pushed his head into the light he was blinded by the sunshine and quickly drew back. So today the mole still lives just beneath the surface of the ground and is still blind. However, now that the mole had made an opening the other creatures quickly enlarged it and hurried to push through. Before all could escape, however, the earth caved in, and so to this day the gophers and badgers and snakes and the other creatures left behind must still live in the ground.

The creatures that had come out safely looked about, but they could not face the sun, so they turned toward the west and moved on. By and by they came to a great body of water. This obstacle they tried to overcome, and they used all their powers trying to cross the water. Those who had wings and could fly had no trouble, but those who could not fly tried to jump or wade or swim to the other shore. Many never reached there; so we still have the water people, such as fishes, frogs, turtles and others.

But those who finally crossed the water on floating logs or bundles of reeds, or who managed to swim across, continued on their way until they came to a dense forest of great trees, and here they were again stopped. By now they were very tired and hungry, but they had not yet learned to kill one another for food and they had not learned what plants could be eaten. So they prayed to the One Who Sits in the Sky and begged him to help them. Some managed to make their way through the forest, but others failed and lost their way and always remained there. These became the deer, the bears, the moose, the foxes, and other forest creatures we have today.

At last the Mighty One in the Sky saw that certain creatures who put their trust in prayers and offerings had overcome all the difficulties in their way. He blessed these people as men and women, and gave them power over all other creatures. He also gave them a sacred medicine bundle and a medicine pipe to be used in praying. He gave them a religion and the power of speech, and taught them how to worship. He showed them the seeds, the nuts, the roots, and the fruits they could eat, and others that would cure sickness and heal wounds. He taught them how to make weapons and traps, and how to kill the other creatures for their skins and flesh, and how to make fire, and all the other things that we know. Also, he blessed all living creatures on earth, even the trees and flowers, the vines and grasses, and he told the people that they must not destroy any of these things without cause or to be used as food. All these things that live on earth and look up at the sun he said were friends of the men and women, and must not be mistreated, that each had its place and must be respected. And it was taught the people that the pipe and the tobacco should be used to offer the smoke to all things He had blessed. And so it has been done from that time until today.

After a time the people found themselves getting crowded, so they divided into families and then into clans, and finally into tribes. And so that they might be known to one another, each dressed in a certain way or wore some mark that would be recognized, and some took up homes on the plains and some in the mountains. Some preferred to hunt and kill wild beasts for food, but others preferred to live in villages and cultivate the plants on which they fed. Gradually, too, their speech changed, and many different tongues were spoken, so they devised sign talk.

Now all the time that the Great Spirit had been talking with His people, and while the smoke offerings were being made, there were two dogs which had been asleep and had been forgotten. When they awoke they were angry because they thought they had been neglected when the smoke offerings had been made to all the other creatures, and they said to the people: "You failed to make any offerings or prayers for us. Therefore to punish you we shall bite you, and yet we never will leave you but will follow you and be with you forever."

The names of these two dogs were Sickness and Death, and, as they said in that long ago, Sickness and Death are always among all living things on earth. All are bitten by Sickness and bitten by Death, as was foretold. It is the same with all things. The sun shines but is overcome by night, the moon becomes full and then wanes, the flowers bloom and then wither, leaves come forth only to be cut down by autumn, the wind blows and then there is calm. Such changes come to all things on earth. We sicken and die, but though the dogs of Sickness and Death may bite, yet He in the Sky sees to it that all things that are bitten return and are reborn.

"My people have a different story," said Smiling Girl. "Would you like to hear it?"

"I certainly would," I told her, so she related the Winnebagos' story of the Creation, and the origin of the Thunder-Bird Clan.

THE ORIGIN OF THE THUNDERBIRD CLAN

A Winnebago Legend

In the beginning the Earth-Maker was sitting in space, when he came to consciousness; and nothing else was there, anywhere. He thought of what he should do and finally began to cry, and tears from his eyes fell down below him. After a while, he looked below him and saw something bright. The bright objects were his tears that had flowed below and formed the present waters. When the tears flowed together, they became the seas as they are now. Earth-Maker began to think again. He thought, "It is thus: if I wish anything, it will become as I wish, just as my tears have become seas." Thus he thought. So he wished for light, and it became light. Then he thought, "It is as I supposed, the things that I wished for came into existence as I desired."

Then again he thought, and wished for the earth, and this

earth came into existence. Earth-Maker looked on the earth and liked it; but it was not quiet, it moved about, as do the waves of the seas. Then he made the grass to grow, but the earth was not quiet yet. Then he made the rocks and stones, but still the earth was not quiet. Then he made the four directions, North, South, East, and West, and the four winds. On the four corners of the earth he placed them as great and powerful people, to act as weights. Yet the earth was not quiet. Then he made four large beings and threw them down toward the earth, and they pierced through the earth with their heads eastward. They were snakes. Then the earth became very still and quiet. Then he looked upon the earth and saw that it was good. Then he thought again of how things came into existence just as he desired.

Then he began his first speech. He said: "As things become just as I wish them, I shall make one in my own likeness." So he took a piece of clay and made it like himself. Then he talked to what he had created, but it did not answer. He looked upon it and saw that it had no mind or thought, so he made a mind for it. Again he talked to it, but it did not answer, so he looked upon it again and saw that it had no tongue. Then he made it a tongue. Then he talked to it again, but it did not answer, and he looked upon it and saw that it had no soul, so he made it a soul. He talked to it again, and this time it very nearly said something. But it did not make itself understood, so Earth-Maker breathed into its mouth and talked to it and it answered.

As the newly created being was in his own likeness, Earth-Maker felt quite proud of him, so he made three more just like him. He made them powerful, so that they might watch over the earth. The first four he made chiefs of the Thunderbirds. He thought: "Some will I make to live upon the earth that I have made." So he made four more beings in his own likeness. Just like the others he made them. They were brothers–Kunuga, Henanga, and Nangiga. He talked to them and said, "Look down upon the earth." So saying, he opened the heavens in front of where they sat, and there they saw the earth down below them. He told them that they were to go down there to live. "And this I shall send with you," he added, and gave them a plant. "I myself shall not have any power to take this from you as I have given it to you, but when of your own free will you make me an offering of some of it, I shall gladly accept it and give you what you ask. This shall you hold foremost in your lives." It was a tobacco plant that he had given them.

He also told them, "All the spirits that I create will not be able to take this from you unless you desire to give it by calling upon them during fasts and offering it to them. Thus only can the spirits get any of it. And this also I send with you, that you may use it in life. When you offer anything, it shall be your mediator. It shall take care of you through life. It shall stand in the center of your dwellings, and it shall be your grandfather." Thus he spoke to them. What he meant was the fire. And then he gave them the earth to live on.

So the four thunder-spirits brought the four brothers down to the earth. The oldest one, Kunuga, said while on their way down: "Brother, when we get to the earth and the first child is born to me, I shall call him Chief of the Thunders, if it be a boy." On they came down toward the earth. When they got near the earth it began to get very dark. The second brother said: "Brother, when we get to the earth and a child is born to me, if it is a girl, it shall be called Dark." They came to a place called Within-Lake at Red Banks (a lake near Green Bay). On an oak tree south of the lake is the place where they alighted. The branch they alighted on bent down from their weight. Then said the third brother to his brothers; "The first daughter born to me shall be called She-Who-Weighs-the-Tree-Down-Woman." Then they alighted on earth, but the thunder-spirits did not touch the earth. Then said the fourth and last brother to his brothers: "Brothers, the first son that is born to me shall be called He-Who-Alights-on-the-Earth." The first thing they did on earth was to start their fire.

Then Earth-Maker looked down upon them and saw that he had not prepared food for them, so he made the animals, that they might have something to eat. The oldest brother said: "What are we going to eat?" Then the youngest two took the bow and arrows that Earth-Maker had given them, and started toward the east. Not long after, the third brother came into view with a young deer on his back, and the youngest brother also came with a young deer about two years old on his back. The deer that were killed were brothers, and those that killed them were also brothers. They were very happy they had obtained food. Then said they: "Let us give our grandfather the first taste." Saying this, they cut off the ends of the tongues, and the hearts, and threw them into the fire with some fat.

The first people to call on them were the War-People. They came from the west. Then came four others. They were the Thunders. Thus they were called, the youngest brothers. Then came those of the Earth. Then came those of the Deer Clan. Then came those of the Snake Clan. Then came those of the Elk Clan. Then came those of the Bear Clan. Then came those of the Fish Clan. Then came those of the Water-Spirit Clan, and all the other clans that exist. Then there appeared on the lake a very white bird—Go-gitchi, the swan, they called it—and after that, all the other water birds that exist came. And they named them in order of their coming, until the lake was quite full. Then the people began to dress the deer meat.

Suddenly something came and alighted on the deer meat. "What is that?" they asked. Then said Kunuga, the oldest brother: "It is a wasp; and the first dog that I possess, if it is black, Wasp I shall call it." Thus he spoke. "And as the wasp scented and knew of the deer-dressing, so shall the dog be toward other animals; and wherever the dog is, and animals are to the windward, he shall scent them."

They made a feast with the deer for Earth-Maker, and threw tobacco into the fire and offered it to him. And to the other clans they showed how fire was to be made, and gave them some. "For," they said, "each of you must make fire for yourselves, as we shall not always lend it to you." There the people made their home. It was just the time of year when the grass was knee-deep, or summertime.

One day they reported that something very strange was near the camp; but they said to themselves, "We will leave it alone." In a little while it moved nearer. Thus it moved toward the camp, and soon it began to eat deer bones. They allowed it to become one of the clans, and took it into their house. It was the dog or wolf. They killed one of them, and made a feast to Earth-Maker, telling him all about what they had done.

In the beginning the Thunder clansmen were as powerful as the thunder-spirits themselves. It was the Thunder-People who made the ravines and the valleys. While wandering around the world the Thunder-People struck the earth with their clubs and made dents in the hills. That is the reason that the upper clans are chiefs of all the others, and that the least of all are the Dog-People. So it was.

One day the oldest of the brothers lay down and did not get up again, and he did not breathe, and he became cold. "What is the matter with our oldest brother?" the three other brothers said. Four days they waited for him, but still he did not arise. So the second brother was asked by his youngest brother what the trouble was. But he did not know anything about it, and told him to ask his third brother; but he did not know either. Then the two older brothers asked the youngest one; but he did not know either. Then they began to mourn for their oldest brother, not knowing what to do or to think. They fasted and blackened their faces as we do now when we are mourning. They made a platform and laid him on it.

When the snow fell knee-deep, the three brothers filled their pipe and went toward the place of the coming of daylight, the east. There they came to the first being that Earth-Maker had placed in the east, or the Island-Weight, as he was called. They came to him weeping, and went into his tent, and placed the stem of their pipe in his mouth. They said: "Grandfather, our brother has fallen, and is not able to rise again. Earth-Maker made you great, and has given you all knowledge, and thus you know all things." He answered and said: "My dear grandsons, I am sorry, but I do not know anything about it. But as you have started to find out, I would send you to the one ahead of me, the North. Perhaps he can tell you."

So, weeping, they started for the corner of the earth where the North lived. When they got there and told him their troubles, he told them he could not help them. "But," he said, "perhaps the one ahead of me knows." So they started for the third one, the West, but from him they could learn nothing. He also referred them to the one ahead or the South. When they reached the fourth and last corner of the earth, they entered the lodge, and behold! there sat the three to whom they had gone before. Here they asked the last one for help, and not only he, but the other three also, answered them: "Grandsons, thus Earth-Maker has willed it. Your brother will not rise again. He will be with you no more in this world. And as long as this world lasts, so it will be with human beings. Whenever one reaches the age of death, one shall die, and those that wish to live long will have to attain that age by being good and doing good. Thus they will live long. Into your bodies Earth-Maker has placed part of himself. That will return to him if you do only good things. This world will come to an end sometime. Your brother shall keep a village in the west for all the souls of your clan, and there he shall be in full charge of all of you. And when this world is ended your brother shall take all the souls back to the Earth-Maker; at least, all those who have acted properly. Thus it was. Now you may go home and bury your brother in the proper manner."

The Thunder-People thanked the four spirits and left their tent. When they got home, they dressed their brother's body in his best clothes and painted his face. Then they told him where he was to go, and buried him with his head toward the west, and with a war-club. They placed a branch of a tree at his grave, and painted a little stick red and tied it to the tree, so that nothing should cross his path on his journey to the spirit-abode.

THE MANDAN STORY OF THE POLE STAR

"How ABOUT telling us a Mandan story?" I asked Red Bear.

"I know only one" he replied. "That is the legend of the Star of the North. Since I heard it from my grandmother, who was a Cree, perhaps it really is a Cree story and not Mandan." He settled himself comfortably in the big chair that creaked with his weight, folded his hands over his paunch, and half closed his eyes as if to peer into the past.

There was no light upon the plains and no light above; for there was no sky and no sun. Upon the plains below, men hunted buffalo and antelope, while spirits hunted the fire-buffalo and the smoke-deer upon the plains above. All men become discontented with their lot in time, and so it was with the men on earth, who watched the hunting of the spirits and envied them and the strange game they took, for how could antelope and buffalo meat compare with medicine meat of the smoke-deer and fire-buffalo? And what was a beaver skin compared to the medicine skin of the sky-eagle?

Then, one day, a man with the strength of three bears, who was named Onowate, threw his war-club into the air and killed the great sky-eagle that to the Indians today is known as the Thunderbird. This made the spirit people angry, and they complained to the Great Spirit, who drew a blue robe between the plains above and the plains below and forever hid the spirit land from the eyes of men.

During the day the sun shone down on the plains below and during the night it shone on the plains above, and men on the earth had to be content to hunt the buffalo and antelope and moose and wapiti, while, for all men knew, the spirit people hunted the smoke-deer and fire-buffalo.

At that long-ago time there was an Indian woman named Ayoo who had more cunning than three mountain lions, and who also had as much curiosity as the magpie. She was curious to see the hunting of the spirit people beyond the blue robe above, and she bribed the men of her tribe to climb up trees and cut holes in the blue robe. In those days the trees were not like trees today, for they were as high as the mountains and almost as large. Even one hundred men, all holding hands, could not reach around the base of one of those trees and could not see the top branches which touched the blue sky-robe. At first the men feared to do as Ayoo wished, for they were afraid of displeasing the Great Spirit, but with the cunning of three mountain lions she urged them and at last they climbed the trees and cut holes in the sky, and when night came the sun shone on the plains above and leaked through the holes and twinkled and became stars. Every night the woman and the men peered through the holes and spied upon the spirit hunters. Then one night Onowate, the man with the strength of three bears, reached through a hole and, catching a fire-buffalo by one leg, he pulled it through. Onowate's arm was burned to his shoulder and his fingers were turned to ashes, but that night he feasted on the dinner of the spirit people.

This made the spirits very angry, and once more they complained to the Great Spirit, but the Great Spirit refused to mend the sky-robe, for while he was very angry with the men below yet he was pleased by their bravery. But in the end he listened to the spirit people, and with a twist of his hand he started the sky-robe spinning. That stopped the men from peeking through holes; no sooner would a man place his eye at a hole than the hole would move, so he either had to stop looking or fall from the tree. In those long-ago times the sky-robe spun much faster than it does today, but if you fix your gaze on the stars in half an hour you will see that they have moved. The spinning sky-robe stopped men from trying to watch the spirit people, and again they hunted buffalo and antelope and moose and wapiti. But Ayoo, the woman as cunning as three mountain lions, was not satisfied, and she went to Onowate, the man with the strength of three bears, who had killed the fire-eagle and had eaten meat of the fire-buffalo, and told him her plan. So one night he went to the biggest tree left on earth, that was named Goriken (which means it cannot be bent). He climbed up this tree to the highest branch, which he pushed into the nearest hole in the sky-robe.

Around and around the sky-curtain whirled, but the branch never moved, for it was part of the Goriken tree that cannot be bent, and it stopped the sky-robe from moving onward. Of course this made the spirit people more angry than before, and again they complained to the Great Spirit. But he was so pleased at the cleverness of the man and the woman that he laughed at the spirit people. So they took the matter into their own hands and sent fire at the man and the woman. The fire burned Onowate's skin and Ayoo's hair, but he beat out the flames and Ayoo put bear grease on his burns, and the Goriken tree still stood straight. So the spirits sent water. This loosened the grip of Onowate, and it filled Ayoo's mouth and it rotted the bark of the great tree, but still the tree held firm. Next the spirits sent stones and then lightning and thunder and hail, but nothing loosed the branch of the tree, and the sky-robe kept on whirling around and around it, and Ayoo was able to satisfy her curiosity. In the end the spirit people complained to the dreaded Snow Spirit whose home is in the Below of Below, and he came up with his cold winds and his snow and his blizzards and ice and beat upon the tree and the man and the woman. Ice froze on the arms of Onowate until they became so heavy and stiff that even with his strength of three bears he could not move them. Hail and snow beat upon Ayoo, until even with her cunning of three mountain lions she could not think. And more and more snow and ice covered the branches of the great tree, until it broke and crashed down and together with the man and woman it was buried deep under the snow.

But even to this time the sky-robe still turns around and around that one point in the north where the light from the land above shines through the hole made by the branch of the Goriken tree, and it never moves. Sometimes under her snow-blanket Ayoo whispers cunning words into Onowate's ears, and with his strength of three bears he tries to lift the great tree once more. Then the spirit-people call upon the Snow Spirit and he comes from his cave in the Below of Below and brings the blizzards we all fear, and buries the man and the woman and the Goriken tree under great drifts of snow so that they cannot ever again stop the hole where the bright star shines that guides men upon their journeys.

THE FIRST FIRE

A Legend of the Cherokees

ALTHOUGH the majority of the Cherokees are among the most highly civilized of Indians and have their own commonwealth, their own legislature and other officials, their own laws, periodicals, and newspapers, there are yet members of the tribe, dwelling in the Great Smokies of the Carolinas, who still keep up some of their old tribal customs on certain occasions and among them there are a few oldsters who know the ancient Cherokee legends and folk stories. It was one of these venerable Indians—an octogenerian named Looks to the Moon—who told me the Cherokee legend of the First Fire.

In the long time ago the world was very cold, for there was no fire anywhere. But the Great Spirit took pity on the animals who were suffering from the cold, and sent the thunder and the lightning that made fire in the bottom of a dead and hollow tree upon an island. The animals all saw the smoke coming from the dead tree and knew there was fire, but on every side there was water so they could not reach it. Then they held a council to try to decide what to do. Every bird and beast that could fly or swim wanted to go to get the fire. First the raven offered to try, for he was strong and big, and as all the others felt sure he would succeed they let him go. Up high in the air he flew, and then across the water to the fire-tree. But then he didn't know what to do or how to get the fire. While he was puzzling about this, a breeze came up, and the flames rose high and scorched the raven until he was black all over, and he was so frightened that he flew back to the council without the fire.

The next to offer to go for the fire was the little screech owl. He flew across the water and came to the tree safely and peered down into the hollow trunk. While he was doing this, hot air came up and nearly burned out his eyes. Although he managed to fly back to the council, he could not see plainly, and he still blinks his eyes when there is much light.

The council decided that it would be best if two creatures went together for the fire, so the hooting owl and the big horned owl flew off across the water together. When they reached the tree it was all ablaze, and the fire was so hot and there was so much smoke and ashes that the owls were almost blinded and the ashes made white rings around their eyes as they are today.

After that none of the other birds wanted to try to get fire, but the Uksuhi snake (black racer) said he would try. He was a good swimmer, and reached the island and crawled through a hole at the bottom of the fire tree. But inside there was so much heat and smoke that he had to get out, but before he managed it his skin was scorched as black as the raven's feathers. Next the great climbing snake, Gule-gi, volunteered to go.

When he reached the island he climbed up the tree, but when he thrust his head into the hollow trunk to look at the fire the smoke choked him and he tumbled into the burning stump, and before he could climb out he was as black as Uksuhi—which is the reason there are two kinds of black snakes today.

So all the creatures held another council, and they were very cold, for they still had no fire to warm themselves, and the birds and snakes and four-footed creatures were all afraid to try to get the fire.

Finally the water spider spoke up. This was the big water spider with downy hair and with red stripes on her body who can dive and swim, and she offered to go. She reached the island easily, but didn't know how she could bring back fire while she swam and dived in the water. Then she had an idea, and she spun her thread and wove it into a Tusti bowl, which she tied on her back. Then she crept carefully through the green grass to where the fire was burning the roots of the tree, and, reaching out a long leg, she managed to get one small coal. Putting this in her Tusti bowl, she ran quickly across the water and brought back the hot coal safely. Very quickly the creatures kindled a fire, and ever since then the big water spider carries on her back the Tusti bowl that is scorched red by the hot coal, and ever since then we have had fire to keep us warm and to cook our food.

HOW CORN CAME TO THE INDIANS

A Legend of the Senecas

In the long-ago time the only food of the people who lived on the bank of a river was game and fish.

One day the people of the village were told by an old woman that she had heard a woman singing on the river. She told them that the words of the song were: *"Fair and fine are the planted fields where I dwell, going to and fro. Fair and fine are the planted fields that we have planted. My grandmother and my ancestors, we planted them."*

For ten nights the old woman heard the singing, and she said to her friends and her family: "Let us go out and see what this singing means. Perhaps some woman has fallen into the water and is singing in the middle of the stream."

Then they went to the river bank, but could see no one. On the tenth night after this the singing was heard again, and again the words were: *"Fair and fine are the planted fields where I dwell, going to and fro. Fair and fine are the planted fields we have planted. My grandmother and my ancestors, we planted them."*

The women of the village again went to the river bank for three nights and sang songs of welcome and recognition. On the third night these women knew that the strange singer was coming nearer. On the next night the women with their children, watching the river and singing, were surprised to see a large number of strange women coming toward them, and one of the girl-children cried: "Oh, Grandmother, do not let these women strike us," and all the children ran from the place. Then the oldest of the village women said: "I alone shall remain here to wait for whatever happens, for I know it is the spirit of my granddaughter that is coming, and she is in need of pity and help."

Then the singer in the river cried: "Oh, my Grandmother! Take me away, for I am able to go where you are now."

Then the grandmother pushed her birch-bark canoe into the water and paddled to the young woman who had been singing in the river. She found her resting on the back of a great beaver that held her high above the water. The singer cried: "Oh, my Grandmother! Take me away." So the old woman placed her in the canoe and paddled to the shore. When they landed the young woman said: "Oh, Grandmother! Leave me here. I will stay here and you must come to me in the morning. Nothing shall happen to me in the night."

So the grandmother went to her lodge and told the others

what had taken place. Early the next morning she went back to the landing place, but there she saw nothing but the growing stalk of a strange plant. Growing on this stalk she found an ear of corn, and breaking it off she carried it to her lodge where she hung it to a roof-pole by the fireplace.

In the night the old woman had a vision in which the young woman who had sung in the river said to her: "Oh, my Grandmother! You must take me from this place, for it is too hot here. You must place me in the ground, plant me and leave me there. Then will I provide for you and your people. Plant me under the ground, my Grandmother."

So the old woman took down the ear of corn and shelled the grains and put them in the ground. The next night the old woman had another vision in which the Corn Maiden said to her: "You and your people must care for me. You must not let the weeds choke me. Then you shall see me sprout and grow to maturity, and in the time to come all the people who shall be born will see that I will provide for them, so you must take good care of me. Soon you and your people will see a great number of other people who are coming here. You will see that I will provide for all during the time the earth shall be. You now know the truth. I am the maize. I am the corn. I am the sweet corn. I am the first corn that came to this earth."

For three more nights the old woman had this same vision, so she knew what she must do with the corn she had planted. When it sprouted she cared for it and kept the weeds away and killed the worms that would eat it. The stalks grew tall, and waving plumes like those of a warrior sprang from the tops of the stalks, and ears of maize grew along the stalks. So in the autumn the old woman and her family harvested the corn and divided it into as many portions as there were families in the village, and to each old woman in each lodge she gave a portion to be used as seed in the springtime, and she told them all how to care for it.

When she went back to her lodge she lay down on her couch to rest for the night, and another vision came to her. This time the Corn Maiden said: "You must tell the people not to waste the corn, for those who do not honor it and care for it properly will always come to want. Unless the act in the proper way toward me, I shall take all the corn away. You must tell all these things to your people, my Grandmother. You must tell them to store what corn they do not eat where it will be safe, where the rats and the squirrels and the birds cannot reach it. You must tell them how to cook the corn, how to roast it, how to grind it into meal, and how to make it pop open over a fire, for there are many ways to eat the maize."

So the old woman told her people all that the Corn Maiden had told her in the vision, and from that time on all the people had maize to eat, and no longer had to depend on game and fish alone.

THE INVENTION OF THE BOW AND ARROW

A Mohawk Legend

LONG AGO the people of the Longhouse did not have the bow and arrow for a weapon. At that time, a spear was the common weapon used in the hunt.

One day a young Mohawk hunter whose name was Ohgweluhndoe left his village in search of bear. His only weapon was a long spear, tipped with flint. Ohgweluhndoe walked a long way. He saw no signs of bear. After a while the thought came to him that perhaps he would find a bear in a thickly forested glen that was not far away. In this particular place there were many wild grapevines. It was at the time of the Moon of Falling Leaves (October). The grapes would be ripe and the bear would, no doubt, be eating them.

Ohgweluhndoe was not wrong in his guess. As he entered the thickest part of the glen, he caught sight of a huge black figure. It was Oh-gwa-li, the bear, and he was busy eating wild grapes. From time to time he would grunt little squeals of pleasure as he gulped the wild grapes down. The young hunter crept very close. He was almost within reach of the bear. Quietly he raised the spear for the death stroke. It would have been a death stroke but for one thing. As Ohgweluhndoe was about to throw the spear, his foot slipped on a rock and he fell sprawling to the ground, almost under the bear's claws. With a startled grunt the hunter looked up. He still held the spear, but now he was in no position to throw it. Oh-gwa-li, the bear, ordinarily would have run away from a human hunter; but the sudden appearance of the young Mohawk startled him, and instead of running away as most black bears do, he turned and started for the hunter. Ohgweluhndoe did not take long getting to his feet. With one jump he was on his feet, and in a moment was heading through the forest. The bear, seeing that the hunter was running from him, gained courage and quickly took after Ohgweluhndoe. For a little while the two, the hunter and the bear, kept the same speed, but in a short time the bear gained rapidly on the hunter.

Ohgweluhndoe knew that in a very little while the bear would have him and that probably he would be torn to pieces. He thought of his wife and son waiting at home for his return. This thought made him determined to kill the bear or die in the attempt. Turning quickly, he made ready to throw his spear at the bear, but the end of his spear had caught on a twisted grapevine which was clinging to the top of a small ash sapling. The hunter tried to pull the spear free from the vine, but he succeeded only in bending the sapling. The bear was almost upon the Indian. Ohgweluhndoe made one more effort to pull the spear loose. As he tugged at the spear he pulled the sapling to the ground. He did not wait long. With a startled yell, he let the spear go and turned to run. He had not run many steps when he noticed that the bear was not following him. He looked back. The bear was on the ground with the spear stuck through his neck. The blood was rapidly reddening the leaves as Oh-gwa-li gave a few final kicks and died.

The surprised hunter went back to see what had happened. The spear which had caught on the vine had caused the sapling to bend, thus forming a bow. The vine had been the bowstring, the sapling the bow. When the hunter had pulled the spear he had caused the sapling to bend. When he dropped the spear the sapling had sprung upright again. The force of this spring had whipped the vine straight, at the same time throwing the spear ahead into Oh-gwa-li's neck.

The hunter again took the spear and put the end of it on the vine. Pulling the vine back, he bent the sapling. When the sapling had bent almost to the ground, he released the spear. It shot through the air. Thus was the bow invented.

In time the Mohawks made smaller bows out of smaller saplings. Instead of grapevile bowstring they used one of rawhide. Instead of a heavy spear, they used an arrow tipped with flint and winged with feathers. The bow became a priceless weapon for the People of Flint, the Mohawks.

AREN AKWEKS (RAY FADDEN)

THE MOHAWK LEGEND OF THE WAMPUM BIRD

LONG AGO a war party of Mohawks captured a young man of the Wampanoag Nation. For some years the Mohawks had been at war with these people. The captive boy was allowed to live, and was given permission to move freely about the Mohawk village. He was closely watched so that he might not escape back to the Wampanoag country.

One day a young Mohawk hunter came running into the village. He was filled with excitement, for he had seen a strange bird in the forest. This bird was covered with wampum beads. Immediately a hunting party was organized, and the hunters set out to try to capture the wonderful bird. The hunters, after walking a short distance, came upon the bird. The bird was as the hunter had described it. It was covered with white and purple feathers. The head chief, as soon as he saw the bird, offered his beautiful daughter to anyone who could get the bird, dead or alive. All the hunters tried to hit the bird with their arrows. They filled the air with their arrows. Occasionally the bird was hit by an arrow, and then off would fly a shower of wampum. Each time, new wampum appeared on the bird to take the place of that which had fallen. Finally, after trying to hit the bird for some time, the best hunters began to get discouraged, and one by one they gave up trying to get the bird.

The young Wampanoag captive, from the unfriendly tribe, asked the chief if he could try his luck. The Mohawk warriors did not approve, and even threatened the boy's life, but the chief interfered and told the boy that he could try. "If warriors have tried and failed, surely a mere boy cannot bring down the bird," said the chief. The warriors finally agreed, and the boy lifted his bow and fitted an arrow. The swift arrow pierced the heart of the remarkable bird and it fell to the earth. Its wampum plumage enriched the people. The boy married the chief's daughter, and with the marriage came peace between the two nations. The boy said, "Wampum shall bring and bind peace, and it shall take the place of blood."

AREN AKWEKS (RAY FADDEN)

THE MOHAWK LEGEND OF CREATION

AFTER Io-no-ko-io-wah-non, the Good Spirit, had made the animals and the earth, he rested. As he gazed around at his various creations, it seemed to him that there was something lacking. For a long time the Good Spirit pondered over this thought, and finally he decided to make a creature that would resemble himself.

Going to the bank of a river, he took a piece of clay and out of it he fashioned a little clay man. After he had modeled it, he built a fire, and, setting the little clay man in the fire, waited for it to bake. The day was beautiful. The songs of the birds filled the air. The river sang a song too, and as the Good Spirit listened to this song he became very sleepy. He soon fell asleep beside the fire. When he finally awoke, he rushed to the fire and removed the clay man. He had slept too long. His little man had baked too long and was burned black. According to the old Mohawks, this little man was the first Negro.

The Good Spirit was not satisfied. Raking a fresh piece of clay, he fashioned another man, and, placing him in the fire, waited for *him* to bake, determined this time to stay awake and watch his little man to see that he would not be overbaked. But the river sang its usual sleepy song. The Good Spirit, in spite of all he could do, fell asleep. But this time he slept only a little while. Awakening at last, he ran to the fire and removed his little man. Behold, it was only half baked! This, says the Mohawk, was the first white man.

The Good Spirit was still unsatisfied. Searching along the river bank, he hunted until he found a bed of perfect red clay. This time he took great care and modeled a very fine clay man. Taking the clay man to the fire, he once more put it to bake. This time, determined to stay awake, the Good Spirit stood beside the fire. After awhile Io-no-ko-io-wah-non removed the clay man. And now it was just right—a man colored like the red color of the sunset sky. This was the first Mohawk Indian.

AREN AKWEKS (RAY FADDEN)

HOW THE EARTH WAS CREATED

A Yuchi Indian Legend

IN THE beginning the waters covered everything. It was said: "Who will make land come?"

Then Look-Chew, the crawfish, said: "*I* will make the land." So he went to the bottom of the water and stirred up the mud with his tail and his claws, and brought up the mud to a certain spot and piled it up.

Then those who owned the mud at the bottom of the water said: "Who is meddling with our mud?" So they kept watch and saw the crawfish. They crept near him, but he saw them and stirred the mud with his tail so they could not see him, and he carried up more mud and piled it up until at last he raised his claws in the air to show all living things that there was land above the water.

But the land was too soft, so they said: "Who will spread this land and make it dry and hard?" Then someone said: "Ah-Yok, the hawk, should spread the soft land and dry it with his wings." But others said: "It should be Yah-Tee, the buzzard, for he has larger wings. He can spread the land and make it dry."

Yah-Tee spread out his wings and tried to dry the earth. He flew above the soft land and spread his great wings over it. He sailed back and forth over the land and spread it out, but after a long time he tired of holding his wings spread so he began to flap them, and this made the hills and valleys because in spots the earth was still soft.

"Who will make the light?" someone asked, for it was all darkness.

Yo-Hah, the star, said: "*I* will make the light." So the star shone, but the only light was close to him.

"Who will make more light?" they cried. So Shar-Par, the moon, said: "*I* will make more light." He made more light, but still it was dark.

Then T-Cho, the sun, said: "You are all my children. I am your mother, so *I* will make the light shine for you." Then she moved to the east, and suddenly light spread over the earth. As she passed over, a drop of blood fell from her to the ground, and from this blood came the first people, the Children of the Sun, the Yuchis.

These first people had no fire, and it was cold, so they wanted to find a fire medicine. But while they were searching for it a monster serpent appeared and killed many people. The others slew him and cut off his head. Next day the head and body were united. So they killed him again. For the second time the head and body joined. Then they cut off his head and placed it in a treetop so the body could not reach it. But the next morning they found the tree dead, and the head fallen and again joined to the body. Once more they killed the great snake and cut off its head, and this time they put it in a higher tree. But again the head and body joined. One by one the people tried all the trees in the forest. At last they placed the head in the branches of Ter, the cedar tree. In the morning they found the tree still alive, but covered with blood that had flowed down from the head. Then someone tried to rub the blood from a branch of the Ter tree and fire came.[1] So in this way the great fire medicine was found.

YOU GREAT WHITE MAN

by Johnny Canoe (Doug Wilkinson)

(Courtesy of *Indian Time Magazine*)

This is the time of year when Christian people's minds turn to commercials of all descriptions. First, they spend money they cannot afford buying presents for other Christians whom they dislike three hundred and sixty-four days of the year. Then their squaws cook food which makes them sick. They also buy huge quantities of firewater, sold to them by the government. They drive cars while drunk and are promptly arrested by the police, whose job it is to maintain the laws made by the government and collect fines which go to one branch of government administration or another—civic, provincial, or federal. If you have no money you go to jail, which in your status of citizen you pay for out of your own pocket in devious forms of taxation. You buy your klootchman a few trinkets, you chop down a tree, buy electric lights and synthetic snow. You kiss under the mistletoe the person you would like to choke. You follow custom blindly. You won't open an umbrella in the house, you won't live in a Number 13 teepee, you fear Friday the thirteenth, and you will not pass under a ladder. Three people will not take a light from one match, your squaw goes and has her teacup read, you wear black when somebody dies, yet all depends on what he left you in his testament. Your churches do not agree, your women wear furs in summer and gauze in winter. You go hunting and kill more than you can eat; you have fine cattle, yet you eat horse; you call yourselves civilized while inventing weapons to destroy

[1] The Yuchis made fire by means of a fire-drill of cedar wood and bark.

yourselves. You put your old people, your father and your mother, in a boardinghouse because they can do it on the old age pension, yet you forget your Number 4 Commandment.

Your newspapers are filled with sordid stories of your children stealing cars, housebreaking, and now using drugs. You are horrified at prostitution and brothels, yet by the simple act of divorce you are able to do the same thing legitimately. You elect a candidate to Parliament, you get dissatisfied at his highhandedness and you question his honesty, yet you elect him again to represent you amid howls of a crooked ballot.

If you dislike anybody, you call him a Communist, yet you cannot see the actual Communist hiding under your bed. You have exchanged your principles for "keeping up with the Joneses," you no longer are individual, you lack the courage of your convictions. You preach one thing and act the total opposite. The proof of this is two wars and an undeclared war.

You protect the health of your murderers to keep them in a perfect condition to hang. Your youth must be physically fit to get shot at in war. You have exploited wherever you went. Now you are being kicked out of Asia and the Middle East. You form the United Nations to protect minorities, you spend a great deal of time and money on discussing this, yet you neglect the Indian, who was the original ruler of the land you live in. You borrowed your God from the Jews, yet you show your gratitude to Jewish people by discriminating against them to the fullest degree. You use your God for profanity. You cannot make up your mind how to worship Him.

You endow anthropology to snoop into Indian culture, and you pay through the nose to decorate your own family tree. You call yourselves democratic, yet you break your necks to be made an Indian chief or princess. You shove down our throats your way of life. You put laws on your books, yet you govern your lives by the taboos of prejudiced public opinion, which often is a complete contradiction of the law. You ridicule other cultures, yet you are internationally reputed to have none of your own, and you write books trying to prove that you have one.

You do research in food, and plan proper diets, yet the cost of living is so high that nobody can eat properly. You waste your national resources to such an extent that you have to appoint commissions at high salaries to look into the matter and excuse your excesses. You are your own downfall.

To an innocent little Indian off the Reserve, it is all very difficult!

JOKES THE INDIANS LOVE

A traveling salesman stopped at a small western town and noticed an old Indian squatting in the street surrounded by his baskets, pottery, and curios. As the stranger had heard that Indians have wonderful memories, he stopped beside the old Indian and asked:

"What did you have for breakfast July 15, 1925?"

"Eggs," replied the Indian.

Two years later the salesman passed through the same town and saw the same old Indian sitting in the same spot. He walked over and by way of greeting said: "How, chief?"

"Fried," the Indian grunted.

"What's your nationality?" the census-taker asked the man.

"Three-quarter Indian," the man replied.

"And what's the other quarter?" the census-taker asked.

"My wooden leg," was the answer.

Down in New Mexico an Indian went to the Office of Internal Revenue to ask for help in making out his income tax report.

"What's your gross income for last year?" the clerk inquired.

"No savvy," the Indian replied.

"Do you have any dependents? Anyone you have to support?"

"No savvy," said the Indian.

"Well," said the clerk, as he closed the book, "if you can't be more cooperative I am afraid I can't help you. I thought perhaps you would have a refund coming to you."

"Haw!" said the Indian. "How much?"

"Is that child Indian?" the eastern woman asked a comely Indian woman standing by the railway station in a western town.

"Half Injun," the woman replied. Then, pointing at the locomotive, she added: "And half Injuneer."

The tourists from the East had been admiring the beaded buckskin garments and eagle-feather headdresses of the Blackfeet camped in one of the National Parks.

"How do you get the eagle feathers?" the lady asked. "I understand that the law imposes a heavy fine for killing eagles."

"We don't kill the eagles," the Indian assured her. "We just make strong medicine so when the moulting season comes the eagles fly over our village and drop their old feathers."

Governor Murray of Oklahoma was entertaining a famous Japanese publisher who was touring the United States. "By the way, did you ever meet a real American Indian?" the governor inquired.

The Japanese admitted he had not.

"Well," laughed the governor, "you're talking to one now."

"If you were not an Indian I'd say you are lost," said the white hunter to his Indian guide after they had tramped for several hours without reaching camp.

"No," replied the Indian, "I ain't lost—but I reckon I am a little confused."

The car stopped before the neat farmhouse with a sign TOURISTS ACCOMMODATED. "Can we get a room for overnight with meals?" the driver asked the man seated in a chair on the porch.

"You sure can," he replied as he rose and approached the car.

"But—but you look like an Indian!" exclaimed the female tourist. "I don't think—"

"I sure am, ma'am," he replied. "But you don't need to be scared. Scalps have gone out of fashion, an' I done lost my scalpin' knife anyhow."

"Is it true that you Indians eat dogs?" the tourist asked a young Pawnee.

"Yes, sir," replied the Indian, "but good eatin' dogs is mighty scarce since the price of sausages has gone up."

The visitor from the east stopped before the old Indian squatting beside his tipi and surrounded by baskets, pottery, and other Indian-made curios.

"How, chief," the tourist greeted him. "Is it true that some Indians can see what is happening in places far away?"

"Huh," grunted the Indian, "Mebbe so. How much you pay for me tell?"

The easterner handed the Indian a five-dollar bill.

Closing his eyes, the aborigine rocked back and forth slowly. Then: "Plenty big fire New York," he muttered. "Plenty people killed. Skyplane hit mountain some place call Virginia. Train plenty smash Iowa place. Big wind call hur'cane hit Florida. No can see more."

"That's wonderful!" exclaimed the tourist. "I never believed it possible. How on earth do you do it?"

"Huh," grunted the Indian with a grin. "Me got radio."

"Why don't you work?" demanded the white man. "You can get a good job."

The Indian dozing in the sun glanced up. "Why?" he muttered.

"So you can earn money," replied the white man. "If you save money and put it in the bank, by and by you will have enough so you won't have to work any more."

"Huh," replied the Indian. "Me no work now."

The motorists from the East stopped at an Indian tipi whose owner was surrounded by Indian curios and handiwork.

"I do not care for your curios," said the tourist, "but I have always wanted to see the inside of a tipi. I will give you a dollar if you will take me inside and show me around."

The Indian showed him his willow back-rest, his buckskin garments and feather headdresses and his weapons and utensils.

"Not bad for a camp," admitted the tourist, "but not a single comfort in it, not even a table or a chair. Why don't you live in a house?" Then, pointing to a house in a grove of trees nearby—"why don't you have a house like that?" he asked the Indian.

"I do," replied the Indian. "I own it. Tipi is my come-on. Tourists pay one dollar to see inside of tipi. No pay one dollar to go inside house."

"Your squaw makeum?" the tourist asked, indicating the baskets, beadwork, and other handiwork on the roadside stand.

"No," replied the Indian in charge. "She don't have time for such things. Too busy teaching in the white kids' school."

"Indeed! And what does she teach?" the tourist demanded.

"Teaches 'em English," replied the Indian.

Entering a diner an Indian aviator ordered a ham sandwich. Lifting the upper slice of bread he asked the counterman, "Did you slice the ham?"

"Yeah," replied the counterman "what is the matter with it?"

"Nothing," replied the Indian, "but I'd call it a 'near miss.' "

At a rodeo, a tourist stopped an Indian wearing a costume of beaded and fringed buckskin. "Are those scalps?" he asked, pointing to the fringes on the Indian's breech-cloth.

"Yes, sir," replied the Blackfoot. "I lifted 'em myself—offen a dead pony."

"Did you ever take scalps?" a tourist asked an Indian.

"No, ma'am," he replied, "but my father took plenty."

The tourist shuddered. "What a terribly barbaric custom!" she exclaimed.

"I dunno about that, ma'am," said the Sioux. "An Indian may scalp his enemy, but more'n one white man skins his friend."

GLOSSARY OF THE PRINCIPAL TRIBES NOW LIVING IN THE UNITED STATES[1]

(English and Indian names and meanings. Racial and linguistic groups. History. Characteristics. Various data. Habits. Original habitat.)

ABBATOTINE. Abba-to-tena, "Mountain Sheep People." Nahane stock. Upper MacMillan, Pelly and Stewart River valleys, Yukon.

ABNAKI. Same as Wabenaki.

ACOMAS. A'-ko-ma, "White Rock People." Keresan group of Pueblo Indians. Rio Grande Valley, New Mexico.

AHTENA. "Ice People." Same as Yellowknives. Athabascan stock. Copper River Basin, Alaska. Formerly hostile.

AKONYE. "People of the Cañon." Athabascan group. A subtribe of the Apaches. Associated with the San Carlos (Arizona) Indians.

ALABAMUS. Alba-Ayamule. "We clear the woods." Muskhogean stock. Alabama. Peaceful, friendly with whites. Now almost extinct.

APACHE. From the Zuñi Apachu, meaning "an enemy," and applied originally to the Navajos, who were formerly savage raiders. The term Apache was used by the whites to designate any or all of various tribes, subtribes, and bands of various stock in the southwest. Among them were the Luerechos, Mescaleros, Jicarillas, Faraones, Llaneros, Chiricahuas, Akonyes, Pinaleños, Coyoteros, Mimbreños, Tontos, Lipans, Kiowa-Apaches, Mohaves, Yumas, and others. Many of these were normally peaceful, while others were born bandits and gloried in warfare and thieving raids on other tribes and white settlers alike. They were famed for their cruelty and tortures inflicted upon prisoners, but, on the other hand, they were loyal to their friends. Many of the so-called Apaches were peaceful, but without discrimination the whites treated all alike. When finally subdued by General Howard, the Apaches took readily to farming, and today many are prosperous ranchers and farmers highly respected by their white neighbors. Many of the men are

[1] Tribes with a majority of members less than three-fourths Indian are not included in this list.

skilled section hands on the railways, while others are expert structural steelworkers.

ARAPAHO. Corruption of the Pawnee Larapihu, meaning "Traders." A plains tribe of Algonquin stock. For many years closely associated with the Cheyennes. They call themselves the Inu-Nyainaor, "Our People," while the Cheyennes and the Sioux know them as the "Blue-sky People." Originally a sedentary, horticultural tribe living in the Red River valley of Minnesota, they trekked westward about the same time as the Cheyennes and became associated with the latter and the Blackfeet. Now divided into the northern Arapahos of Wyoming and the southern branch on the Arkansas River. Friendly with the whites, the Sioux, the Blackfeet, the Cheyennes, the Kiowas, and Comanches, but enemies of the Utes, Pawnees, Crows, and Shoshones. Among themselves they recognize five divisions or groups, each with a slightly different dialect and probably representing five original tribes. Unlike most of the plains tribes, they buried their dead in the ground. Never troublesome except for a time when some of the tribe allied themselves with the Cheyennes in the latter's war with the government.

ARIKARA. From Ariki, a "horn," derived from their custom of wearing the hair twisted in hornlike form on either side of the head. Caddoan stock. Linguistically almost identical with the Pawnees. Once associated with the Skidi band of Pawnees. Originally inhabited the Missouri Valley as far south as Omaha, but migrated north into Sioux territory. Friendly toward whites except on one occasion, when there was a short conflict over treatment by traders.

ARIVAIPA. From Arivapah, meaning "girls." A very warlike and savage tribe included among the "Apaches," whose home was the Arivaipa Cañon of Arizona. Now on the San Carlos and Fort Apache reservations.

ASSINIBOIN. A-Sin-A-Pwan, or "Those who cook by using stones." A Siouan tribe once allied with the Yanktons. Originally about the headwaters of the Mississippi, but moved north and joined the Crees about 1670. At present mainly on reservations in Montana.

ATHABASCAS or FOREST CREES. From Athap-Askaws, meaning "Grass or reeds about." A large tribe of northwest Canada and the United States border. The tribe from which the linguistic stock name of Athabascan is derived.

BANNOCK. A tribe of Shoshonean stock formerly of Idaho and Wyoming. Now mainly on reservations. Friendly except for one outbreak in 1878 when the tribe was half starved from lack of food on their reservation (two and a half cents per capita per day allowed). A few whites were killed, but peace was made, and conditions improved a few months later.

BLACKFEET. See Siksika.

BLOODS. A subtribe of the Blackfeet.

CADDO. A confederation of several tribes of Caddoan stock. Originally in the lower Red River area of Louisiana. Spread north and west. Peaceful agriculturalists, they often aided the whites against the raiding Comanches, but their lands were seized and the settlers planned a wholesale massacre of the tribe. With great difficulty they were safely transferred to Oklahoma. During the Civil War they were loyal to the Union, thus incurring the hatred of the Confederates, who were in the majority in the Caddo area.

CAHITA. A small group of tribes of Pima stock who inhabited northern Mexico and a narrow area of the United States just north of the border. The three principal tribes were the Cahitas, Mayos, and Yaquis. All were sedentary Indians with permanent villages and small farms. They differed greatly in their characteristics, however. Whereas the Mayos were peaceful and desired only to be left alone, the Cahitas and Yaquis were warlike and carried on a desultory war with the Mexicans until subdued by President Diaz, who deported many of them to Yucatán and southern Mexico. As it turned out, the deportees were benefited by their exile. Although virtually slaves at first, they became freemen with the passing of the Diaz regime, and in the warm climate with its rich soil they prospered. Many of their fellows voluntarily migrated and joined them. Many are miners, others are *vaqueros,* others truck and bus drivers, while others are seamen or pearl divers. They are considered the best in each profession and are industrious, honest, and trustworthy. Many have heavy bushy beards. (See further details under Yaquis.)

CATAWBA. A Siouan tribe of the western portions of northern Georgia and the Carolinas. Now considerably mixed with both white and Negro blood. But still retaining their tribal language and many of the old ways, dances and ceremonies.

CAUGNAWAGA. From Ga-Hna-We-Ge or "At the Rapids." A division of the Iroquois, originally occupying northwestern Vermont and northeastern New York and Canada near Montreal. Closely related to the Mohawks, the two dialects being practically the same. In 1763 many of the tribe migrated to the Ohio Valley near Sandusky. About 1755 they had established a settlement near St. Regis, N. Y. Some moved west, and by 1820 a number were with the Salish, while others reached the mouth of the Columbia River in

Oregon and as far north as the Peace River in Athabasca. Throughout the west they were known as Iroquois. At the present time mainly in the vicinity of Montreal, at St. Regis, and about Lake George. They have played a very important part in the building of bridges, skyscrapers and other steel structures throughout the world, the men being considered the best of all structural steelworkers. They have had a part in the erection of the Empire State Building, the George Washington Bridge, the Storm King, Golden Gate, and other great bridges.

CAYUGA. From Kwenyio-Guen or "Place where locusts were taken." An Iroquois tribe of the Six Nations, originally about Cayuga Lake, N. Y.

CAYUSE. A tribe of Waiilpation stock, formerly of Oregon and Washington. Always famed for bravery and for the superiority of their horses, which became known by the tribe's name. Almost wiped out by smallpox in 1847. Survivors joined the Nez Percés.

CHEMEHUEVI. A Shoshonean tribe inhabiting the valleys of the Colorado westward to California.

CHEROKEE. From the Choctaw Chiluk-Kior, "Cave People." A very large and powerful tribe of Iroquoian stock. Formerly holding the entire mountain area of southwestern Virginia, North Carolina, South Carolina, Georgia, Tennessee, and Alabama. Today thoroughly civilized. The one tribe with a printed language of eighty-six characters, invented by an illiterate Cherokee named Sequoia. One of the "Five Civilized Tribes" of Oklahoma. A number still remain in the Great Smoky Mountains and other areas in the east. They retain many of their old dances, ceremonies, and traditions and are mainly engaged in farming. At one time hostile, they fought practically all other tribes and the United States until finally conquered by Andrew Jackson.

CHEYENNE. From the Sioux Shahi-Yenna, or "People of Red Talk," meaning an alien language. Their own name is Tisi-Tsi-Istas, or "Our People." The sign-language gesture for Cheyenne is drawing the right forefinger rapidly across the left forefinger; and they are known to other tribes as "Cut fingers," owing to their custom of cutting off the fingers of the left hand, or the entire hand, of those they killed, and preserving them as "fetish" trophies. When first known, they inhabited the prairie lands of Minnesota and were a sedentary agricultural tribe. Pressed by the Chippewas, they were forced westward and became fused with the Sutaio tribe, which was completely absorbed, the language being lost. Crossing the Mississippi, the Cheyennes occupied the Black Hills of Dakota.

They were harassed by the Assiniboins, Crows, and other tribes, but became fast friends of the Sioux and Blackfeet and, later, the Arapahos. For a time they maintained more or less permanent villages, but took to a nomadic life and depended upon the buffalo for a living. However, as recently as 1860 many cultivated small farms and dwelt in earth- or sod-covered houses rather than in tipis. After they came in contact with the peace-loving Arapahos the two tribes became allies, although not assimilating. About 1832-35 the tribe became divided into two principal groups—the northern Cheyennes about the headwaters of the Yellowstone and North Platte rivers, while the southern Cheyennes occupied the valley and vicinity of the Arkansas.

Here they were constantly at war with the Kiowas and Comanches but in 1840 a council was held and peace established, after which the Cheyennes, Kiowas, Comanches, Kiowa-Apaches, Arapahos, and Sioux became allies.

In 1849 great numbers died of the cholera, nearly two-thirds of the tribe being wiped out. At times they raided as far south as Mexico, but until forced by the actions of the whites they were peacefully disposed toward the settlers and others. Even among the other Indians the Cheyennes have always been famed for their bravery, fighting ability, horsemanship, and pride. They are also famous for their kindly treatment of prisoners and for adopting them into the tribe. On one occasion prisoners of twenty-eight different tribes were among the Cheyennes, and all but a few became members of the tribe voluntarily. Also, many white prisoners joined the Cheyennes and married Cheyenne women. They were very strict morally, with a high regard for women.

They were ruled by a council of forty-four elected chiefs, of whom four had power to appoint one of their number as head chief. The tribe was divided into numerous bands or subdivisions, and had innumerable secret and "medicine" societies, each with its own secret dialect and its medicine bundles, fetishes, etc. They were very fond of ceremonies, the most important of these being the sun dance with its self-tortures, and the fire dance in which the Indians walked barefooted over red-hot coals. At the present time there are from twelve thousand to fifteen thousand Cheyennes of more than three-quarters full blood, distributed on various reservations and on farms and ranches of their own.

CHICKAHOMINY. From K'chick-aham-min-nough: "The Coarse-Pounded Corn People." A Virginia tribe that belonged to the Powhatan confederacy. Once large and powerful. At present numbering about 250, mainly of mixed Indian and Negro blood, but still retaining some tribal organization and a chief. The majority in New Kent and Charles City counties, Virginia.

CHICKASAW. One of so-called "Five Civilized Tribes": Cherokees, Choctaws, Creeks, Seminoles, and Chickasaws. Muskhogean group related to Choctaws in language and customs, although formerly mutually hostile. Originally inhabiting northern Mississippi and the area where Memphis, Tennessee, now stands. An agricultural tribe with well-built permanent villages. Noted for bravery, independence, and warlike character. Constantly at war with Creeks, Choctaws, Cherokees, and other tribes. In 1732 annihilated a war party of Iroquois who invaded their territory. Enemies of the French but inclined to be friendly with the English, and victors in various engagements with the former. In 1715 allied with the Cherokees and drove the Shawnees from the Cumberland. In 1769 at war with Cherokees, whom they drove away. About 1822 began to migrate west, and by 1834 were mainly in Indian Territory (Oklahoma). In the early days they numbered about four thousand. In 1904 there were about five thousand. Now thoroughly civilized, with their own political organization, municipalities, etc.

CHINOOK. The best-known of the Chinookan family group. Originally north of Columbia River, Washington, to Gray's Bay. Numerically a small tribe of a few hundred individuals. Now fused with the Chehalis, whose language has been adopted, the original Chinook having become extinct. However, it formed a basis for the Chinook-English trade jargon used from California to Alaska.

CHIPPEWA. Corruption of Ojibway, meaning to "pucker up," because of the puckered seam on their moccasins. One of the largest tribes in the United States, with many in Canada. Formerly occupying both shores of Lakes Huron and Superior across Minnesota to North Dakota. An Algonquin group that included the Ottawas and Pottawattomies, but later separated into divisions, although still maintaining more or less of a confederacy, while north of Lake Superior they are so closely affiliated with the Crees and Muskogee that they are scarcely distinguishable. Frequently at war with the Sioux, Sauk and Fox, and other tribes, in order to protect their wild rice fields which were, and still are, of paramount importance to them. Eventually they drove the Sioux across the Mississippi, and began a westward migration until many settled about the headwaters of the Red River in the Turtle Mountains. At the same time they spread over the peninsula between Lakes Huron and Erie, forcing the Iroquois to withdraw. Warred with the white settlers up to the end of the War of 1812. In 1815 they signed a treaty that has never been broken. At the present time they number about thirty thousand, of whom about fifteen thousand live in the United States on reservations and on their own farms.

CHIRICAHUA. Meaning "Great Mountain." One of the "Apache" tribes of southeastern Arizona. The most warlike and cruel of the various Apache bands who made frequent raids across Arizona, New Mexico, and into Mexico. Most of the famous Apache chiefs and warriors were Chiricahuas, among them Cochise, Vitorio, Loco, Chato, Nachi, Bonito, and Geronimo. Although they were inveterate bandits and gloried in murder, yet their ordinary facial expression was open and pleasant. They were also hospitable, and food was free to anyone. In trade and monetary affairs they were honest, and invariably paid their debts. Once they made a friend, whether red or white, they remained steadfast, and there are many instances of such leaders as Cochise placing a guard about the home of some friendly settler to stop the raiders from molesting the white occupants. They would not eat fish or pork, but considered unborn calves and entrails as delicacies. Largely they subsisted on flour from various seeds, cacti fruits and other desert products, together with what game they could kill. Their favorite beverage was *tizwin,* made from ground-sprouting corn fermented in water. Deficient in most arts, they wove superior water-tight baskets, often of large size. They were fond of dances, especially "devil dances" with clowns, masks, and huge, elaborate headdresses. In 1872 they made a treaty with the United States, and about one thousand settled on the Chiricahua Reservation. In 1875 they were removed to the San Carlos Reservation. Oddly enough, they took readily to farming, and today the majority are respected farmers and ranchers who are on equal terms with their white neighbors. Many are skilled railway section hands, and others are expert structural steelworkers.

CHOCTAWS. One of the "Five Civilized Tribes." An important Muskhogean tribe formerly inhabiting northern Mississippi and southern Georgia. Related to the Chickasaw, Huma, and other Muskhogean tribes, the dialects being practically identical. First known to whites by contact with De Soto, whom they attacked with fury. When the French began settling in their area, the Choctaws became their allies against other tribes. Later they split into two factions, one allied with the French, the other with the English. After the Revolutionary War, many of the tribe moved west across the Mississippi, where they battled with the Caddos.

Always on friendly terms with the whites, the Choctaws deeded much of their land to the government and moved into Indian Territory. At one time they practiced artificial head-flattening. The dead were skeletonized and the cleaned bones were deposited in boxes or baskets in the "bone houses." Now thoroughly civilized. Some still live in Louisiana and Mississippi, while the majority, about seventeen to eighteen thousand, are in Oklahoma.

CHUMASH. A group of California Indians inhabiting the coastal area. Also known as "Santa Barbara" Indians. Now true Mission Indians with very few if any of pure Indian blood. In the past noted for their friendly, hospitable character, and their comparative wealth and abundance of food. Largely relying upon seafood, but also cultivating many food plants. They dwelt in dome-shaped grass houses of large size, each housing fifty or more people, often of several families. Their canoes were made of planks lashed together and caulked. Coiled baskets, stone carving, and painted posts, as well as carved wooden dishes, were unique, and like their canoes were totally unlike anything made by other California tribes. They were addicted to unique shell ornaments, and asphalt inlaid with abalone shell. No true tribal divisions, the basis of the organization being family groups.

COCHITI. A Keresan tribe with its pueblo, San Felipe, on the west bank of the Rio Grande twenty-seven miles southwest of Santa Fé. Formerly had several pueblos.

COCOPAS. A division of the Yuman group originally living in villages about twenty-five miles above the mouth of the Rio Grande and in the mountains of Lower California. Very similar to the Yumas. Although primarily agricultural, they were inclined to be warlike, and were often included with the Yaquis in their depredations. Very few now living within the borders of the United States.

COMANCHES. A term applied to several bands of Shoshonean stock. Considered a fairly recent offshoot of the true Shoshones of Wyoming, as the same dialect is spoken, and until quite recently friendly with the Shoshones. Also, their traditions tell of their former home in the northwest. During the early part of the nineteenth century they roamed over the plains from Kansas, Colorado, Oklahoma, and Texas as far north as the headwaters of the Red, Trinity, and Brazos rivers. For over two centuries they waged a steady war on Mexico, raiding as far south as Durango. As a rule they were friendly toward the whites, but bitter foes of the Texans, who had taken possession of their best hunting grounds. For nearly forty years they were at war with the Texans. In 1835 they made their first treaty with the government, but it was not until 1874-75 that, with their allies the Kiowas and certain Apache bands, they settled on their reservation between the Washita and Red rivers in Oklahoma. Never a large tribe, their numbers appeared far greater than they were because of the wide area they covered and the rapidity of their movements. During the epidemic of smallpox and cholera, many died. At the present time there are not over one thousand, mainly on the Kiowa Agency reservation, Oklahoma. A proud and brave race, they were noted as the finest horsemen of the plains. They were as steadfast friends as they were implacable foes, and had a high sense of honor. Their language became the trade jargon of the Southwest, and is rich, sonorous, and not as difficult as most Indian tongues.

COYOTEROS. One of the Apache groups, divided into the Pinal and White Mountain Coyoteros (or Apaches), whose habitat was the area about the present White Mountain Reservation in Arizona. Like the other related bands, the Coyoteros ranged over practically all of Arizona and New Mexico and into Mexico. Noted for their ferocity and fighting ability, yet they took readily to agriculture, and are now respected and prosperous farmers and ranchers.

CREES. Name contracted from the French Kristinaux, corrupt form for their own name: Kenistenoag. An Algonquian tribe whose true habitat was Canada, but which occasionally ranged southward to northern Minnesota and the northwestern states. Always friendly to the whites, they were foes of other tribes. Many ethnologists consider them an offshoot of the Chippewas.

CREEKS. A very large confederation of Muskhogean Indians whose name was given them by the English because of the number of streams in their territory. Originally inhabiting much of Alabama, Georgia, and Florida. Although they successfully drove off all other Indian tribes, they were always friendly allies of the English and other whites until General Andrew Jackson's actions brought on the "Creek War" of 1813-1814. Later the majority of the tribe, together with the Seminoles and the Indians' Negro slaves, were removed to Indian Territory. Today they are one of the so-called "Five Civilized Tribes." The nation in Oklahoma is divided into forty-nine townships, three of which are wholly inhabited by the Negro descendants of former slaves. The capital is Okmulgee. Their legislature is made up of a House of Kings or Senate, and a House of Warriors similar to our House of Representatives. The chief executive is a head chief duly elected. They have published several volumes of their laws, they have their own schools, papers, churches and hospitals, and are very progressive and up-to-date.

CROWS. The name is a corruption of their own tribal name Absaroke, meaning a sparrow hawk, or in other words, "The hawk people." A Siouan tribe of the Hidatsa group. Warlike and nomadic, the Crows were constantly at war with the Sioux, Blackfeet, and Cheyennes. Although they raided and robbed the whites, whom they despised and regarded as inferiors, they seldom killed them unless in self-defense. At present the majority of the Crows are on the reservations, although many are prosperous farmers and ranchers, and all live amicably with their former enemies.

DAKOTAS, LAKOTAS, NAKOTAS. Depending upon the Santee, Teton, and Yankton dialects, but all meaning "Allies." The largest and best-known of all the groups, and commonly referred to as the "Sioux." Dialectically the confederation can be divided into the Santee, Yankton, Teton, and Assiniboin, although the latter is a distinct tribe. Originally the Dakotas inhabited practically all the territory from the Mississippi westward through Minnesota, the Dakotas, parts of Montana, and Wyoming, and southward to Colorado, Nevada, Kansas, and Nebraska. Nomadic and relying mainly upon the buffalo for a living, the Dakotas were almost constantly at war with the Chippewas, Crows, Gros Ventres, Utes, and other tribes, but were friendly with the whites and were allies of the English during the War of 1812. Their first serious outbreak against the whites was the Minnesota massacre of about seven hundred settlers and one hundred soldiers by the Sisseton and Wahpeton tribes under Little Crow in 1862. However, the main body of the Dakotas had no part in this. It was not until treaties were broken by our own government, and the Indians robbed of lands in the Black Hills, that the long and relentless "Sioux War" began. In many respects the Dakotas are the highest type of all the western tribes, both mentally and physically as well as morally. No one, white or Indian, has ever questioned their bravery. At the present time they are mainly on or near the various reservations. Many are well-to-do farmers and ranchers. They have numerous books printed in their own language, and there are regular newspapers in the Dakota tongue.

DELAWARES: The Leni-lenape or "The Real Men." A large tribal confederacy of the Algonquian stock made famous by Cooper's *Leatherstocking Tales.* Originally inhabited eastern Pennsylvania, southeastern New York, with most of New Jersey and Delaware. To all of the near-by Algonquian tribes they were referred to as the "Grandfathers" out of respect for their admitted priority politically. Many of these other tribes, as well as the Nanticokes, Shawnees, and Mohicans, claimed blood relationship with the Delawares. The Leni-lenape proper consisted of three principal tribes, the Munsees, Unamis and Unalachtigos. Each had its own territory and dialect. The Delawares were the first to make the treaty with William Penn. The great chief of that time was Tamenend, for whom Tammany Hall was named. Although the tribes had always been friendly with the whites, yet the colonies permitted the Iroquois to take dominion over them. Crowded from their homes by the whites, most of the Delawares moved to the Susquehanna and Wyoming valleys in Pennsylvania about 1742. By invitation of the Hurons, many went farther west to Ohio, and within a few years the bulk of the Lenape, together with the Munsees and Mohicans, were living in Ohio and were consolidating with the Hurons. War with the Iroquois followed, and they also fought the ever-encroaching white settlers. Later, by permission of the Spanish in 1789, many of them moved into Missouri and Arkansas. As early as 1820 the Delawares and their Shawnee allies were in Texas. A number also trekked west across the Mississippi into the Dakotas, while others became affiliated with the Caddos and Wichitas in what is now Oklahoma. By 1850 they had reached the great plains and had become true horse Indians, following the buffalo for a living like the true plains tribes. Many of them migrated to the far northwest and settled in Oregon and Washington where some still remain. In the Southwest they spread across Texas and Arizona to the Mexican border. Always born traders, the Delawares, who were friendly with both whites and other Indians, had free access to the villages and camps of hostile tribes, and were often employed as scouts by the Army officers. At the present time the majority are on their reservation in Oklahoma, with scattered groups elsewhere while large numbers are in Canada associated with the Hurons and Canadian Iroquois.

DIEGUEÑOS. A Spanish name for a tribe of Indians living in the vicinity of San Diego, California. They were of Yuman stock, and were a mixture of remnants of several allied tribes. Among the earliest of the California Indians to become Christians, the few hundred still living are mission Indians, although few are of pure blood. One small group of about 30 still remain at the ancestral home in Monmouth, New Jersey, where they are known as "Sand Hill Indians" although surrounded on all sides by whites for over

200 years they retain their language, tribal organizations, ceremonies and arts.

DIGGERS. A name given a small tribe in southwestern Utah. First applied to them because they were agriculturists, and later used to designate any Indians who dig edible roots or tubers. Hence the term included many tribes of California, Oregon, Idaho, Utah, Nevada, and Arizona, even though the tribes were not even distantly related. As farming was considered a lowly occupation by both the whites and the nomadic Indians, the term "Digger" became one of opprobrium.

FLATHEADS. A term applied to any Indians who artifically deformed or flattened their heads. In the southeastern states it was at times applied to the Choctaws and Catawbas, as well as other Muskhogean tribes, most of whom flattened the heads of their children to some extent. In the northwest it was applied to the Chinooks and others. Strangely enough, the Indians to whom the name is officially applied, the true Salish, never were addicted to the practice, the name *"Tetes-Plates"* having been given them by the French, who saw slaves from the coast with deformed heads among the Salish.

FOXES. So named by the French, who met a hunting party of Indians and asked their name. The Indians replied "Wahgosh" (Red fox), which was the name of their clan and not of the tribe, which was the Wesh-kwa-hihug or "Red Earth People." An Algonquian tribe inhabiting the area about Lake Winnebago, Wisconsin. Closely affiliated with and related to the Sauk tribe. The only northern tribe with whom the French waged war. They were naturally a warlike and aggressive race, and were enemies of all the surrounding tribes, at times extending their depredations as far south as Louisiana. They formed an alliance with the Iroquois on the one side and with the Sioux on the other, and thus became almost unconquerable. Their power was finally broken by the combined efforts of the Menominees, the Pottawattomies, the Chippewas, and the French. Now scattered in Kansas and the Mississippi Valley and on reservations.

GROS VENTRES. "Big Bellies." A name employed by French and later by others to two distinct tribes: the Atsinas, a band of the Arapahos, and the Hidatsas, of Siouan stock. The name as applied to the Atsinas refers to the gesture indicating the tribe in sign language, by sweeping both hands in front of the abdomen. On the other hand, the Hidatsas formerly tattooed parallel stripes across the chest, and the gesture sign to indicate this was so similar to the name sign of the Atsinas that both became known by the same name. As a matter of fact the gesture has nothing to do with the abdomen, but means "many lodges," or "spreading tipis."

HANOS. From Anopi, or "Eastern People." A Pueblo tribe now largely intermarried with the Hopis. Their pueblo is the most easterly of Tusayan in northeastern Arizona.

HAVASUPAI. "People of the Blue Water." A small isolated Yuman tribe who dwell in the Cataract Cañon of the Rio Colorado in northwestern Arizona. At one time developed a pueblo culture and built permanent adobe villages. Owing to enemy inroads they abandoned these, and took to the inacessible mountains, where they occupy caves in winter and wattled houses in summer. A peaceful, sedentary, strictly agricultural people. They make excellent baskets, are famous for their tanned buckskin, but have no good pottery, obtaining what they need by trade with the Hopis and other Pueblo Indians.

HIDATSAS. A Siouan tribe known to the Mandans as Minitari or "They Crossed the Water," because of their traditional crossing of the Mississippi. The Sioux call them the Hewaktokto, or "Tipis in a row," a name by which they are also known to the Arapahos and Cheyennes. To the Crows they are the "Amashi" or "Earth Lodge People," while they are commonly referred to as Gros Ventres by the whites. Because of disease and attacks by enemy tribes, the Hidatsas were so greatly reduced in numbers that they were forced to join the Mandans and Arikaras, by whom they were completely absorbed. At the present time they are on a reservation on the site of their old village on the northeastern side of the Mississippi.

HOPIS. A corruption of Hopitu, "Peace People," or Hopitu-shinumu, "Peaceful All People." A group of Shoshonean stock with six pueblos in northeastern Arizona. Sometimes erroneously called "Moquis," a word meaning "dead" in the Hopi language. Probably the best known to tourists of any of our Indians, as, like other Pueblo tribes, they cater to the tourist trade, selling curios and handicraft, staging dances, etc. Famous for their blankets, textiles, and pottery.

HUNKPAPAS. "Those Who Camp at the Entrance." A name given them because of their priority custom of setting up their tipis at the entrance or head of a camp. A Siouan tribe of the Dakotas and a division of the Teton Sioux. At one time the most dreaded of all the plains Indians.

HUPAS. An Athabascan tribe that occupied the valley of the Trinity River in California from the south fork to the Klamath River, including the Hupa Valley. Agriculturists, they are self-supporting farmers and ranchers.

HURONS. "Rough Hair," from their former custom of wearing the hair in an upright roach. A confederation of four Iroquoian tribes that formerly occupied the area about Georgian Bay, Ontario, some living within the boundaries of the United States. Frequently raided the Iroquois, who were traditional enemies. About 1700 they were conquered by the Iroquois. Many fled to Illinois, but soon had trouble with the Sioux. As a result they moved back to Wisconsin and joined the Ottawas. At war with the French until 1748. The tribe then moved to the vicinity of Detroit and Sandusky, where they became known as Wyandottes, and gradually obtained control of the Ohio Valley and neighboring lake districts.

IOWAS. "Sleepy People." A Siouan tribe closely related to the Otos. Believed to be an offshoot of the Winnebagos. An agricultural tribe in what is now Iowa south to the Platte River and to the Missouri River, also portions of Minnesota. Friendly toward the whites, they were enemies of the Sioux. In 1824 ceded lands on the Missouri, and in 1836 were given a reservation in northeastern Kansas. In 1890 they were given an additional reservation in Oklahoma.

IROQUOIS, from the Algonquian Irinakhoiw or "Real Adders." Often referred to as Mingos, a corruption of Mingwe, the Delaware name for the Iroquois. A confederation of tribes known as "Six Nations" and consisting of the Mohawks, Oneidas, Senecas, Cayugas, Onondagas, and Tuscaroras. They occupied the greater part of New York State, and were famed for their prowess in war and for their political and social organization. They were sedentary agricultural people with large villages of well-made log houses. (See chapter on the Six Nations.)

JICARILLAS. "Little Baskets," so named by the Spanish on account of their beautifully made baskets. An Athabascan tribe included among the "Apaches," although hereditary enemies of Mescaleros and Navajos but allied with the Utes and the Taos Indians. Noted for their hostility to the whites, their raids, murders, and cruelties, until a peace treaty was made after their defeat by U.S. troops in 1854. In 1878 their rations and annuities were suspended in order to force them to move southward to a new reservation, and as a result they took to stealing cattle and almost anything they could use. Now peaceful and well-to-do farmers.

KAIYHKHOTANA. The most westerly Athabascan tribe of Alaska, located on the banks of the Yukon between the Anvik and Koynkung Rivers.

KANSAS. A southwestern Siouan tribe whose dialect is closely related to the Osage and Quapaw languages. They occupied western Kansas. A peaceful tribe, they are now on a reservation in Oklahoma.

KAROKS. "Upstream People." Occupied the neighborhood of the Klamath River in northwestern California.

KAWIAS. A Shoshonean-stock tribe of California. Now mainly Mission Indians with others on their reservation.

KICHAI. An almost extinct tribe of the Caddo group, with a dialect similar to that of the Pawnees. Formerly occupying northwestern Louisiana and Texas. Nomadic and often at war with the Apaches. Friendly with the whites. The few survivors are now associated with the Wichitas.

KICKAPOOS. From Kiwigapaw-a: "He who moves about, standing now here, now there." A tribe of Algonquian stock forming a division with the Sauks and Foxes, with whom they are linguistically connected, and distantly related to the Miamis, Shawnees, and Menomines. There seems to be a good deal of confusion regarding the history and original location of the tribe. As early as 1667-70 they were reported by Allouez as being in what is now Columbus County, Wisconsin. Other early explorers and missionaries also reported the Kickapoos in that area. After the destruction of the Illinois Confederacy in 1765, the tribe moved to the vicinity of Peoria. They spread south and west, many taking to the nomadic life of the horse Indians of the plains. They aided Tecumseh in his campaign against the United States, and fought as allies of Black Hawk in 1832. In 1837 about one hundred of the Kickapoo warriors were employed by the government to fight the Seminoles in Florida. In 1809 they ceded their lands on the Wabash and Vermilion Rivers to the United States, and all their lands in Central Illinois in 1819. Later they moved into Missouri and Kansas. About 1852 a large number, together with some Pottawattomies, migrated to Texas and thence into Mexico, where they became known as "Mexican Kickapoos." In Mexico they became raiders and a terror to the settlements and ranches, but in 1873 a portion returned and settled in Oklahoma. More than half their number remained in Mexico and are living on a reservation granted them by the Mexican government, in the Santa Rosa Mountains of eastern Sonora. Originally the Kickapoos had fixed villages and were agriculturists, but they often raided the Comanches and other tribes, and after acquiring horses they took to the nomadic life of the true plains tribes. At present the majority are on their reservation in Oklahoma.

KIOWAS. From Ka-i-gwa, or "Principal People." A tribe of distinct linguistic stock whose home was the area about the upper Yellowstone and Missouri rivers, but who later moved southward and were mainly about the upper Arkansas and Canadian rivers in Colorado and Kansas. Up to 1840 they were allied with the Crows but at war with the Cheyennes and Arapahos. At that date a peace treaty was made, and the Kiowas were allies of their former enemies. Together with the Comanches, they carried on constant warfare with the frontier settlers of Texas and Mexico, extending their raids as far south as Durango, Mexico. Among the plains tribes they were noted for their ferocity, fighting spirit, and as the most bloodthirsty of all the Indians. In proportion to their numbers they killed more whites than any other tribe, and were even more dreaded than the Apaches, with whom they were often confused.

In 1837 they signed their first treaty with our government, and were placed on a reservation, together with the Kiowa-Apaches and true Apaches. In 1874-75 they again went on the warpath, joining the Comanches, Kiowa-Apaches, and Cheyennes. Never a numerous tribe, they were decimated by war and epidemics, and in 1852 about three hundred died from the measles. The survivors now live on lands allotted to them, and are a peaceful lot engaged in ranching and farming.

KIOWA-APACHES. Often confused with the Kiowas and the Apaches, this tribe is of Athabascan stock, and although from time immemorial allied with the Kiowas they retained their distinct language and customs. Their own name was Na-i-shan-dina meaning "We (or our) people." To the Pawnees they were known as the Kaskaia or "Bad Hearts," and to the Kiowas as Semat or "Thieves." They have no direct relationship to the various Apache tribes, and had never even heard of the latter until about 1800. Although now on friendly terms with the Mescaleros, they were formerly their enemies. Like the true Kiowas, the tribe came from the northwest plains region and joined the Kiowas for mutual protection. Unlike the Kiowas, they have remained friendly with the whites since 1874.

KLAMATHS. A Lutuamian tribe of southwest Oregon. Their own name is the Eukishikni, or "People of the Lake." A peaceful tribe, always friendly with the whites, and had no part in the brief Modoc Wars of 1872-73. Like the Modocs, the Klamaths made frequent raids on the tribes of northern California for the purpose of capturing women and children as slaves. In 1864 they ceded most of their territory to the United States and settled on a reservation.

KNAIAKPTANAS. An Athabascan tribe inhabiting Kenai Peninsula, Alaska. The only northern Athabascan tribe on the Pacific Coast. Customs very much like those of the neighboring Eskimos.

KUTCHAKUTCHINS. "Giant People." A Kuutchin tribe inhabiting the banks of the Yukon River, Alaska. A seminomadic tribe depending upon hunting and trapping for a living. Born traders. Their standard of values was the Nakieikor strings of beads seven feet long. Each string had the value of one or more beaver skins, depending on the color of the string, the total of seven strings having the value of twenty-four skins. Houses inverted cup-shape, made of skins on curved poles. The few living are at Fort Yukon.

KUTCHINS. A group of Athabascan tribes of Alaska and British Columbia in the Yukon district. Formerly female children were frequently put to death to prevent a surplus of women. Noted for their hospitality, often entertaining visitors for months, each head of a family taking his turn of feasting the whole band while etiquette requires him to fast himself.

KUTENAI. A tribe of distant linguistic stock inhabiting northern Idaho and Montana and British Columbia. According to their traditions, they once dwelt east of the Rocky Mountains in Montana, but were driven west and north by the Siksikas. The two tribes are now affiliated. They are rich in folklore and legends. At one time they were great buffalo hunters. Famed for their watertight baskets woven of roots.

KWAKIUTLS. "Smoke of the World." A group of closely related tribes of British Columbia and the adjoining borderland of the United States. Probably the most Mongolianlike of the northwestern tribes.

LAGUNAS. A Keresan Pueblo tribe, whose best-known pueblo, Laguna, is on the San José River in New Mexico about fifty miles from Albuquerque. The tribe is composed of people of several linguistic stocks, the Shoshonean, Keresan, Tanoan, and Zuñian.

LASSIKS. A California tribe of Athabascan stock almost exterminated by the whites, who placed a bounty on the Indians' heads and captured children, whom they sold into slavery.

LIPANS. One of the so-called Apache tribes. Their own name is Naizhan, or "Our People." Formerly occupying New Mexico and northern Mexico from the Rio Grande eastward through Texas to the Gulf Coast. A nomadic tribe famed for their depredations among the white settlements of Texas and Mexico. From 1845 until 1856 they were constantly at war with the Texans, and suffered heavy losses, finally being driven back to Coahuila, Mexico, where they joined the Kickapoos. The nineteen known survivors were brought back to the United States in 1905 and were placed on the Mescalero Reservation in New Mexico, where there were a few others. They took readily to civilization and agriculture. Only a few now survive.

LUISEÑOS. The most southerly Shoshonean group in California, originally inhabiting the coastal area from Las Animas south to San Marcos and inland. Now mainly on reservations and at various missions.

MAHICANS or MOHICANS, also sometimes spelled MOHEGANS. The name means "The Wolves." An Algonquian tribe made famous by Fenimore Cooper in his *Leatherstocking Tales.* Originally occupying the Hudson River Valley almost to Lake Champlain. Also in the Housatonic Valley eastward into Massachusetts and Connecticut. That portion of the tribe that occupied the lower valley of the Connecticut River were usually known as "Mohegans," while those of New York were commonly called "Mahicans." Usually at war with the Mohawks. Friendly with the whites, they sold most of their lands to the settlers and the majority moved to the Wyoming Valley in Pennsylvania, and later went to Ohio, where they merged with the Delawares. The group that still remained in the Berkshires Mountains of Massachusetts became known as the Stockbridge Indians. Another group remained near Litchfield, Connecticut, while more were near Norwich, Connecticut, where they still reside. Although the Mohicans are always lauded as friends and allies of the white settlers, while the Pequots are villified as bloodthirsty savage foes, yet the two tribes had been joined until about fifty years prior to the arrival of the white settlers. At the present time there are quite a number of the tribe dwelling near Norwich, Connecticut, near Stockbridge, Massachusetts, in Litchfield County, Connecticut, and at various places on the Hudson River. All, however, are so thoroughly civilized that they are usually unrecognizable as Indians.

MAKAHS. The only tribe of Wakashan stock in the United States, and the most southerly of the group. Inhabited Washington about Cape Flattery. At present mostly on a reservation at Ozette.

MANDANS. The name is a corruption of the Dakota word Mawatani. Their own name was Numakiki, or "The People." A Siouan tribe that occupied the valley of the upper Missouri River. Although linguistically closely related to the Winnebagos, they have always been most intimate with the Hidatsas. Before the Lewis and Clark expedition the whole Mandan tribe dwelt in villages of log and earth lodges partly underground, the whole being enclosed by a log palisade. They were agriculturists, peacefully inclined, and have always remained friendly to the whites. Ravaged by the smallpox epidemic, they were reduced from several thousands to less than one hundred individuals, and joined the Hidatsas. As their villages were of a type the early explorers had not hitherto seen, as among the Mandans there were a number of blonds or semi-albinos (as is common in many tribes) and as some of their words were allegedly understood by Welsh members of the same expedition, the Mandans were believed to be descendents of survivors of a Welsh expedition that landed on the Atlantic Coast, moved westward, and was never heard from again. However, there is no evidence in support of the theory. The Mandans still living are among the Hidatsas and Arikaras on reservations, although some are farmers on their own allotted lands.

MARICOPAS. A Yuman tribe living near the Rio Grande and Gila rivers in Arizona. Now mainly on reservations.

MARTHA'S VINEYARD INDIANS. Commonly known as Gay Head Indians. Once very numerous, but today few in number and mainly of mixed white, Negro, and Indian blood. Probably none are of pure Indian blood.

MASKEGONS. From Muskigok, meaning "People of the Swamps." An Algonquian tribe considered a branch of the Crees. Known to the traders as "Swampy Crees." Mainly inhabiting Canada.

MIDEWAKANTON. From Mde-wakan-otonwe, or "Sacred Mystery Villagers." A subtribe of the Santee Sioux. A powerful tribe of the Dakota confederation.

MENOMINEES. From Menominiwok-ininiwok, or "Men of Wild Rice." An Algonquian tribe of Michigan and Wisconsin. A peaceful semiagricultural tribe, but enemies of neighboring Algonquin tribes.

MESCALEROS. An Apache tribe of southern New Mexico and northern Mexico. Never as warlike as the other Apaches. Now on a reservation with a few Lipans in southern New Mexico. Many are farmers and ranchers.

MIAMIS. An Algonquin tribe originally inhabiting the vicinity of Green Bay, Wisconsin. Also where Chicago now stands, and later in Indiana and Ohio. Took a prominent part in the wars in the Ohio Valley until the end of the War of 1812. Sold their lands to whites and moved to Kansas and thence to Oklahoma, some remaining in Wabash County, Indiana, on land allotted to them. In the old days the men were addicted to tattooing the entire body. They were hard-working farmers, affable, mild, and sedate. Although they hunted the buffalo, they were never horse Indians. Their homes were cabins covered with rush mats. Very fine thread was spun from buffalo hair and woven into bags and other objects.

MICMACS. From Migmak, meaning "Allies." An Algonquian tribe that occupied Nova Scotia, a few living within the borders of Maine. Although they were near neighbors of the Maine Wabenaki, the Micmac dialect is more closely related to the language of the western plains tribes than to that of the eastern Algonquins.

MIMBREÑOS. An Apache tribe who dwelt in the Mimbreño Mountains of New Mexico, but who roamed and raided from the Rio Grande into Mexico. Now farmers and ranchers.

MINGO. From Mingwe, meaning "Treacherous." A term often applied to the Iroquois.

MINNECONJOUS. "Those who plant by the stream." A division of the Teton Sioux. Regarded by the whites as the most unruly and most troublesome of all the Sioux tribes.

MISSOURIS. A tribe of the Chiwere group of the Siouan family, although their dialect was partly Algonquian. Closely related to the Otos and Iowas. The few survivors are now with the Otos on their reservation.

MODOCS. From Moatokni, meaning "Southerners." A Lutuamian tribe of Oregon. Mainly famed for the short but rather bloody so-called Modoc Wars, the result of broken promises and treachery on the part of the whites, which resulted in the murder of the officers of the state and other murders and crimes. The hostiles, led by Captain Jack, took refuge in the lava beds and for a time kept the soldiers and civilians at bay. Eventually captured, Jack and the other leaders were hanged.

MOHAVES. The largest and most warlike of the Yuman tribes. Inhabited both sides of the Rio Grande. Physically a very fine race, famed for the elaborate painting of their bodies. Tattooing was also universal, but was confined to small areas. Primarily agriculturists, they dwelt in square houses with low walls and flat roofs covered with brush and sand.

MOHAWKS. From Mohowauuck. A Narraganset word meaning "Man-eaters," from the fact that they once held cannibalistic ceremonies. The most easterly tribe of the Iroquois Confederation and the most dreaded by the white settlers and by other Indians of New England. At present the Mohawks, like the other Iroquois, are thoroughly civilized, and are mainly in the vicinity of St. Regis reservation near Hogansburg, N. Y. In their lives, industries, houses, and all other respects, they are indistinguishable from their white neighbors.

MOHICANS. See MAHICANS.

MONTAUKS. An Algonquin tribe once very numerous and inhabiting Long Island, N. Y., especially the eastern portion. The few living survivors are mainly of mixed blood. Until 1875 they maintained more or less of a tribal organization. Their last "king" or sachem, David Pharaoh, died in 1875. The handful of those still living are officially recognized by the State of New York as constituting a "tribe."

NARRAGANSETS. "People of the Small Point." An Algonquin tribe of Rhode Island and eastern Connecticut. At one time one of the most powerful tribes of New England, numbering several thousand members. During the King Philip War they lost nearly one thousand killed and captured. All but a few of the survivors joined other tribes. Those who still live in Rhode Island, Cape Cod, and Connecticut are mainly of mixed Indian, white, and Negro blood.

NAUSETS. An Algonquian tribe formerly living on Cape Cod, Massachusetts. A part of the Wampanoag tribe. Allies of the whites during the King Philip War. The few who survive are of mixed Indian and white blood.

NAVAHO (NAVAJO). Not of Spanish derivation but from Navahu, meaning a large area of cultivated land. A tribe that occupied parts of Arizona, New Mexico, and Utah. They were the original "Apaches," the Zuñi name for the Navajos being Apachu, meaning "an enemy," and noted for their savage and warlike character. They were probably the largest of all the far west tribes, and were pastoral and agricultural. Until their territory came under control of the United States they maintained almost constant warfare with other tribes and with the whites. In 1846 a treaty of peace was arranged, but as usual was not carried out by the whites. Hostilities then continued, and in 1849 a military expedition invaded Navajo territory, and another treaty was made, which was also violated. In 1863 a military force under Kit Carson drove the Navajos as far as Cañon de Chelly, their original home and stronghold, and induced the Indians to surrender after having destroyed most of their sheep. The tribe was then sent to Fort Sumner on the Bosque Redondo, New Mexico, where they remained as prisoners until 1867, when they were restored to their original home and given a supply of sheep and goats. At this time they numbered about six thousand. Although classed as of Athabascan stock, the Navajos are a composite race of several stocks, because of various tribes who became fused with and absorbed by them. They are famed for their wool textiles and blankets, their sand paintings, and silver work. They have suffered much from the government's failure to provide schools, medical assistance, and other things, as promised, and by the curtailment of their flocks and grazing lands allotted to white ranchers. Many have been forced to live in abject poverty, but with the discovery of uranium on their lands their lot will probably be greatly improved. Now the largest tribe in the United States, numbering about forty-five thousand.

NEZ PERCÉS. So called by the French, who applied the term to several tribes who used nose ornaments. The name is now confined to a Shahaptian tribe that never pierced the nose. Originally dwelling in portions of Idaho, Oregon, and Washington. Inclined to be friendly, the Nez Percés were finally forced to hostilities by the actions of the white settlers and our government. After several victories, the Indians, under youthful Chief Joseph, decided to migrate to Canada. Joseph's amazing and masterly retreat is famed as one of the epics of our history. Again and again Joseph outwitted and outfought the troops sent to capture and bring back the Indians, yet on their long trek toward Canada no whites were molested, no outrages committed other than cattle being taken to provide food. After their final surrender they were taken to Indian Territory, but later the majority were returned to their reservation in Washington, where they still remain.

NIANTICS. From Naintuk-ut, meaning "At a land on an estuary." A small but important Algonquian tribe formerly occupying the coastal lands from Niantic Bay to the Connecticut River. These were subject to the Pequots, and were almost exterminated during the Pequot War. The survivors were placed under the rule of the Mohicans. No known Niantics now exist, although a few persons of mixed blood living with the Mohicans and Pequots near Norwich, Connecticut, call themselves Niantics. As far as known the last pure-blooded Niantic was a woman from the vicinity of Niantic, Connecticut, who died a generation ago. (See illustration.)

OGLALA. A tribe of the Dakotas.

OMAHAS. "Those who move against the wind." One of the group of the Dhegiha of the Siouan family, the others being the Quapaws, Kansas, Poncas, and Osages. Formerly occupied the area about Pipestone, Minnesota, parts of Iowa, Nebraska, and South Dakota. Friendly with the other Sioux tribes, but later at war with them. In 1854 and 1865 they ceded their land to the United States, and in 1882 they were given lands in severalty and were granted citizenship. Those remaining are prosperous farmers and are increasing in numbers.

ONEIDAS. A tribe of the Iroquois "Six Nations" confederacy.

ONONDAGAS. A powerful tribe of the Iroquois.

OOHENONPAS. "Two boilings" or "Two kettles," meaning "always plenty of food." A division of the Teton Sioux commonly called the "Two Kettle Sioux." Not a warlike race, they were friendly with the whites, and treated traders and settlers with respect. Even during the Fort Kearney uprising they took no part in the hostilities, and in 1865 they agreed to never attack either whites or Indians except in self-defense, and to settle on lands allotted to them. They now live on or near reservations in South Dakota, and are mostly farmers and ranchers.

OSAGES. A French corruption of their own name; Wazhazhw. The most important of the southern Siouan group. Friendly with the whites, but usually at war with other tribes. In 1808 they ceded the United States all their lands, amounting to the greater portion of what is now Arkansas and Missouri, and retained much of the northern part of Oklahoma. In 1870 boundaries of their present reservation were established. In 1906 this contained 1,470,058 acres. The Osages are the richest tribe in the United States, due largely to the oil fields on their lands.

OSSIPEES. A small tribe of the Wabenaki, who formerly inhabited eastern New Hampshire and Oxford County in Maine, where they were known as Passaconnoways, after the name of the famous chief, but called themselves Pascatawayas. The last of the tribe resided near Norway, Maine, on the banks of the Androscoggin River. The last member of the tribe, Indian John, died in 1877.

OTOS. One of three Siouan tribes forming the Chiwere group, the other two being the Iowas and Missouris. Formerly inhabited portions of Iowa, Wisconsin, Missouri, and Kansas. Affiliated with the Pawnees. Never a warlike tribe, they fought only to defend themselves against other tribes. They were an agricultural tribe friendly with the whites. At present they are on their reservation in Oklahoma.

OTTAWAS. From Adawe, or "Traders," because of their fame as traders with other tribes and with the whites. An Algonquian tribe of the area about the Great Lakes. They lived in substantial log houses and were agriculturists. Now joined with the Chippewas and other tribes.

PAIUTES. A name that has been applied to a number of the Shoshonean tribes of Utah, Idaho, Arizona, Oregon, Nevada, and California. The name, a corruption of Pa-Ute or "Water Ute," properly belongs to the Corn Creek tribe of Utah. As a rule they have been peaceful and friendly with the whites, although during the 'sixties they had a number of affrays with miners and emigrants who wantonly attacked the Indians without discrimination. They are industrious, and are mainly employed on ranches by white owners. They make top cowhands, and have great mechanical ability. According to those who know them best, they have steadily resisted the vices of civilization, and have become a necessity of the farmers and ranchers. Although dressing in conventional clothes and outwardly civilized, many still prefer to live in their wickiups almost bare of even the simplest furnishings. Thanks to their healthy lives and the good food they are able to buy, they are steadily increasing in numbers.

PAPAGOS. From Papah-Ootam, or "Bean People." A Piman tribe whose home was Arizona, especially in the vicinity of Tucson and extending southwest into Sonora, Mexico. They subsist by agriculture, maize, beans, and cotton having been their chief crops which they irrigated. Many wild desert plants are eaten, especially the mesquite beans, the fruits of cacti, and a syrup made from fruit of the giant Sahuaro cactus. Nowadays they cultivate wheat and barley to a large extent. At one time they had a large trade in salt, which they obtained from great inland salt lakes. They also raise stock, and many of the men are employed as workmen on the railways and irrigation systems of the whites. They are dark-skinned, tall, and hardy, and are considered honest and industrious. Always a friendly race.

PASCATAWAYAS. See Ossipees. The Indian name for the "Passaconnoways."

PASSACONNOWAYS. See Ossipees.

PASSAMAQUODDY. From Pesked emakaddi, "People of Polluck," or Pestumokadyk, meaning "Pollock-Spearers." An Algonquian tribe of the Wabenaki, but whose dialect closely resembles that of the Canadian Malecites. Formerly occupying all of the Maine and New Brunswick coasts from St. Andreas, New Brunswick, to Calais, Maine. Now on a small reservation at Pleasant Point near Eastport, Maine. Famed for their skill in handling birch canoes in the open sea, where they shoot porpoise and spear pollock. Like the closely related Penobscot (or, correctly, Tarratine) Indians of Panawamske Island near Old Town, Maine, they have the right to send a representative to the state legislature. The tribe has mixed somewhat with the whites and Negroes, but there are still a number of full-bloods.

PAWNEES. From Paeriki, meaning a horn, from the Pawnee custom of wearing a scalp-lock of hair stiffened with grease and paint so it stood erect like a horn above the head. The Pawnees' own name for themselves was Chah-ikisic-hahiks, or "Men of Men." A tribe or confederation of Caddoan stock inhabiting the River Platte valley in Nebraska. Tribally the Pawnees were divided into the Skidi, Pitahauerat, Chauti, and Kitkehahki. At one time the Pawnees raided as far south as New Mexico, mainly to steal horses, and rarely molesting the whites except in self-defense. Always a friendly tribe, the Pawnees never made war with the United States, but a number of them served the Army as scouts against hostile tribes. They agreed to submit all grievances to the federal authorities for settlement, and in 1892 nearly all went to Oklahoma, where they acquired private lands and became citizens. Unlike the majority of the plains tribes, the Pawnees had permanent villages with log huts, and cultivated a variety of crops, although also relying upon the buffalo for hides and much of their food supply.

PENNACOOKS. From Pena-Kuk, meaning "At the base of the Hills." An Algonquian tribe that occupied the Merrimac Valley in New Hampshire, Massachusetts, and southern Maine. Usually classed with the Mohicans linguistically. Their most famous chief was Passaconnoway, after whom the Passaconnoway tribe of Oxford County, Maine, was named. In 1676, after the treacherous attack by the whites, most of the tribe fled to Canada, while others went westward only to be overtaken by the British at the Housatonic River, where nearly all were killed. The few survivors joined the Mohicans in the Hudson River Valley and finally settled at Scaticook, N. Y. Those who reached Canada were given land near St. Francis. Smarting under the wrongs they had suffered, they became implacable foes of the English, and aided the French during the French and Indian War. Quite a number still live in

Canada, and there are a few among the Mohicans of New York State.

PENOBSCOTS. A popular name for the Tarratine tribe of the Wabenaki living on Panawamske Island near Old Town, Maine, on the Penobscot River. At one time the most numerous of Wabenaki tribes, occupying a large area on both sides of the river. Under Baron de St. Castine, a French nobleman who joined the tribe and married a daughter of Chief Madokawando, the Tarratines allied themselves with the French and played havoc with the English settlements. Since 1749 the treaty has never been broken. They elect the chief by vote and have a representative in Maine legislature. Many are employed in factories at Old Town. Others act as guides. Their baskets are famous and are in large demand. It is compulsory for all children to learn French, English, and Wabenaki. First Catholic Church north of Florida is on the island. About four hundred living, with very few of mixed white and Indian blood, and none with Negro blood.

PEQUOTS. From Paquatauog or "Destroyers." An Algonquian tribe of eastern Connecticut. The most dreaded of all New England tribes, and always enemies of the whites; yet less than fifty years before the arrival of the English, the Pequots and Mohicans had been one tribe. Owing to a dispute between Sassacus and Uncas, the Mohican chief, the tribe divided, the Mohicans or Mohegans going inland. In a short time they had virtual control of all the interior of Connecticut, Rhode Island, and Massachusetts, and became friends and allies of the whites. The Pequot War, which started with the murder of a trader who had cheated the Indians, resulted in the almost complete extermination of the occupants of their principal village, about eight hundred dying in the flames or being shot down. The remainder of the tribe fled westward and were everywhere hunted like wild beasts. Many were killed near Fairfield, Connecticut. Some reached the Mohawks only to be killed. One of their chiefs fled to the vicinity of Guilford, Connecticut, where he was overtaken by a Mohican, killed, and beheaded. His head was placed on a pole near the shore, in commemoration of which the locality is now named Sachem's Head. Nearly all the Pequot prisoners taken were sold as slaves in the Bahama Islands, where a number, with an intermixture of Negro blood, still remain. Others were given to the Mohicans, and many were made slaves by the colonists. Today a few still live near New London, Connecticut, and other localities; nearly all are of mixed blood, although retaining their tribal name.

PIEGANS. A tribe of the Blackfeet or Siksika confederation.

PIMAS. A tribe occupying the valleys of the Gila and Sant rivers in Arizona. The ruins called Casa Grande and other massive pueblo groups were built by ancestors of the Pimas. Pastoral and agricultural, the Pimas had extensive irrigation systems. Their houses are of poles covered with sod and grass. In the past they suffered greatly from raids by other tribes. Now allied with the Maricopa, with whom they intermarry. Always a peaceful tribe, but courageous in battle when attacked. Never scalped their fallen enemies. Believed that their foes, and especially the Apaches, were possessed with evil spirits, and never touched the bodies of those killed. No enemy males were spared, but women and children were taken prisoners and treated kindly and with consideration, and these often married into the tribe. The women are famed for their fine, beautifully woven, water-tight baskets. Mainly subsisting on their crops and cattle, the Pimas yet use great quantities of the mesquite beans and the fruits of the Saguaro cactus.

PIÑAL COTEROS. A division of the Coyotero Apaches who inhabited the Pinal mountains north of the Gila River in Arizona. Now on reservation or their own farms and ranches. Were allied with the Pueblo people. Never as savage or warlike as the other Apache tribes, they caused little trouble, and since the treaty of 1873 have devoted themselves to agriculture and ranching. They are noted for their soft and musical voices and the beauty of their women. They are a light-hearted, rather timid race, and are known for their honesty and industry.

PONCAS. One of the so-called Dhegiha tribes of the Sioux group, forming with the Omahas, Osage, and Kansas the upper Omaha division. The language is the same, the only differences being a few dialectic variations. The early history is the same as that of the Omahas. The combined tribes moved from the mouth of the Osage River, the Osages settling farther up the stream, while the Omahas and Poncas crossed the Missouri and finally settled near the pipestone quarries of Minnesota. Originally they had permanent villages of earth houses, and cultivated the soil, but also hunted the buffalo. When the soil was exhausted and game became scarce, they moved to a new village site. On the Big Sioux River they built a strong palisaded fort as protection against the Sioux. But the Dakotas finally forced them to flee until they reached Lake Andes in South Dakota. From there they ascended the Missouri to the mouth of the White River, where the Iowas and Omahas remained, while the Poncas went on to the Black

Hills. Eventually they returned, and with their allies went down the Missouri to the mouth of the Niobrara River. Peace was made with the Sioux, and the two became more or less affiliated, but in 1877 the two tribes were at war and the Poncas were removed to Oklahoma. This led to an investigation, and as a result a portion of the tribe returned to their home on the Niobrara, while others elected to remain in Oklahoma. During their wanderings the Poncas became nomadic, lived in tipis, and hunted the buffalo for their living. They are mainly famed for the religious ceremony of the sun dance, although it was common to a great many of the western tribes. The self-torture for which this dance was noted was practiced by many tribes, although the Kiowas forbade any torture or bloodshed. It often consisted of fastening thongs to lacerated breast or back muscles, and pulling against the weight of a dragging buffalo skull, or throwing oneself away from a post to which the thongs were attached. Just why the dance should have become associated with the Poncas is a puzzle. Today many tribes have abandoned the dance, while others still hold it—although in most cases without self-torture.

POTAWATOMIS (POTTAWATTOMIES). From Potawatamink or "People of the Place of Fire." An Algonquian tribe, allied with the Chippewas and Ottawas who originally dwelt near Green Bay, Wisconsin. In 1846 they moved across the Mississippi, although in the early part of the nineteenth century they were in possession of much of Michigan, Illinois, Wisconsin, and Indiana. In early days they were allies of the French against the English; during the Revolutionary War they were allies of the British, and again during the War of 1812 they were hostile to the United States, until the final treaty was made in 1815. Some of the tribe went to Canada, while others went to Kansas and Iowa, where they were known as Prairie Pottawattomies. In 1846 all were united on a reservation in Kansas, and in 1861 a number took lands in severalty and became citizens. More kindly and humane than most of the other tribes, they were quick to become Christians. They were not addicted to liquor, and were noted for their hospitality. Like the other Indians of the middle west, they had permanent villages and were agriculturists. According to educated members of the tribe, the Pottawattomie language is completely lost, except for ceremonial uses. Their traditions relate that they originally came from Tiahuanaco in Bolivia. In many of their religious beliefs and other matters, they are similar to the tribes of the Gulf Coast and Mexico. In view of the Pottawattomie tradition that the tribe came from north-eastern Mexico, it seems highly probable that *"Indios Quinque"* which appeared in Sonora on some of the older Mexican maps, was the Spanish name for the Kindewa or "Eagles," one of the largest and most important of the clans or divisions of the Pottawattomies. Moreover, along the route which the tribe would have followed on the northward migration, we find artifacts, carvings, incised tablets, and metal plaques with figures and designs almost identical with those from the Spiro Burial Mound, Spiro, Oklahoma. Some even depicting the plumed serpent god, Quetzalcoatl. The complete history of the tribe as known to its members has been written by Chief Shup-She (Mr. Howard L. La Hurreau) of Fort Wayne, Indiana.

POWHATANS. From Pawa Tan or "Where falls the water" (rapids). A group or confederacy of Algonquian Indians who occupied Virginia and who are mainly famous because of the romantic story of Pocahontas and her father, Chief Powhatan. Although Pocahontas may have saved Captain John Smith's life, she married an Englishman, John Rolfe, and later resided in England. At that time the confederacy consisted of seven tribes. At first friendly, the Indians were so badly treated by the whites that they became hostile. Finally they made a concerted attack on the settlements, killing over three hundred whites and burning every house and settlement except those close to Jamestown. The whites then started a war of extermination, killing every Indian, man, woman and child they met, and burning their villages. The war continued for fourteen years until General Wyatt massacred over one thousand Indians and destroyed their principal village. For a time there was peace, but off-and-on hostilities were resumed. Today there are only a few survivors of the once-great confederacy. These are the Pamunkeys, Chickahominies, and Rappahannocks, who still live in Virginia, although few if any are of pure Indian blood.

PUEBLOS. Any one of numerous tribes who dwell in fixed villages of well-built adobe houses. Usually employed to designate the Indians whose pueblos or villages are of the older type, with blind walls and the houses accessible only by means of ladders. Some of the compact villages are on mesas, others on level ground. Neither are all the Pueblo Indians of one tribe or linguistic stock. Those of the Nambe, Tenuque, San Ildefonso, San Juan, Santa Clara, Hano, Sandia, Taos, Picuris, Jemez, and Senecu pueblos are of Tanoan linguistic stock. Those of San Felipe, Santa Ana, Sia, Cochiti, Santo Domingo, Acoma, Laguna, are of Keresan stock, while those of Walpi, Sichomovi, Michongnovi, Shipaulovi, Shongo-povi, and Oraibi, all commonly known as Hopis, are of Shoshonean stock.

QUAPAWS. From Ugakhpa, or "People down the River." A southwestern Siouan tribe. First described by De Soto (1539). At that time the Quapaws lived in large, well-built villages surrounded by palisades of logs and with towers for the defenders. The whole was surrounded by a moat. Their principal villages were then on the west bank of the Mississippi in what is now Arkansas. They were agriculturists and had large, well-tilled fields. They were mound-builders and built mounds of a distinctive type. Some of these are in Indiana on the Ohio River near the mouth of the Wabash. After migrating to various localities up and down the Mississippi Valley, some went to Texas, others to Louisiana, and in 1877 they were placed on a reservation in Oklahoma. According to all of the older accounts, they were honest, gay, peaceful, and very different from other tribes in many ways. They buried their dead, sometimes in mounds and sometimes in houses. Comparatively few of the Quapaws survive, as during the past they have mixed with the Caddos, Osages, and other tribes.

QUILEUTES. A Chimakuan tribe of distinct linguistic stock living at the mouth of the Quillayute River on the coast of Washington. A warlike tribe, they held their own against neighboring tribes. Noted for their skill in sealing and whaling. Mainly dependent upon seafood and wild plants and berries, they do little hunting on land.

QUINAIELTS. A Salish tribe of the Washington coastal area.

SALISH. From Salst, meaning "The People." A tribe of the Salishan family of western Montana in and about Flathead Lake. Commonly known as Flatheads, not because they artificially deformed the head but because they left their heads in natural form or flat on top. Mainly a hunting tribe. In 1856 ceded lands to the United States and signed the peace treaty. Quite distinct from the Salish Indians of the Pacific coast.

SAN CARLOS APACHES. Not a distinct tribe. Applied to the Apaches who lived on the Gila River and were placed in the San Carlos Agency. Often carried on raids and desultory war with the whites as well as with other tribes.

SANONAS. A division of the Teton Sioux comprising the Sans Arcs, Sihasapa, Oohenonpa, and Hunkpapa.

SANS ARCS. From Itazipa-Cho, or "Without Bows." A band of the

Teton Sioux. (See Sioux.) At peace with the whites since the treaty of April 29, 1868.

SANTEES. From Isan-Yati, or "They camp at Knife Lake." A division of the Dakotas (Sioux) comprising the Midewakanton, Wahpekute, Wahpeton, and Sisseton bands.

SAUKS. Osa-kiwag, or "People of the Yellow Earth." An Algonquian tribe who originally occupied the eastern peninsula of Michigan. The name Saginaw, Sagi-na-we, means "Country of the Sauks." Although residing in an agricultural area they were nomadic, ranging through the forests, dependent upon hunting, and were more savage and warlike than other Indians of the area. Migrating westward, the Sauks met and fought the Sioux, but later became their allies. Often attacked the French settlements. Joined the Fox tribe and moved southward, so that by 1777 they had reached Spanish territory of Missouri. Friendly to the Spaniards, who gave them presents. Also friendly with the English. Tricked into making over their lands to the whites, the Sauks and Foxes became hostile, and the Black Hawk War resulted (1832). However, the Sauks did not enter into the conflict wholeheartedly, but fought savagely with the Sioux, Omaha, and Menomine tribes. The Black Hawk War ended the power of the Sauks and Foxes as far as the whites were concerned, but in Iowa they won a decisive victory over the Sioux, the Omahas, and the Menominees, finally driving the Sioux from the area. In 1837 made final cessions of Iowa territory, and were given lands across the Missouri in Kansas. Later given lands in severalty, which caused the Sauks and Foxes to separate, the latter returning to Iowa, where they bought land and settled down as farmers, becoming prosperous. In 1867 the Sauks ceded their Kansas lands to the government, and in exchange were given a tract in Oklahoma, where in 1889 they took up lands in severalty and are now well-to-do farmers and ranchers.

SCATICOOKS. From P-ska-tituk, or "At the River's Fork." A small tribe that inhabited the Housatonic Valley near Kent, Connecticut. Most of them moved in 1730 to Dover Plains, New York. The tribe consisted mainly of refugee Pequots combined with Paugussets, Uncowas, and Potatucs. By 1860 only a dozen or so of full blood survived, while the remainder, less than fifty, were of mixed blood. In 1870 the chieftainess, Eunice Mahwee, died, leaving only one man of full Indian blood and with a knowledge of the language. Today only a few, more of Negro and white than Indian blood, consider themselves Scaticooks.

SEMINOLES. From the Creek Sim-a-no-le, meaning an outlaw or runaway—since the Seminoles were made up of fugitives and emigrants from the Creeks of northern Florida. First known under their present name in 1775. There are two principal bands or divisions, one calling themselves Ikaniuksalgi, the others Mikasukis. In addition to the Creek blood there is considerable Yuchi and Tamassee blood in the Florida Seminoles, as well as a large percentage of African blood because of the many runaway slaves who joined the Indians. There is also some admixture of white blood. Mostly famed for the fact that they were never conquered by the United States after fighting the longest, bloodiest, most disastrous and most costly war, in comparison with numbers involved, in our history. The war, which was caused by the government's trying to force the Indians to move to Indian Territory, lasted from 1835 until 1842 with a loss of 1,500 American troops, a cost of over twenty million dollars, and not a single victory for the government. At the close of the war many Indians withdrew into the swamps and Everglades, while others were taken to Oklahoma, where they organized the Seminole Nation and became thoroughly civilized and progressive and are now one of the so-called Five Civilized Nations.

SENECAS. A powerful tribe forming one of the Iroquois or Six Nations confederation. Originally living in Ontario County, New York. Later moved west to Lake Erie and into northern Pennsylvania. Became the largest of Iroquois tribes. Now mainly living in Tonawanda, Cattaraugus, and Alleghany reservations, New York. One of the last to suppress cannibalism and to accept the principles on which the confederation was founded. In the wars between British and colonists they were allies of the English. Many very prominent men have been members of the tribe, among them General Eli Samuel Parker, who was an eminent civil engineer, and secretary to General Grant during the Civil War, as well as a general in the Union Army.

SHASTAS. From Susti-ka, after a chief. A group or confederacy of several small tribes of Shastan linguistic stock of northern California and southern Oregon. A sedentary agricultural people living in clusters of rectangular, partly subterranean plank houses. The tribe is now practically extinct.

SHAWNEES. From Shawunogi, or "Southerners." An Algonquian tribe originally occupying South Carolina, Tennessee, Pennsylvania, and Ohio. They were wanderers, hunters, whose tribal affinities are unknown. The most southerly of the eastern Algonquins. A warlike tribe, the Shawnees fought the Cherokees, Iroquois, Catawbas, and others. One group were known as the Savannas, after whom Savannah, Georgia, is named. Friendly toward the whites, they were reported by Governor Archdale as "good friends and useful neighbors." The British, however, favored the Catawbas, and at the instigation of the French a few bands of Shawnees attacked the British settlements, but were repulsed. During the Revolutionary War the Shawnees were allies of the colonists, and boasted of having killed more English than had any other tribe. After the war a number were granted lands on the Delaware, where they were received by the Iroquois as "brothers" and by the Delawares as "grandsons." Later they were at war with the more western Iroquois and the Cherokees, and many joined the Creeks. For nearly forty years the Shawnees were almost constantly at war with the English or the Americans, and were regarded as the most hostile tribe of the central states. Favored by the Spanish, who offered them lands in Missouri in 1793, a number migrated to that area. During the Tecumseh war the Shawnees took no active part. Soon after, a number moved into Texas and others went to Kansas. In 1869 they agreed to join the Cherokees in Oklahoma, although a few still remained in Kansas and elsewhere.

SHOSHONIS or SHOSHONES. From the Cheyenne name meaning "Snake People," from their home on the Snake River, Idaho. They also occupied portions of Wyoming, Nevada and a small area near Great Salt Lake in Utah. A tribe of Shoshonean linguistic stock. Broadly speaking, they were divided into two groups, the more northerly and easterly group being horse Indians and buffalo hunters leading a nomadic life and noted as warriors. The more westerly group were sedentary, living in a poor area, had no horses, and led a rather hand-to-mouth existence, depending upon salmon, wild plants and berries, and some agriculture. They were often referred to as "Digger Indians." The nomadic plains group dwelt in tipis, whereas the western group used brush houses or shelters, often merely a roofless circular pile of brush affording little protection. Usually friendly toward the whites, the Shoshones gave little trouble, and as early as 1909 large numbers were enrolled in the various reservation schools. They did not suffer so much from epidemics as the other plains tribes, and are still numerous.

SIAS. A small Keresan tribe of the Pueblo Indians inhabiting a single pueblo on the Jemez River near Bernalilo, New Mexico.

SIKSIKA or BLACKFEET. From Siskina-ka. Uncertain if used because of a custom of wearing black-painted moccasins, or because of a war party returning with moccasins blackened by the ashes of a prairie fire after having had their ponies stolen. An important Algonquian confederation of the Siksika, the Bloods, and the Piegans. Closely related and allied with them were the Atsinas and Sarsis. They held a vast territory, extending from the North Saskatchewan River in Canada to the Missouri River in Montana and west to the Rocky Mountains. Now mainly on reservations in Canada and Montana, although many are well-to-do farmers and ranchers. Also a number are camped in tipis in the national parks, where, dressed in their native costumes and regalia, they are a drawing card for tourists. They were plains nomads, depending upon the buffalo, and were noted for their bravery and fighting ability. Traditional enemies of the Crows, they also fought the Crees, Dakotas, Assiniboins, Flatheads, and Kutenais, but never engaged in hostilities of importance with the whites. Each tribe of the confederation had its own customs, dress, dances, and elected chief, and each was divided into several bands totaling nearly fifty. Like many other tribes, they were primarily sun worshipers. Once very numerous, they were decimated by disease and warfare. Altogether they were and are a fine race, with many admirable qualities, and were noted for their fondness for revelry, joking, laughter, and merrymaking. Many of the women married white men, who were adopted as members of the tribe.

SIOUX. A name used to designate any of the many tribes of the Dakota group or confederation, all of Siouan linguistic stock. Once the most numerous of all the plains Indians. Widely distributed, some of the Siouan group inhabiting the southeastern and middlewestern areas. Those usually referred to as Sioux were the Midewakantons, Wahpekutes or Santees, the Sissetons, Wahpetons, Yanktons, Tetons, Brûlés, Sans Arcs, Mineconjous, Oohenonpas (Two Kettles), Oglalas, Hunkpapas, and Assiniboins. The Blackfeet, once the enemies of the Sioux, eventually became allied with them. In addition to the above the group now includes the Mandans, Arikaras, and Hidatsas. Famed for their horsemanship, military skill, and prowess, for their long wars with the whites, their many famous chiefs, and their social codes and etiquette. Today the majority are on reservations, but many are prosperous, independent farmers and ranchers, while others are scattered over all the states, many in the great eastern cities, where they pass unnoticed and unrecognized.

SISSETONS. One of the seven original tribes of the Dakota confederation. They formed a link between the eastern and western Siouan tribes, but were more closely related to the eastern than the western groups. Originally in western Minnesota and eastern Dakota. Less warlike than other Dakota tribes, they gave little trouble to the whites after making numerous treaties, and in 1800 were given lands on the Minnesota River, where they became farmers.

SKIDIS. A tribe of the Pawnees. The name is a corruption of Tskiri, or "wolf." Sometimes called the Wolf Pawnees. Their dialect is quite unlike that of the other Pawnees. According to tradition they were once united with the Arikaras. Originally mainly on the Loup River, Nebraska. The first of the Pawnee group to push northward, and have always retained their tribal organization, traditions, and rites. In 1770 many were in Texas, and by 1862 they had settlements in northeastern Texas. Never hostile to the whites, they made frequent raids on other tribes, mainly to obtain horses, for a man's wealth was measured by the number of his ponies. Many were employed as scouts by the Army during the Indian campaigns. They finally settled in Oklahoma, where they took lands in severalty and became citizens and well-to-do farmers and ranchers.

SKITSWISH. A Salish tribe of northern Idaho. They were noted for their industry, self-respect, and peaceful behavior.

TACHIS. A large tribe of the Yokuts or Mariposan group about Tulare Lake, California. Now mission Indians, with a few others living in Kings County.

TAHLTANS. The most southwesterly tribe of the Nahane group, whose home was the basin of the Stikine River, as far north as the Iskut River and westerly into Alaska. Hunters and salmon fishers, they are a quiet, honest, industrious lot, kindly and agreeable. Many are employed as guides, others work for the trading companies, and they took so readily to white men's ways that they now have villages of well-built log houses and have all the luxuries and gadgets of civilization.

TAWAKONIS. A Caddoan tribe of the Wichita group, formerly inhabiting the Brazos and Trinity river valleys in Texas. At one period a very powerful tribe, they are now on reservations incorporated with the Wichitas.

TETONS. From Tito-n-wa-n, or "Prairie Dwellers." The most westerly and largest tribe of the Dakota confederacy. They included the bands west of the Missouri.

THILINGITS. A name applied to any Indians of the Koluschan linguistic family. Inhabiting the coast and islands from the mouth of the Portland River to the Bering Straits.

TOLOWAS. An Athabascan tribe of extreme northwestern California, along the coast. A diminishing and demoralized tribe because of close association with the whites.

TONKAWAS. Once a powerful tribe of Texas and northern Mexico. A distinct linguistic group. Although savage fighters and deadly foes of the various Apache tribes, they were uniformly friendly with the whites. Among the other tribes they bore an evil reputation as horse-stealers, and were accused of being cannibals. On October 25, 1862, while camped at the Andarko Agency, the Tonkawas were attacked by a number of Delawares, Shawnees, and Caddos, who killed two agency employees and massacred 137 men, women, and children of the Tonkawas, or over one-half of the tribe. After several years of wandering, the few remaining Tonkawas were gathered together and placed on a reservation at Fort Griffin, Texas, and later were removed to Oklahoma, where the few dozen survivors mixed with the Lipans and other friendly tribes.

TONTOS. One of the so-called Apache tribes, but the name is so indiscriminately applied it is almost meaningless. It is used to designate the Yavapai, Yumas, Mohaves, and the Pinaleño Apaches who were placed on the San Carlos Reservation. Also used when referring to the Coyotero Apaches and to mixtures of all. In fact Tontos was used when referring to practically all Indians between the White Mountains of Arizona and the Rio Grande, but especially the Yavapai, who were also known as Apache-Mohaves. Those officially called Tontos are of Athabascan linguistic stock, and were a seminomadic lot, not particularly warlike or hostile. They are now mostly on the San Carlos reservation, but many are well-to-do farmers and ranchers on their own lands.

TUSCARORAS, TUSCARAUAS. From Skaru-reny or "Hemp gatherers," because they harvested the Indian hemp—*not* the introduced plant from which marijuana is prepared but the native *cannabium,* valued for its fibers, which were used for bowstrings, weaving, textiles, etc. A large and important confederation of Algonquian tribes who originally occupied parts of the Carolinas. Regarded as mild, friendly, and peaceable, the Tuscaroras were abominably treated by the whites, who regarded all Indians as little better than beasts. They were abused, killed, and many were sold into slavery, with the result that they became implacable enemies of the white men. A disastrous war followed in which large numbers of whites were killed, and many settlements destroyed. Finally migrating north in 1712-1715, they joined the Five Nations of the Iroquois, making the confederation the Six Nations. (See Iroquois)

TUTUTNIS. A tribe of Athabascan stock that dwelt on the lower Rogue River in Oregon as well as on the coast at the river's mouth. Although known by a common name, yet the various villages were often at war. One of their unusual customs was to bury widows alive in the graves of their husbands. A rather quarrelsome and warlike tribe, they were known to the settlers as the "Rogues," or "Rogue Indians." They were removed to the Siletz Reservation in 1856 as prisoners of war. Today they are respected farmers and businessmen, scarcely distinguishable from their white neighbors.

UINTAS. A division of the Ute tribe in northeastern Utah. Also known as "Elk Utes."

UTES. An important group of tribes of Shoshonean stock. Formerly occupied all central and western Colorado, eastern Utah, much of Nevada, and parts of New Mexico. A warlike race with no agricultural tendencies. Gave only minor troubles to the whites, but were addicted to raiding other tribes to obtain women and children as slaves or to be held for ransom. Many were employed by the government as scouts, and a number were added to U. S. troops by Kit Carson during the campaign against the Navajos. In 1861 a treaty gave the Uintah Valley to the Uinta Utes, and in subsequent treaties many were assigned to various reservations. Later, many were allotted severalty lands, and acquired citizenship. Although prior to this the Utes had committed numerous depredations, murders, and burnings, there had been no serious war such as that with the Sioux and other tribes. Very largely the tribes were restrained by Chief Ouray, who was always friendly and desired peace. At present the Utes are ranchers and farmers, and with the discovery of oil on their lands they have become wealthy.

WABENAKI. (Also Abenaki.) A very large group of Algonquian tribes of northern New England. (See Chapter on People of the Dawn.)

WACOS. One of the divisions of the Tawakoni, whose main village was on the site of Waco, Texas. The houses were of grass sod, and the tribe was thoroughly agricultural. In 1824 they had over two hundred acres of cultivated land well fenced in. Never troublesome, they were given reservations, and in 1902 received allotments of land, becoming citizens and prosperous farmers and ranchers.

WAHPEKUTES from Wah-pe-kute, or "Leaf shooters." One of the tribes of the Dakotas or Sioux.

WAHPETONS. From Wahk-pe-tonwan, or "Living among leaves." One of the Sioux or Dakota tribes. Generally classed with the Sisseton Sioux. Originally occupied parts of Minnesota and Wisconsin.

WAILAKIS. An Athabascan tribe of Round Valley, California. Now almost extinct. They dwelt in circular houses and subsisted by fishing and gathering wild plants, nuts, and berries, and by hunting. At one time numerous, they were hostile to neighboring tribes, and were good fighters taking the entire heads of the vanquished as war trophies.

WALAPAIS. A Yuman tribe of Arizona occupying Hualapai, Yavapai, and the Sacramento valleys of the Aquarius Mountains. An inferior race physically, they lived by hunting and on wild plants, and even after being provided with schools they made little progress and did not take kindly to agriculture.

WALLAWALLAS. Meaning "Little River." A tribe of Shahaptian stock, formerly living on the eastern banks of the Columbia and Snake Rivers, and nearly to Umatilla in Oregon and Washington. Their language is closely related to that of the Nez Percés. By treaty made in 1855 they were removed to the Umatilla reservation in Oregon, where they have intermarried with the Nez Percés, Umatilla, and Cayuse Indians.

WAMPANOAGS. "Eastern People." In colonial days one of the principal tribes of New England, occupying the eastern shores of Narraganset Bay and parts of adjacent Massachusetts. Ruled all the coast, as well as Nantucket and Martha's Vineyard. Their chief, Massasout, made the first treaty of friendship with the colonists, which was faithfully kept until his death. He was succeeded by his son, King Philip, whose war with the whites is famous. It was brought on by the colonists, who did not abide by the treaty. The Wampanoags were almost exterminated, and many were sold into slavery, while the few survivors fled for sanctuary to other tribes of the interior. Those on Nantucket and Martha's Vineyard had no part in the war and were not molested. The so-called Gay Head Indians, now mainly of mixed African and Indian blood, are descendants of the Wampanoags, and some of the Stockbridge and other tribes claim to be of Wampanoag blood.

WASCOS. From Wacq-to, the name of a small cup-shaped rock near the tribes' principal village in the vicinity of the Dalles in Wasco

County, Oregon. They were a sedentary people, depending upon salmon, wild plants, and some hunting for a livelihood. They were skilled wood- and horn-carvers, made excellent baskets, and tanned hides to perfection. Their houses for winter use were partly underground and were of cedar planks, while the summer homes were large and made of poles covered with brush, grass, reeds, etc. They practiced the artificial flattening of the children's heads. They had slaves who were often buried alive so they might accompany the dead chief to the spirit world.

WASHOS. A small tribe of distinct linguistic stock who formerly lived in the Truckee River area of Nevada, as well as the valley of the Carson River to below Carson City, the borders of Lake Tahoe, and as far west as the Honey Lake area of California. Conquered by the Paiutes, they were driven from their lands and took to a parasitic vagabondish life about Reno and other towns. Now almost extinct.

WHITE MOUNTAIN APACHES. A division of the Coyoteros, the name given them because of their home in the White Mountains of Arizona. Later applied to all Apaches under the Fort Apache agency, consisting of Arivaipa, Tsiltaden, Chillion, Chiricahua, Coyotero, Mimbreño, and Mogollon Indians. Now peaceful, trustworthy, and industrious, many are railway section hands, structural steelworkers, farm and ranch hands, etc.

WICHITAS. A Caddoan confederacy related to the Pawnees. Formerly ranging through Kansas and Arkansas to the Brazos River in Texas. Now residing mainly in Caddo County, Oklahoma. Known to the Sioux as Black Pawnees, to the early French as Tattooed Pawnees, to the Kiowas and Comanches as Tattooed Faces. Among the tribes of the confederacy were the Wichita proper, the Tayovaya or Taweha, Waco, Yscani, Ajwesh, Aisidahetsh, Kishkat, and Korishkitsu. The only divisions now existing are the true Wichitas, the Wacos, and the Tawakonis. The earliest missionary work undertaken among the plains Indians was in 1541 by the Franciscan Father Juan de Padilla and a few other priests who had been attached to the Coronado expedition. They were killed by the Indians, who were jealous of the missionaries' labors, with an enemy tribe. Originally friendly toward the whites. They were cannibals and devoured their prisoners as a religious ceremony. Took part with the French against the Spanish. In 1760 asked for peace and a mission. Being refused, they attacked the Spaniards about San Antonio. After being decimated by smallpox they allied themselves with the Tawakonis and Wacos. In 1835 made their first treaty with the United States, with whom they had been friendly, agreeing to dwell peacefully with the whites and with the Osages. Settled down north of Lawton, Oklahoma. Because of the determined hostility of the Texans, the tribes were removed to the Washita River area in Oklahoma. Acted as scouts and allies of the whites against the Comanches. In 1902 given allotments of land in severalty, and became citizens and prosperous farmers. They were naturally a sedentary tribe, with small farms, and dwelt in permanent villages of conical houses of poles covered with grass thatch, but when away from home used the skin tipi of the plains nomads. Many were tattooed from head to foot, hence the name given them by the French.

WINNEBAGOS, from Wini-py-a-gohag, or "People of the muddy water." A large Siouan tribe of Minnesota and eastern Dakota, especially about Lake Winnebago. They were beginning to lead a civilized life when the Sioux War broke out in 1862 and the people of Minnesota demanded the removal of the Indians. They were taken to the Crow Creek reservation in Dakota, where they suffered greatly from disease and ill treatment, and finally fled to the Omahas' reservation for protection. Were then assigned to a reservation in northeastern Nebraska, where they have acquired lands in severalty and have prospered as farmers and ranchers. Usually peaceful, the Winnebagos sided with England during the Revolutionary War and the War of 1812, but otherwise have had no trouble with the whites.

WYANDOTTES. See Hurons.

YAKIMAS. From Ya-ki-ma meaning "runaway." A Shashaptian tribe formerly living on both sides of the Columbia River and on the Yakima River in Washington. The name Yakima is commonly used to designate any of the tribes, such as the Paloos and others, who are in the area of the reservation of the Yakima. Naturally quiet and peaceful, the Yakimas were employed by the settlers as boatmen, laborers, and lumbermen, but were demoralized by vile liquor supplied by the whites and were robbed and cheated at every turn.

YAKUTATS. A Thilingit tribe whose home was the coastal area of Alaska and southward to Washington. Mainly noted for their carved horn and wooden objects, their canoes and fishing abilities, and the priests' strikingly Oriental costumes. Now civilized, and scarcely distinguishable from their white neighbors.

YANKTONS. From Ihanke-yony-wan, or "End village." One of the Dakota tribes. Never having any serious troubles with the whites, they often refused to join the other Sioux tribes in the Indian wars. (See Dakotas.)

YANTONAIS. A Sioux tribe closely related to, if not merely a branch of, the Yanktons.

YAQUIS. An important division of the Cahitas who dwelt on both banks of the Yaqui River, largely on Mexican territory. They were a sedentary, agricultural race who cultivated many food plants as well as cotton, which they spun and wove into excellent cloth. They were noted for their serapes. Originally at peace with the Spaniards, the treatment they received caused them to revolt, and a more or less desultory warfare with the Mexicans was carried on until 1906-1907, when President Porfirio Diaz had many deported to Yucatan and southern Mexico. Here, as it turned out, they have been better off and more prosperous than on the desert borderland. All those who have had first-hand dealings with the Yaquis have spoken highly of their capabilities and characters. Of all the North American tribes who, for several centuries, have been completely surrounded by the whites, they are the only tribe that was never subdued until the Diaz campaign. Those who still remain along the border are all quiet, civilized, and mainly Christian, with farms and ranches. Many are employed as ranch hands or *vaqueros,* and others as farmers and miners, while others have their own farms and ranches. Only a few come under the United States tribes. They are physically a fine race, strong and of medium size, and have quite heavy beards. They work silver to some extent and find ready sale for their baskets, mats, hats, etc. Many of the raids and atrocities laid to the Yaquis were in reality committed by the Apaches of the border.

YAVAPAIS. Also known as Mohave-Apaches. A Yuman tribe of Arizona.

YUCHIS. A tribe also known as Westis, who lived in the vicinity of Savannah, Georgia. A sedentary agricultural tribe living in well-built houses in large compact villages. They used the blowgun for hunting. In 1836, in company with the Creeks, they went to Oklahoma.

YUMAS. From Yamayo or "Son of the chief," because their chieftainship was hereditary. In their own language they call themselves the Kwichan. Dwelling on both sides of the Colorado River about fifty miles from its mouth. A fine race physically, brave and good fighters, they were not warlike, and dwelt in villages, where they cultivated food plants and tobacco. Never troublesome to the whites, they yet are often included among the so-called Apaches.

YUROKS. From Ur-uk or "Downstream people." A tribe of Weitspekan linguistic stock living on the lower Klamath River in California. Unknown to the whites until 1850. Never at war with the settlers, although there were a few frays with the miners in some areas. A much larger and finer race physically than other California tribes. They had no chiefs, the prominence of a member depending upon his wealth (mainly consisting of *Dentalium* shells, which were their medium of exchange). They also valued the scalps of woodpeckers and large "coins" of obsidian. Their costumes of leather were often very beautifully decorated with shells, bright-colored feathers, woodpeckers' scalps, quills, and beads. They made beautiful spoons and other objects of horn and wood, often inlaid with *Haliotis* (abalone) shell. Their canoes were made of redwood and were square or scowlike at both ends. A sedentary race, they dwelt in villages of houses constructed of split and dressed planks. Usually they were square or octagonal in shape, with a subcellar and gabled roof, and were from twenty to thirty feet square.

ZUÑIS. The common name of a pueblo tribe of Zuñian linguistic stock occupying the Zuñi Pueblo on the north bank of the Zuñi River, New Mexico. Their own tribal name is A-shi-wi or "The flesh," or, broadly interpreted, "People of the flesh country." The name Zuñi is a Spanish corruption of the Keresan Sunyitsi. The Zuñi pueblo is one of the most popular, and frequently visited by tourists. The tribe has always been friendly with white Americans but suspicious of the Spanish, and hereditary enemies of the Navajos. They are industrious, quiet, and good-natured, and adhere closely to their ancient religion and their many secret ceremonies and dances.

BRIEF BIOGRAPHIES OF FAMOUS INDIANS

ADOETTE. Ado-e-et, or Big Tree. A Kiowa chief born 1845. In the fall of 1868 the Kiowas and confederated tribes were compelled to go on the reservation in Oklahoma, but they still carried on raids into Texas despite the establishment of Fort Sill in their midst. In May 1871 a war party led by Set-t-ain-te (Santanta) or White Bear, together with Satank or Set-angya (Sitting Bear) and Adoette, attacked a wagon train and killed seven men and made off with forty-one mules. For their part in this raid the three chiefs were arrested at Fort Sill to await trial in Texas. Sitting Bear resisted, and was killed by the guard, while the other two were locked up in the Texas prison until October 1873, when, upon promising to prevent hostilities on the part of the tribe, they were released. Later, White Bear was arrested merely on the suspicion that he was planning trouble, and committed suicide in prison. The result was an outbreak of the Indians in 1873-74. Although other chiefs had not taken part in it, they were believed to be hostile, and Adoette with these chiefs again was arrested and confined in Fort Sill. After that the Kiowas remained at peace. Adoette became a Christian, and spent the rest of his life farming on his allotment on the former reservation.

AMERICAN HORSE. Washechun-tashunka. Oglala Sioux chief and associate of Red Cloud in the Sioux wars. In 1887 he signed a treaty with the Crook commission reducing the reservation to half its former size. The majority of the tribe objected, and, being still further excited by the murder of Sitting Bull, they considered going to war. While the Indians were gathered at the agency to treat with the commissioners their cattle were stolen. With the promise that their beef rations would be restored, they signed the agreements, but with the drought ruining their crops and with no increase in their meat they were actually starving to death. Taking up arms, a number went to the Bad Lands determined to make war on the whites. American Horse, however, induced them to surrender. In 1891 American Horse headed a delegation to Washington that resulted in the issue of adequate rations and fairer treatment of the Sioux.

ATTUCKS, CRISPUS. An Indian-Negro half-breed of Framingham, Massachusetts. Leader of the famous Boston Massacre of March 5, 1770, and the first to be killed by the British, and therefore the first American fatality of the Revolutionary War. A monument to his memory was erected on Boston Common in 1888. A giant in stature, Attucks was a sailor by profession, and was the son of a Negro father and Indian mother. His family name was that of his mother, Ahtuk, meaning "A small deer."

AWASHONKS. The chieftainess of the Seconet (Narragansets) of Rhode Island, whose name was signed to the Plymouth treaty of 1671. She was loyal to King Philip, but later made peace with the English.

BIG JIM. Wapameepto, or "Gives light as he walks." A famed Shawnee leader born on the Sabine reservation, Texas, in 1834. Became chief of the Kispicotha band commonly called "Big Jim's band of Absentee Shawnees." Grandson of Tecumseh. His father was a signer of the Sam Houston treaty between the Cherokees and other tribes, and the Republic of Texas, made on February 23, 1836. Probably the most conservative of his tribe, believing the earth was his mother and must not be wounded by tilling the soil, he was one of the last to accept an allotment of land in Oklahoma and always resisted all attempts at civilization of his people. Endeavoring to find some spot where he and his band would be free from molestation, he went to Mexico in 1900 and died of smallpox while there.

BIG MOUTH. Brûlé Sioux chief, although an Oglala by descent. Noted for his manly and warlike character. An opponent of Spotted Tail in the latter's efforts to maintain amicable relations with the whites; this made him gain popularity with the antagonistic members of the tribe. When Spotted Tail returned from his visit to Washington and other eastern cities, he found that Big Mouth's influence would inevitably result in war. Calling at the tipi of Big Mouth, he killed him with a revolver shot.

BLACK BEAVER. A Delaware born at present site of Belleville, Illinois, in 1806. Died in Anadarko, Oklahoma, May 8, 1880. A noted guide and interpreter, he was the first to arrange a conference between the Comanche, Kiowa, and Wichita tribes, and Col. Richard Dodge, in 1834. From then until his death he was constantly employed by the government, and proved valuable to scientific and military expeditions. On nearly all of the early transcontinental expeditions Black Beaver was the most trusted and efficient scout and interpreter.

BLACK HAWK. Ma-katawimesheka-kaa "Great black hawk (eagle)." A famous chief of the Sauk and Fox tribe, and leader in the Black Hawk War of 1832. Born at a village at the mouth of Rock River, Illinois, 1767. Distinguished himself in war when fifteen, and was head of a war party at seventeen, when they attacked an Osage camp of one hundred Indians and came out safely with scalps. On his next raid he found the enemy camp deserted, and all but five of his party left him. With these he attacked the Osages and took two scalps. At nineteen he led two hundred of his tribe on a desperate attack on several hundred Osages and killed twenty-seven, but lost seven, including his father. For five years he took no part in war. Then he destroyed an Osage camp of forty lodges and killed nine men himself. On another raid he found only five Cherokees, four men and a woman. He carried off the latter and released the men, as he considered it no honor to kill so few. In the War of 1812, Black Hawk with most of his tribe joined the British and raided many border settlements. Later, in opposition to the chief Keokuk, he made friends with the colonists. Following the war, the number of settlers moving west forced the Sauks and Foxes to move across the Mississippi, but Black Hawk refused to go, declaring he had been deceived by the treaty, and he endeavored to induce the Winnebagos, Pottawattomies, and Kickapoos to oppose the whites. By 1831 matters were so serious that Governor Reynolds called out the militia, who marched on Black Hawk's village, only to find it deserted. On June 30, Black Hawk and twenty-seven of his band signed a treaty agreeing to move peacefully across the Mississippi. The following spring it was found that after killing some Menominees, Black Hawk and his followers had recrossed the river, and again the militia was called out and followed the Indians up the Rock River, where they had gone to join the Winnebagos and Pottawattomies. In their first encounter they were routed; the Indians attacked the settlements, and also defeated Major Delment's battalion. However, a little later, while trying to cross the Wisconsin, Black Hawk's band was attacked and lost sixty-eight killed and wounded. From then on he and his tribesmen met with one disaster after another. Crossing the Mississippi, they were shelled by the steamer *Warrior*. Troops killed over 150 of the Indians, and the Sioux attacked and massacred them. Black Hawk and chief Neapope escaped, only to be captured by the Winnebagos. Black Hawk was sent east and confined at Fortress Monroe,

Virginia, but was taken on a tour of principal cities, where he aroused great interest. After his release he settled near the Des Moines River, where he died October 3, 1838. His body was placed upon the surface of the ground according to tribal custom, dressed in a military uniform presented by General Jackson, and with a sword given him by the general, together with a cane presented by Henry Clay and medals from John Quincy Adams and the City of Boston. The body was stolen in July 1839 and carried to St. Louis, where it was skeletonized and the bones sent to Quincy, Illinois. Following a protest by Governor Lucas of Iowa, the skeleton was restored, but Black Hawk's sons permitted the bones to remain in the office of the governor until they were turned over to the Burlington Historical Society. They were destroyed when the building was burned down in 1855.

BLACK KETTLE. A Cheyenne warrior and chief in 1864. His village on Sand Creek, Colorado, was treacherously attacked without reason by Colonel Chivington and his troops, who massacred men, women, and children, tortured the wounded, and mutilated the bodies. The Indians were unarmed and had come in to hold a council with Major Wyncoop. A few of the Cheyennes escaped by burying themselves in the sand by the creek. Among them was Black Kettle, carrying his wife, who had been shot through the body eight times. She eventually recovered. Traveling at night, the refugees started north with no food, no adequate clothing, and no blankets. It was bitterly cold, and they had to move slowly, as Black Kettle was burdened with his wounded wife. Almost starving, they finally met some buffalo hunters and, obtaining meat, continued on their way. Eventually, more dead than alive, they found their fellow Cheyennes after traveling over two hundred miles.

BLACK THUNDER. Makatan-anama-ki. A Fox chief and patriarch of his tribe who was at the council held at Portage, Wisconsin, in July 1815. His eloquent repudiation of charges brought against him won the Indians' claims. He signed the treaty of St. Louis on Sept. 14, 1815.

BLOODY KNIFE. A famed Arikara warrior and chief long in the service of our government. His father was a Hunkpapa Sioux and his mother was an Arikara, but he was born on the Hunkpapa reservation. When he was still a youth his mother returned with him to her tribe. At that time the overland mail carriers were so often killed by hostile Sioux bands that no one could be found to carry the mail through the Sioux territory. Bloody Knife volunteered, and successfully got the mail through on time. Later he was chief of scouts at Fort Lincoln, North Dakota. He took part in the battles on the General Stanley expedition to the Yellowstone in 1873, and accompanied Custer to the Black Hills in 1874, as well as in 1876. On the day of the famous Battle of the Little Big Horn, Bloody Knife was with Reno's command and was killed while fighting.

BLUE JACKET. Weyapiersenwah. A Shawnee chief noted mainly as the leader of the Indians in the battle with General Wayne, August 20, 1794, at Presque Island, Ohio. After the defeat of the Indians, Blue Jacket signed the treaty at Greenville, Ohio, and also that made at Fort Industry, Ohio, on July 4, 1805.

BOSWORTH, MARY. A Creek Indian woman also known as Mary Mathews and Mary Musgrove. She caused a great deal of trouble for the colonial government of Georgia in 1752, and roused the Creeks to war against the English. She held a very high place among the Creeks, as she was related to the chiefs of both the Upper and Lower Creeks. She possessed a complete knowledge of English, and was employed by Governor Oglethorpe as interpreter and go-between with the Indians at a salary of five hundred dollars per year. Her third white husband was the Reverend Thomas Bosworth, whom she married in 1749. Because of his close association with the Indians, he was given a commission as agent by South Carolina. This proved to be a most unfortunate act, for, being heavily in debt he induced his wife to assume the title of "Empress of the Creek Nation," and to make claim to vast areas of land. Notifying the governor that she was coming to claim her lands, she led a large force of Indians against Savannah. A troop of cavalry met the Indians outside the town and compelled them to surrender their arms before entering. The ex-preacher, clad in canonical robes, headed the procession, with his "Queen" by his side. They were received with full military honors, including a salute of cannon, and a council was arranged. During the meetings the Creeks somehow managed to secure their weapons, and a massacre was averted only by the seizure of Mary and her husband. Both were held in prison until they made full apologies and promised good behavior, whereupon they were released and the Indians were given presents. Nothing is known of her subsequent career, but undoubtedly she and Bosworth had "lost face" with the Creeks and probably left in disgrace for more congenial surroundings.

BRIGHT EYES. Real name Susette La Flesche. Eldest child of Eshtamaza or Joseph La Flesche, head chief of the Omahas. Born in

Nebraska in 1850, she attended the mission school on the Omaha reservation and later went to a private school in Elizabeth, New Jersey. After her return she was a teacher in the government's day school on the reservation, and was active in progressive movement on the part of the young people. In 1877-78 the Poncas were forcibly transferred to Oklahoma (Indian Territory), and her father went there to help the sick and dying Poncas. Susette accompanied him. The heroic effort of Standing Bear to win justice, and the Indians' terrible march of six hundred miles, followed by his arrest (see Standing Bear), resulted in the indignation of the citizens and it was arranged for the chief, together with Susette and her father, to go east and relate the story of their wrongs. It was at that time she was given the name Bright Eyes, and it was largely due to her eloquence and her vivid representation of the Poncas' treatment that the public and the press demanded that the government should restore the Poncas' lands and that no more forcible removals of the Indians should be made. She was married to Mr. T. H. Tibbles in 1881, and together they visited England and Scotland and gave many public addresses regarding the Indians. After her return she resided at Lincoln, Nebraska, and busied herself writing until her death in 1902.

CANONICUS. A Narraganset chief who died at the age of eighty in 1647. In 1622 he sent the Plymouth Colony a declaration of war as a matter of form, but cultivated the friendship of the English. When Roger Williams went to Rhode Island he entered the territory of Canonicus, and from him received the title to the land. Canonicus was at war with the Wampanoag tribe until 1635, when Roger Williams arranged for peace between the two. Although always on friendly terms with the colonists, he never trusted them and aside from Williams the whites were suspicious of the chief's good faith.

CATAHECASSA. Ma-ka-tawikasia, or Black Hoof. A head chief of the Shawnees, born 1740. One of the greatest and most famed leaders of the warlike tribe throughout the period when they were dreaded as inveterate and merciless foes of the whites. He had a leading part in Braddock's defeat in 1755 and in the desperate battle with the Virginia troops as Point Pleasant in 1774. He always resisted the encroachments of the settlers west of the Allegheny Mountains, and constantly battled with both troops and civilians until the victory of General ("Mad Anthony") Wayne ended in the peace treaty of August 3, 1795. Convinced of the hopelessness of his cause, the chief gave up fighting, and became noted as an orator, advocating friendship and lasting peace with the whites. When British agents endeavored to stir up rebellion among the Indians during the War of 1812, Black Hoof held his tribe in restraint and sided with the colonists, although Tecumseh and his band became allies of the British. He died at Wapkoneta, Ohio, in 1831.

COCHISE. A Chiricahua Apache chief who was the son of Nachi, and his successor. One of the most famed of the "Apache" chiefs, Cochise, although constantly warring with the Mexicans, was friendly with the Americans until 1861. Then he went with other chiefs under a flag of truce to a camp of U. S. troops to deny the charge of having abducted a white child; the commanding officer treacherously had the chiefs seized and forced by torture to confess. One of the Indians was killed, and Cochise was wounded, but despite three bullets in his body he escaped by cutting through the tent. His companions who, despite the "third degree," maintained their innocence, were hanged. Cochise at once began hostilities to avenge his comrades and relatives, and the troops were forced to retreat. Cochise and his band then determined to drive the whites from his territory, and settlements, homes, and wagon trains were wiped out, until the country was laid waste. When the troops were withdrawn at the outbreak of the Civil War, and the forts were abandoned, Cochise was convinced that he and his men could prevent whites from settling in his territory. With chief Mangas Coloradas, the Indians defended Apache Pass in Arizona when Californians under General Carleton strove to reopen communication between the Pacific coast and the east. However, the artillery of the whites forced the Indians to retire, and when Regular Army troopers returned to Arizona at the close of the Civil War, they declared a war of extermination against all the so-called "Apaches," regardless of tribe. Unspeakable cruelties were committed by both sides until Cochise surrendered in September 1871. When orders came to transfer his people to the new reservation in New Mexico, he escaped with two hundred warriors in 1872 and was joined by about five hundred other Chiricahuas. After the Chiricahua reservation was established in 1872, he and his band came in and became ardent farmers. He died peacefully in 1874, and was succeeded as chief by his son Taza. Although a ferocious fighter and noted for his bravery and military genius, Cochise would never have been troublesome had the settlers kept their faith with him and his fellows. He was inherently honorable, he was as steadfast in his friendship as he was implacable in his hatred, and on more than one occasion he safeguarded settlers who had been kind to him and posted a guard about their homesteads to protect them.

COCKENOE. An Algonquin name meaning "Interpreter." A Montauk Indian who was captured by the Pequots during the war of 1637. He afterward became the interpreter for John Eliot, the missionary and translator of the Bible, and taught Eliot the language of the Massachusett Indians. He rendered inestimable service to the colonists as well as to the authorities. Without him the Eliot Bible would never have been written. He died about 1790.

COLBERT, WILLIAM. A Chickasaw chief who aided the colonists during the Revolutionary War and joined the army of General St. Clair, leading his tribesmen against the hostile Indians. Famed as the greatest war chief of the Chickasaws, he served nearly a year with the regular infantry and then returned to his tribe and led the warriors against the Creeks, whom he drove from Pensacola to Apalachicola, killing many and returning to Montgomery, Alabama, with eighty-five prisoners. When, as leader of the Chickasaw delegation, he visited Washington in 1816, he was addressed as "General" by the President. On the treaties ceding Chickasaw lands to the government his name is signed as "General Colbert," with the exception of some signed "Piomingo," a name that was also borne by a Chickasaw captain in the St. Clair expedition. It was also used as a pen name by John Robertson, a Muscogulgee warrior who wrote *The Savage,* published in Philadelphia in 1810.

COLORADO. A chief of the White River Utes and leader of their outbreak in 1879. The cause of this was the Ute agent, N. C. Meeker, who believed he could force the Indians to labor and who meddled in their tribal quarrels and affairs. The result was the resentment aroused in Colorado's band. When Meeker moved the agency to the Utes' pasture lands and started plowing the grazing land, the Utes stopped him by force. When Meeker complained, troops under Major T. T. Thornburgh were sent to the agency. After a parley the Utes were assured that the troops would not enter the Indians' land, and when they broke their promises and moved on they were ambushed. Thornburgh and a number of his men were killed. The Utes, now thoroughly aroused, then killed the male employees of the agency and made prisoners of the women. The head chief Ouray (which see) who had always been an advocate of friendship with the whites, forced his tribe to cease all hostilities, and the matter was settled amicably.

COMCOMLY. A Chinook chief who received Lewis and Clark hospitably when they reached the mouth of the Columbia River in

1805. When the Astor expedition arrived to take possession of the country for the United States, Comcomly cultivated the friendship of the whites and gave his daughter in marriage to Duncan M'Dougal, a Canadian who was leader of the expedition. Although Comcomly was under suspicion of secretly plotting to kill the garrison and steal the stores, yet when a British ship arrived in 1812, planning to capture the fort at Astoria, he offered his services with eight hundred warriors to defend the settlement. But the colonists had concluded a peaceful sale and transfer to the British, who won the chief's friendship by gifts and promises. At the time of his heyday Comcomly when visiting Vancouver was preceded by three hundred slaves, who carpeted the pathway from the fort to the governor's house, a distance of several hundred feet, with beaver and otter skins.

CORN PLANTER. Kaiiontwa Kon, or "By what he plants." A chief of the Senecas also known as John O'Bail, born about 1735 on the Genesee River, New York. One of the warriors at the battle and defeat of Braddock in 1755. His father was John O'Bail or Abeel, a white trader. All that is known of Corn Planter's youth is contained in a letter he wrote to the governor of Pennsylvania in which he tells of playing with the Indian boys. His mother, a full-blooded Seneca, told him his father lived in Albany. The youth called on him and was treated kindly, but was not told that the United States was about to rebel against England. His letter says he was married prior to his visit. A signer of the various treaties in which vast areas of land were ceded to the government, he became so unpopular with his tribe that his life was in danger, and in 1790, accompanied by Halftown, he went to Philadelphia and laid the Indians' complaints before General Washington. For his many valuable services to the whites he was given a commission in the Continental Army and a large grant of land in Pennsylvania, where he resided. In his old age he declared the Great Spirit had told him to have no further dealings with white men or to keep any presents given him by them. He therefore burned his uniforms, belts, and other articles, and broke his magnificent sword. For a time he received a government pension of two hundred and fifty dollars per year. He died on Feb. 18, 1836, when 101 years of age. A monument to him was erected on his reservation by the state of Pennsylvania in 1866.

CORNSTALK. A celebrated chief of the Shawnees, born about 1720, who died in 1777. He was mostly famed for his leadership of the Indians at the battle of Pleasant Point, October 10, 1774. Although the Shawnees were defeated in the day-long battle, his generalship and prowess won the highest praise of the whites. After the battle he made a treaty with Lord Dunmore in November 1774. Later in the year he notified the settlers that he might be forced into war by malcontent members of his tribe. He and his son were held prisoners as hostages and were murdered by some vindictive soldiers. As a result, the Indians declared war that lasted for seven years and wrought havoc with the settlers. A monument to Cornstalk was erected in the courthouse yard at Point Pleasant in 1896.

CRAZY HORSE. The name is an incorrect translation of his Indian name of Tashunkewitko, meaning "a man like a wild horse." He was an Oglala Sioux chief, bold, adventurous, courageous, and a noted warrior, and a leader of the southern Sioux, who scorned life on a reservation and constantly raided the Crows and the Mandans. When the Sioux war broke out because of the government's breaking the treaty in which it was agreed that the Black Hills would be left to the Indians, Crazy Horse was the leader of the Sioux warriors. Although General Reynolds and General Crook in the winter of 1875 surprised the Indians' camp and captured all their horses, Crazy Horse and his band managed to stampede the herd in a blinding snow storm and recovered their mounts. Later, Crazy Horse was joined by numerous other chiefs and their warriors, until the united Sioux and Cheyenne forces annihilated Custer and his men at the Little Big Horn. Followed by General Miles, the Indians split up, but not until the troops used heavy artillery did Crazy Horse and two thousand followers surrender. Although there was no evidence to support the suspicion that he was plotting another revolt, he was arrested on September 7, 1877, and was shot when he tried to escape from the guard.

CROW DOG. Kangisanka. A Sioux chief. He took an important part in the Sioux war of 1876, but when, in 1881, the question of a new treaty arose and Spotted Tail was a strong advocate for maintaining peace with the whites, Crow Dog was leader of the opposition. Fearing the peaceful faction would win, he shot and killed Spotted Tail. He was arrested and sentenced to be hanged, but the Supreme Court ordered his release on a *habeas corpus* ruling that the federal courts had no jurisdiction over crimes committed on the reservations secured to the Indians by treaties. When the ghost-dance craze excited the Sioux, Crow Dog induced his band to go to war, and in 1890 he led them in a flight from Rosebud Agency into the Bad Lands, where they were faced by General Brooke's force. When friendly Indians tried to persuade Crow

Dog to surrender, he was inclined to do so, although the more hostile of the band threatened to shoot those who wavered. Finally even the most violent realized their cause was hopeless, and returned to the agency peacefully.

CROW KING. A Hunkpapa Sioux chief who became famed for his courage in defying the power of the medicine men who had formed a guild or merger until they threatened to control the tribe. He was also a noted and fearless warrior. During an attack on the Crows he was wounded by an arrow through the lungs. In order not to hamper his men by carrying him to their camp, and convinced he had but a short time to live, he had them leave him behind. Provided with a blanket and with his horse near, he was left in a ravine beside a creek. In his delirium he had a vision in which a spirit appeared and told him that if he would humble himself and become a dog for a day, and in company with his wife, Red Bird, would move on all fours about the village and eat like dogs, he would live. Making a vow that he would do this, he felt stronger, and, dragging himself to the stream, he drank and then managed to mount his horse. When, several days later, he rode into the village the Indians thought him a ghost. He told Red Bird of his vow and the two went on all fours with the dogs at night, barking and snapping and eating scraps, but at dawn returned to their tipi as man and woman. Crow King rapidly recovered from his wound, but Red Bird, feeling too deeply shamed to remain in the village, eloped with an Indian of another village. Crow King assured her that he felt she was justified in leaving him, and sent the couple presents and best wishes for their happiness. About this time his brother, High Bear, became ill and the most powerful of the medicine men was summoned. Knowing that Crow King was the richest of the band, with many horses, blankets, and guns, the wily shaman demanded exorbitant fees and accomplished nothing, but insisted he must have the aid of his fellows. Time passed, High Bear showed no improvement, and Crow King's wealth was rapidly diminishing. Finally High Bear died, and according to custom the medicine man's life was forfeit. But instead of killing him, Crow King invited all the medicine men to a feast and ordered them to bring their medicine bundles with them. When all had gathered he asked each in turn to show his "medicine" and describe its powers. When this had been done Crow King seized the bundles and denounced the shamans as a set of frauds, grafters, and charlatans. Then, to the amazement of everyone, he threw the magic bundles into the fire, and failed to drop dead as all expected. After that demonstration, faith in the medicine men's powers rapidly decreased and the band turned to agency doctors. His defiance of the occult powers of the shamans was the most courageous deed in Crow King's life—in some ways one of the bravest acts of any Indian of history.

DUCOIGNE, JEAN-BAPTISTE. A Kaskaskia (Peoria) chief of the early nineteenth century famed for his unwavering friendship for the whites and his loyalty to the United States. Not a full-blooded Indian, he had a strong tendency to live and act like a white man. In his memoirs, General W. H. Harrison, who knew Ducoigne well, states that he was "a gentlemanly man not given to drink" and in Harrison's letter to the Secretary of War he stated: "His [Ducoigne's] long and proven friendship has gained him the hatred of all the other chiefs, and ought to be an inducement with us to provide as well for his happiness as his safety." The chief often boasted that neither he nor any of his people had ever shed the blood of a white person. He signed various treaties, the last of which, made at Vincennes in 1803, provided that the government would build him a house and give him one hundred acres of fenced land. He had two sons, Louis and Jefferson, and a daughter, Ellen, who married a white man and in 1850 lived in Indian Territory (Oklahoma). Ducoigne died in the autumn of 1832, and his name is perpetuated in the name of the town of Duquoin, Illinois.

DULL KNIFE. Tah-me-la-pash-me. Chief of a band of northern Cheyennes, and one of the tribe who signed the treaty at Fort Laramie between the United States and the northern Cheyennes and northern Arapahos. In 1876 he and his warriors attacked Washakie's band of Shoshones and won the day. Because of the violation of the treaty by the United States and the crooked dealing of an Indian agent who rationed inedible beef and charged the government for prime beef, the Cheyennes became hostile, and Dull Knife and his band joined the Sioux under Crazy Horse and Sitting Bull in the uprising. He and his braves had a part in the Custer battle, and it was largely Cheyennes rather than the Sioux who annihilated Custer and his men, although all the available Sioux joined the Cheyennes in wiping out the Custer command. For a further account of Dull Knife and his band, see Glossary. Dull Knife was killed January 9, 1879, while trying to escape from Fort Robinson, Nebraska.

EASTMAN, CHARLES ALEXANDER. Ohiyesa, or "The Winner." A Santee Dakota (Sioux) physician, professor, and author, born

1858 near Redwood Falls, Minnesota. His father was a full-blooded Sioux named Many Lightnings. His mother was the half-blood daughter of a well-known Army officer. She died soon after his birth, and he was reared by his Indian grandmother and an uncle, who fled with him to Canada after the Minnesota war of 1862. He lived the primitive life of a wild Indian until fifteen. His father, having become a Christian and civilized, then brought the boy back to Flandeau, South Dakota, where some Sioux had homesteads and farms. Young Eastman was placed in the mission school at Santee, Nebraska, where he progressed so rapidly that in two years he went to Knox College, Galesburg, Illinois, and from there to Dartmouth College. Graduating from there, he entered the Boston School of Medicine, and in 1890 received the degree of M.D. He was soon appointed government physician at Pine Ridge agency, North Dakota, where he served for three years, including the time of the ghost-dance disturbances. Went to St. Paul, Minnesota, in 1893, and practiced medicine, also serving as secretary of the Y.M.C.A. among the Indians. Later became attorney for the Sioux in Washington, D. C., and still later served as government physician at Crow Creek, South Dakota. In 1903 he was appointed by the Office of Indian Affairs to carry out the revision of the allotment rolls and to select permanent family names for the Sioux. Author of several books: *Indian Boyhood,* 1902; *Red Hunters and the Animal People,* 1904; *Famous Indian Chiefs, True Stories of Indians,* etc. In 1891 married Elaine Goodale of Massachusetts. They had six children.

EASTMAN, JOHN. Mah-Piya-Wakan-Kidan, or "Sacred cloud worshiper." Born March 1849 at Shorkopee, Minnesota. Brother of Dr. Charles Eastman. A college-educated Presbyterian clergyman prominent in religious work among the Indians. In 1874 he married Miss Mary J. Faribault, a half-blood Santee. Served as delegate of his people in Washington.

FRANCISCO. A Yuma chief. When, on March 18, 1850, the Tonto Apaches killed Royse Oatman at Gila Bend, Arizona, they carried off the two youngest children—Olive, twelve, and Mary, seven years of age, and sold them to the Mohaves. Here they were well treated until the time of famine, during which Mary died of starvation. The girls' brother, Lorenzo, who had been left for dead, survived and tried to interest the people of California in searching for his sisters. This was done, but the searchers sent out from Fort Yuma found no trace of the captives. Upon their return to the Fort they met Francisco, who said he had some knowledge of the girls and would rescue the surviving sister if he were given four blankets and some beads to pay for her. When he reached the Mohave village the Indians denied all knowledge of Olive, having disguised her by staining her skin. But she spoke and told Francisco who she was. He thereupon "told the Mohaves off," as we say, and warned them of what might follow if they refused to release her. On the very day he had set, he arrived at Fort Yuma with the missing girl. Because of his services in rescuing her, and the rewards and presents he received from the whites, he was chosen head chief. He remained always friendly with the whites, although his tribe attributed their misfortunes to his friendship when in 1857 they made a raid on the Maricopas. The latter, reinforced by the Papagos, killed all but three of the seventy-five Yuma warriors, and these survivors killed Francisco, who had led them to disaster.

GALL. Pisi. A Hunkpapa-Teton Sioux chief. Born in the Moreau River area, South Dakota, 1840. Died at Oak Creek, South Dakota, December 5, 1894. Of humble birth and an orphan, he was reared with the kindness accorded all orphans by the Sioux, and when still a youth became noted as a warrior. He possessed great military ability and at the Battle of the Little Big Horn proved this when he led the Sioux forces. Although he acted as a lieutenant of Sitting Bull, his superior leadership placed him at the head of his warriors. After this battle he fled to Canada with Sitting Bull, but in 1880 he and Crow Chief withdrew with their bands from Sitting Bull, and they surrendered to Major Igles at Poplar River, Montana, on January 1, 1881. He then settled down as a farmer on the Standing Rock reservation. He became a firm friend of the whites, and denounced Sitting Bull as a fraud and a coward. He was very active and influential in inducing the Indians to submit to the plans of the government and the education of the children. He was a man of strikingly noble appearance, and was highly esteemed by the whites for his honesty and candor. He played a large part in the ratification of the act of May 2, 1889, by which the huge reservation was split up into several separate reservations. From 1889 until his death he was a judge of the court of Indian offenses at Standing Rock Agency.

GARAKONTHIE. Ga-ra-kon-ti-e, or "Moving Sun." Known to the whites as Chief Daniel. An Onondaga chief during the middle of the seventeenth century. Died at Onondaga, N. Y., 1676. A steadfast friend of the whites throughout his life. In 1658 he protected and aided the French, and soon became recognized as a protector of Christians and an advocate of peace. In 1661 he induced the

Onondagas to send an embassy to Quebec and to return their French captives. He accompanied the prisoners to Montreal, where he was well received, and secured the freedom of a number of his tribe who had been captured by the French. In 1662 he dissuaded his people from an attack on the whites and frustrated a plot to murder the French missionary at Le Moyne. During the war that followed he protected the French, and in 1669 was baptized as a Catholic in the cathedral at Quebec and was given the name of Daniel. He was everywhere famous as a humane, able, and friendly leader, and as an orator. Although his firm friendship with the whites lessened his influence with the hostile faction of his tribe, yet when any embassy was sent to either the French or the English his services were always in demand.

GELELEMEND. ("A leader.") A Delaware chief born about 1722, and commonly known as Killbuck, the name of his father, who was one of the best-educated Indians of his time. Having won a reputation for sagacity and discretion, he was chosen chief to succeed White Eyes in 1778. He strove always to maintain peace with the whites, and was assured of government aid in civilizing and educating the Indians if lasting peace could be arranged. However, the hostile faction under Hopocan had the majority vote in the tribal council. As a result, the officer in command of the Pittsburgh garrison invited Gelelemend to move his band to an island in the Allegheny River where they would be under the protection of the soldiers. However, they were not protected from a party of white murderers who, having massacred nearly one hundred Christian Delawares at Guadenhutten in 1782, fell upon Gelelemend and his band and slaughtered all but a few. Gelelemend was among those who escaped, but the documents given the Indians by William Penn were destroyed. He rendered valuable services in inducing a general peace, but the Munsee band held him to blame for the tribe's misfortunes, and to escape their vengeance he remained at his Pittsburgh home long after peace was declared. He finally joined the Moravian Church, and was baptized William Henry. He died in January 1811.

GLIKHIKAN. A noted Delaware warrior and orator. Accusing the French priests in Canada of having refuted the Christian doctrine, he challenged the Moravian missionaries to a debate in 1769, his idea being to win the Indian Christians from the Church. To everyone's amazement, he himself was converted, and went to live with the United Brethren. During the Revolutionary War his diplomacy saved the Christian settlements from annihilation by the Hurons under Half King, and when the Hurons captured him and the German missionaries their chief saved him from the vindictive Munsees. Despite his friendship with the whites, the fact that he was a Christian, and the services he had rendered, Glikhikan was murdered and scalped by the white raiders under Col. David Williamson at the massacre of Guadenhutten on March 8, 1782.

GERONIMO. Goyathlay, "One who yawns." Nicknamed Jerome (Geronimo) by the Mexicans. A famous Chiricahua Apache medicine man and chief who acquired fame by opposing the authorities and by sensational publicity and advertising. Born in 1834 at the headwaters of Gila River, New Mexico, son of Taklishim, "The Gray One." In 1876, when the government decided to remove the Chiricahuas from their reservation because the Mexicans complained of Apache depredations across the border, it was planned to move the Chiricahuas to San Carlos. Geronimo and some of the younger men fled to Mexico, but when they returned they were arrested at Ojo Caliente, New Mexico, and taken to the San Carlos Agency. Here they settled down, peacefully took to farming and ranching, and were doing well, but became discontented when the government refused to help irrigate their lands. Their crops failed, most of their cattle were stolen by white rustlers, and matters came to a head when the government tried to prevent the Indians from making their corn liquor or *Tiswin*. At that time Geronimo had the best farm at San Carlos, and was perfectly peaceable, yet whenever there was any trouble with the Indians the government made him the scapegoat, arresting him frequently. During his enforced absence from his farm practically all his horses and cattle were stolen, his fences cut, and his growing crops destroyed. Disgusted with the treatment he had received, Geronimo, in 1884-85, gathered a small band of hostiles and terrorized the inhabitants of all of Arizona, New Mexico, and Sonora and Chihuahua in Mexico. As a matter of fact, many of the tales of the depredations were spread by Geronimo himself in the well-founded belief that fear would accomplish more than actual violence. General Crook was sent with orders to capture or kill Geronimo and his men, but in March 1886 a truce was made, at which time the terms of surrender were agreed upon. But meantime the wily Geronimo had slithered away and was over the border. General Miles was then placed in command, and the following August Geronimo again surrendered. By this time Geronimo's name had become a household word, and he was regarded as the epitome of all that was savage, cruel, and treacherous. After their surrender the entire band of 340 warriors, together with Geronimo and Nachi, the hereditary chief, were deported as prisoners of war to Fort Marion, St. Augustine, Florida, then to Alabama, and finally back to Fort Sill, in Oklahoma, where they remained for the duration of their lives. Strange as it may seem, although technically prisoners of war, they took to peaceful pursuits, became industrious workers, made money and prospered, and were noted as keen traders. Probably none of the famous Indian chiefs of our past history have had as little real claim to fame as Geronimo. He was a thorough believer in the old adage that "He who fights and runs away will live to fight another day." Rarely did he engage in a stand-up battle, yet he caused the authorities more headaches than did many other leaders whose names have been forgotten, and he always managed to be one jump ahead of our troops until he saw fit to surrender and thus save his skin.

GRAND SOLEIL. The French rendering of the title Great Sun always borne by the head chief of the Natchez, the subchiefs being called "Suns." A noted chief of the Natchez in the early part of the eighteenth century, he, like the rest of his docile tribe, was a friend of the whites until the French commandant demanded the site of the Indians' village of White Apple near the present town of Natchez. The chief refused to comply, and told the commandant that his people had occupied the village for "more years than there were hairs in the governor's wig." The commandant then ordered the Indians' growing crops confiscated unless the Indians paid him for what they needed. The chief then sent bundles of sticks to the Natchez villages, in order, so he said, to indicate the various quota of the tribute. In reality the bundles were messages declaring war on the French, and indicating the number of days that were to pass before making concerted attack on the whites. The French never dreamed of the docile, friendly Natchez stirring up trouble, even though an Indian woman warned them. On November 30, 1729, the attack came, and every white person in the settlement, a total of about seven hundred, was killed. Grand Soleil and his warriors then proceeded to devastate the French plantations in Louisiana until the governor of the colony raised a force of Frenchmen and Choctaw Indians and recaptured the fort at Natchez. The chief then agreed to peace and the tribe broke up, various bands going in different directions. Grand Soleil and his band went nearly two hundred miles up the Red River, where he was attacked by the French. After a desperate battle he surrendered and was taken to New Orleans, where, with his men, he was put to death. All the women and children who survived an epidemic were transported as slaves to Haiti.

HAIGLER. The principal chief of the Catawbas about the middle of the eighteenth century. Commonly known to the English as "King Haigler." A friend of the whites and disposed toward peace, he yet offered the services of his tribe to the governor of South Carolina when the Cherokee war broke out in 1759. He joined Colonel Grant's forces and took an active part in the desperate battle of Etchoe. The victory of the whites largely resulted from his assistance. He was considered a man of sterling character, honest, truthful, courageous, just, and a father to his people, by whom he was beloved. He realized that they were being demoralized by liquor, and sent a letter to Chief Justice Henley on May 26, 1756, requesting the prohibition of sales of liquor to the Indians. As a result of this he was waylaid, killed, and scalped by the Shawnees when returning with a single servant from Waxaw. Among his descendents was his grandson, Col. Samuel Scott, who was chief of the Catawbas in 1840, and who signed the treaty with South Carolina on March 13th of that year.

HALF KING. Scruniiyatha. A Seneca chief born 1700. Died at the home of John Harris at the site of Harrisburg, Pennsylvania, October 1, 1754. A prominent leader, he was consulted for information, advice, and assistance by the white officials and even by George Washington. He accompanied Washington on the latter's journey of 1753-1754. He claimed that he personally had killed the French officer Jumonville, in revenge against the French who, he claimed, had killed, boiled, and eaten his father. He was a born diplomat, and when Ensign Ward was ordered to surrender by Contracaeur, Half King advised the ensign to reply that his rank did not empower him to do so, thus causing a delay that proved vital. For his services he was decorated by Governor Dinwiddie and given the honorary name of the governor, which he adopted with a great deal of pride. He has been greatly confused with the Huron Half King of Ohio, the Oneida Half King, and other chiefs of the same English name.

HALF KING. Petawontakas or Dunquad. Delaware name Pomoacan. A Huron chief of Sandusky, Ohio, during the latter part of the Revolutionary War. Employed by the British, he aided the Delawares in their opposition to the encroachment of white settlers beyond the Allegheny Mountains, and he saved the Moravians at Lichtenau from the hostile Indians in 1777. He was the leader of a combined force of Hurons, Ottawas, Chippewas, Shawnees, and others, with some French, and managed to maintain order and discipline among them. Numbering over two hundred, they camped about the mission, but were so silent that their presence was hardly noticed. He wisely prohibited all liquor. He also insisted upon the removal of the Christian Indians from the vicinity of Sandusky as a precautionary measure, and when the Moravians went to Detroit he sent a protective guard with them. His name appears on various treaties, sometimes signed "Petawontakas," at other times "Dunquad" or "Half King."

HIAWATHA. Haion-hwa-tha, or "Maker of Rivers." The name and title of hereditary chiefs of the Tortoise clan of the Mohawks. The second on the roll of chieftainships of the Iroquois confederation. The first known man of the name was a great reformer, legislator, statesman, and medicine man famed as one of the founders of the Iroquois league about 1570. With Dekanawida, the two strove to end all strife, murder, and war, and to promote universal peace and well-being. The confederation of the various tribes was one step; another was to establish the price of ten strings of wampum, each a yard in length, as the value forfeit for taking a human life. It was also decreed that the murderer forfeited his life to the family of his victim and that twenty strings of wampum must be paid to them to save his life. Although by birth a Mohawk, Hiawatha began his reform work among the Onondagas, but was met with opposition by their tyrannical leaders, who destroyed his daughters. He then turned to the Mohawks, but made his first real headway with the Oneidas. The Mohawks and Cayugas then formed a tentative union with the Oneidas, and induced the Onondagas to join the league when the Senecas also came into it. As the Onondaga chief was reputed to be a great magician, the Indians believed that he had been outdone by Hiawatha's magic. In time the personality and character of Chief Hiawatha became interwoven with the mystical deity of the same name who was one of the chief gods of the Iroquois. It was in this mystical form that he became the central figure of legendary lore and was immortalized by Longfellow.

HIAWATHA. A mythical titular deity of the Iroquois and other Algonquian tribes. He was believed to be the humanized form of the Creator's son, or his visual manifestation. This purely spiritual Hiawatha has become greatly confused with the famous Mohawk chieftain of the same name, undoubtedly borrowed from this deity.

HILLIS HADJO. Hilis-hadso, or "Crazy medicine." A Seminole

leader of the early part of the nineteenth century, known to the whites as "Francis the Prophet." He took an active part in the Seminole war, and was suspected of being an instigator of the second uprising. Convinced by some English traders that the Treaty of Ghent of 1814 provided for the restoration of the Seminole country to the Indians, he went to England hoping to obtain aid against the Americans. He was received with great interest and attention, and was hailed as a hero who had fought gloriously in the British cause during the War of 1812. He was described as being dressed in a splendid costume of red and gold, and carrying a tomahawk adorned with gold. His mission of course led to no practical result. In 1817 an American named McKrimmon was captured by the Seminoles and brought before Hillis Hadjo, who ordered him burned to death. At the last minute the captive's life was saved by the chief's daughter Milly, who declared she would throw herself in the flames if the sentence were carried out. Soon after this episode the chief was captured and hanged by the Americans. His wife and several daughters surrendered at St. Mark's, where Milly, who had saved McKrimmon's life, was kindly received, although she refused to marry the man she had saved until convinced that his offer was not made solely out of gratitude.

HOBOMOK. A Wampanoag chief who was a lifetime friend of the English, whom he met at Plymouth in 1621. He aided in strengthening the friendship of Massasoit for the colonists. He became a Christian, and died sometime before 1642 as a member of the Plymouth colony. He repeatedly warned the settlers of plots among the Indians, and when there was fighting he proved a great warrior and performed valorous deeds. His name is synonymous with Hobomoko made famous by John Greenleaf Whittier. Hobomoko, however, was actually an evil spirit of the Massachusetts and other Algonquian tribes.

HOLE IN THE DAY. Bag-wun-ag-ijik, or "Opening in the sky." A Chippewa chief of the warlike Bear Clan, who succeeded Curly Head as war chief in 1825. Already had been recognized as chief by the government because of his bravery and fidelity to the Americans in the War of 1812. Most of his life was devoted to fighting the Sioux, driving them across the Mississippi, and bringing an end to the struggle that had endured for centuries over the control of fisheries and hunting grounds of the Lake Superior region. On one occasion George Copway, a white friend of the chief, traveled 270 miles in four days to warn Hole in the Day of a Sioux raid. The chief was so impressed that he promised to become a Christian after one more battle with the Sioux, a promise that he kept. He died in 1846 and was succeeded by his son of the same name. At the time of the Sioux uprising in 1862 the son was accused of plotting a similar revolt, but there was no evidence to justify the suspicion. He was murdered by members of his tribe at Crow Wing, Minnesota, June 27, 1868.

HOLLOW HORN BEAR. A Brûlé Sioux chief, born in March 1850 in Sheridan County, Nebraska. When only sixteen years old he accompanied a band led by his father against the Pawnees, and distinguished himself by his bravery. In 1868 he joined a band of Sioux in an attack on United States troops in Wyoming and another attack in Montana. The next year he led a raid on the laborers constructing the Union Pacific Railroad. Later he became friendly, and was made captain of the Indians at Rosebud, South Dakota, and arrested Crow Dog for the murder of Spotted Tail. Five years later he resigned and was made second lieutenant under Agent Spencer but was forced to resign because of ill health, the result of old wounds. In 1889, when General Crook was sent with a commission to Rosebud to make an agreement with the Indians, the Sioux chose Hollow Horn Bear as their representative and spokesman. At the time of the inauguration of President Theodore Roosevelt on March 4, 1905, he took part in the parade at Washington.

HOLOTAMICO. Commonly known as Billy Bowlegs. The last Seminole chief of prominence to leave Florida for the reservation in Oklahoma. Born about 1808. After the removal of the first lot of Seminoles he became the recognized chief of those remaining and the leader of hostilities in 1855 to 1858. Although only twenty-five years of age and not then a chief, he was one of the signers of the treaty of Payne's Landing, May 9, 1832, by which the Indians agreed to move to Indian Territory. Numerous other Seminoles have been known as Billy Bowlegs.

HOPEHOOD. A chief of the Norridgewock known to his tribe as Wahowa. He was the son of the Indian known as Robin Hood, and took part in the King Philip's War. He led an attack on a house filled with women and children at Berwick, Maine, but all escaped except a woman and two children who barricaded and defended the door. In 1685 he joined Kankamagus and other chiefs in a protest to Governor Cranfield of New Hampshire, claiming the English were inciting the Mohawks to attack them. On March 18, 1690, he joined the French under Hertel in the massacre of Salmon Falls, and in May 1690 he attacked Fox Point, New Hampshire, burning several houses, killing fourteen persons, and carrying away six prisoners. Not long after this he penetrated Iroquois territory, where some Canadian Indians, mistaking him for an Iroquois, killed him and several of his men. At one time he was a captive of the English and served as a slave in Boston.

HOPOKAN. Koni-esch-guan-okee, or "Maker of daylight," but known to the whites as "Captain Pipe." A Delaware chief of the Wolf division, war chief of his tribe. Famed for his wisdom and oratorical ability. During the French war he fought against the English with great skill and courage. In 1764 he tried to capture Fort Pitt by strategy, but failed and was captured. After the termination of the war he settled with his clan in Ohio, and with the outbreak of the Revolutionary War he joined the British against the colonists, but notified the British commander at Detroit that he would not act savagely toward the whites, as he had no interest in the quarrel other than to obtain subsistence for his people—adding that he expected that when peace was made the Indians would be punished for any acts they had committed against the whites, regardless of which side they had been on. However, when Hopokan's band captured Col. William Crawford, who had led a party of whites and had massacred the Moravian Christian Indians, Crawford was put to death by torture. At the close of the war Hopokan in 1780 settled on land on the Upper Sandusky, at a site known as Pipe's village. He died peacefully in 1794.

HORNOTLIMED. A Seminole chief who became famed through a single act during the Seminole War of 1817-18. His home was at Fowl Town, but at the outbreak of the war he fled to Mikasuki. On November 30, 1817, three vessels arrived at the mouth of the Apalachicola River laden with supplies for the garrison up the river. Unable to ascend the stream because of adverse winds, the ships anchored offshore. Lieutenant Scott with forty men was sent in a boat to offer assistance, and upon their return they were ambushed by Hornotlimed and a few warriors, who killed all but six soldiers. These saved their lives by swimming to the opposite shore. The Indians then attacked the vessels, killing twenty soldiers left to guard them, more than twenty women, and the ill. The scalps were displayed on the red sticks which the Mikasuki erected in their villages. Soon afterward Mikasuki was attacked by the troops, but the majority of the Seminoles escaped, although Hornotlimed was taken prisoner and hanged. General Jackson in his report referred to Hornotlimed as "Homattlemico the old red stick."

JOLLY JOHN. Ah-ilud-egi, or "Throws away the drum." A Cherokee chief who was the adopted father of General Samuel Houston. Later he became chief of the Arkansas band of Cherokees. His early life was spent in Tennessee near the mouth of the Hiwassee River, where an island still bears his name. It was at this spot that Houston came to live with him, remaining for three years and acquiring a lifetime friendship for his adopted people. In 1818, Jolly John moved to the other side of the river and joined the Arkansas band, whose chief he became upon the death of Chief Tollunteeskee.

JONES, PETER. Ka-ke-wag-wonnaby. A Missisauga chief, missionary, and author of mixed blood, born January 1, 1802. Died June 29, 1856. His father was a Welshman named Augustus Jones, and a close friend of Joseph Brant. Peter's mother was Tuhbenahneeguay, the daughter of Wahbanosay, a chief of the Missisaugas on Credit River, Ontario, on land now known as Burlington Heights. Here Peter and his brother John were born. Until he was sixteen years of age, Peter lived the life of the tribe. At that time his father, who was a government surveyor, had the boy baptized by the Reverend Ralph Leeming, an English Episcopalian minister of the Mohawk church near Branford, Ontario. Peter took an active part in religious affairs, joined the Wesleyan Methodist Church, and was sent on a missionary tour in 1827 to various outlying Indian villages, although he had not been ordained. He had by this time begun his literary career, his first book being a hymnbook he translated into the Chippewa language. In 1830 he was made a deacon of his church, and a minister in 1833. The rest of his life was devoted mainly to missionary work among the Missisaugas and Chippewas, and to some extent among the Iroquois. As he was a chief and a minister of the gospel, he had great prestige and influence with the Indians. He visited New York and England in behalf of his people, and perfected titles to their lands. In addition to his volumes of hymns, he wrote an Ojibway spelling book in 1828, and translated part of the New Testament in 1829 and the first book of Moses in 1835. Other books included *The Life and Journals of Kah-ke-wa-quona-by* in 1860, and *A History of the Ojibways* in 1861. He was a man of strong personality, robust and athletic in build, a sound and fervent preacher, and with a vast store of wide knowledge on many subjects. He married an Englishwoman, who, with four sons, survived him. His seventh, who bore his father's Indian name, was editor of the magazine *The Indian,* published at Hagersville, Ontario, in 1885-86. Although inured to out-of-doors life and hardship, Peter Jones's health finally yielded to excessive exposures, and he died near Branford in 1856. A monument was erected to his memory by the Ojibways and other tribes in 1857.

JOSEPH. Hinmaton-yalatkit, or "Thunder from the water." A Nez Percé chief who became famous for his amazing and masterly retreat toward safety in Canada. Although his mother was a Nez Percé his father was a Cayuse who was given the name Joseph by his teacher, the missionary Spalding who was with Doctor Whitman and went to Idaho about 1839. The name was handed down as a family name. Joseph was undoubtedly one of the most remarkable Indians within the United States. He and the Nez Percés had always been friendly with the whites; but the treaty of 1863, by which the whites obtained rights to the Wallowa Valley, Oregon, the ancient home of Joseph, it was not recognized by him, for he claimed—and rightly—that in making the treaty the whites had used trickery and deception and that he knew nothing of the treaty, his first knowledge being an order to vacate within thirty days. He therefore continued to occupy the land. Although several minor collisions took place between the whites and the Indians, there was no serious trouble until the government attempted to remove the Indians to the Lapwai agency in Idaho. Even then the matter might have been carried out peacefully had it not been for the outrageous acts of some white settlers who wantonly killed several Indians, stole their horses, and burned houses. As a result, some of the more hotheaded Indians attacked the whites, and several of the latter were killed despite Joseph's efforts to prevent an outbreak, for his father on his deathbed had made him promise never to make war on the whites. He was scarcely more than a youth and was faced with a momentous problem. The only solution seemed to be for him to lead his band northward to Canada, where they would find sanctuary. The retreat was one of the most remarkable if not the most remarkable strategic action in the history of the world. Unaccustomed to war, lacking proper weapons, with inadequate supplies, and encumbered with women, children, the aged, and the ill; and opposed by trained soldiers under Generals Miles and Howard, and Colonel Sturgis, together with hundreds of volunteers, Joseph and his band outgeneraled and outfought his enemies at every turn. Attacked by Howard's troopers, the Indians killed and wounded a number of soldiers and drove them for ten miles. Reinforced by volunteers led by Colonel Gibbons, the troops attacked at Big Hole Pass, but were forced to retreat. At Tash Pass the Nez Percés were victors, yet never did the Indians injure or kill a white settler, nor did they commit any depredations other than to commandeer horses, cattle, and food. Finally, when within fifty miles of the border, they were headed off by the thousands of soldiers under Miles and Howard, and Joseph realized he must surrender—after covering 1,300 miles in fifty days with a loss of less than two hundred men. The white officers were loud in their praise of the military and tactical skill of Joseph, and the fact that noncombatants had been unmolested. Under the capitulation agreement it was promised that the Indians would be taken back to Fort Keogh, Montana, for the winter, and then to the reservation in Idaho. Instead, the 431 Nez Percés were taken to Fort Leavenworth, Kansas, and thence to Oklahoma. At Fort Leavenworth sanitation and food was so bad that a large number died, and the survivors found even worse conditions in Oklahoma. After many appeals to the government, backed up by white sympathizers, a party of 33 women and children were returned to their old home, to be followed the next year (1884) by 118 other members of the tribe. The remainder, 150 altogether, including Joseph, were never permitted to return to Idaho, but were sent to the Colville reservation in Washington. Joseph lived to visit President Theodore Roosevelt and General Miles in Washington in March 1903. He urged the education of the Indian children, discouraged gambling and drunkenness, and died on the reservation, a discouraged, broken-hearted man, on September 21, 1904.

KAMIAKAN. The principal chief of the Yakima and confederated tribes of eastern Washington in 1855 and leader in the war that lasted for three years. Because of the heavy increase of settlers and gold-seekers, Governor Stevens was instructed to negotiate treaties to obtain the Indians' land and place the tribes on reservations. Led by Kamiakan, the Indians naturally opposed this, but eventually, persuaded by the Nez Percés, a few tribes agreed. However, the entire Cayuse, Yakima, Wallawalla, Paloos, Spokan, and others were determined not to give up their land and homes and be confined to reservations. Although no treaty had been made, white immigrants continued to take possession of Indian lands, and frequent collisions resulted. In September 1855 war began when the Indians killed special agent Sohon while he was on his way to try to arrange a conference with Kamiakan, who declared he would keep all whites from his territory and would declare war on any tribe refusing to join him. Repeated battles with both civilian and regular troops followed, usually with the Indians the victors. In 1857 the uprising west of the Cascade Mountains was put down and several of the Indian leaders hanged. At one time the Indians even attacked Seattle, and the town was saved only by a naval vessel stationed in the harbor at the time. On May 17, 1858, a strong force of cavalry under Colonel Steptoe was defeated, but a few months later the war was ended by two battles involving over seven hundred cavalry troops plus a large force of infantry and artillery. Kamiakan was among the wounded Indians. Realizing their cause was hopeless, the tribes bowed to the terms made by Wright; but despite the fact that they were prisoners of war, and the promises made by the victors, twenty-four of the chiefs were hanged or shot. Kamiakan still refused to sue for peace, and fled to British Columbia, where he remained until his death.

KANAKUK. A famed prophet and chief of the Kickapoos. When, in 1819, the tribe ceded its lands covering practically half of Illinois, they could not go to the reservation assigned them in Missouri, as it was still occupied by their enemies, the Osages. About half the tribe then emigrated to Mexico. The others were planning to follow when the government intervened. Trouble was avoided by Kanakuk, who exhorted them to remain where they were, promising that if they lived worthily, abandoned their superstitions, avoided quarreling, obeyed the law of the white men, and refrained from alcohol they would at last inherit a land of peace and plenty. He was at once elected chief, and many of the Pottawattomies of Michigan joined his disciples. To further impress the Indians he exhibited a chart showing a road passing through fire and water which the virtuous must travel to reach the promised land. He also supplied his followers with sacred prayer-sticks carved with religious symbols. Even when in the end the Kickapoos were removed to Kansas, Kanakuk went with them, and remained their chief, still managing to maintain prohibition among them. He finally died of smallpox in 1852.

KICKING BIRD. Tene-angpote. A Kiowa chief, the grandson of a captive Crow who had been adopted into the tribe. A very intelligent man, he fully realized the hopelessness of fighting the whites, and used all his influence to induce the tribe to submit to the inevitable conditions. He signed the treaties establishing the Kiowa, Comanche, and Apache reservations in Oklahoma, and had no part in the outbreak of 1868 and the Kiowa raids into Texas.

When, in 1873, the federal authorities failed to keep their promises to release the Kiowa chiefs imprisoned in Texas, Kicking Bird lost all faith in the government and planned to join in a raid on the Tonkawas and the white buffalo hunters in Texas. But when Lone Wolf joined the hostiles and defied the United States troops, Kicking Bird induced two-thirds of the tribe to return with him to Fort Sill, where he was recognized as the head chief of the Kiowa, Lone Wolf's offer to surrender being ignored. Kicking Bird asked for, and assisted in the establishment of, the first school among the Kiowas, in 1873. He died suddenly, apparently from poison, May 5, 1875 and was buried with Christian rites.

KING PHILIP or METACOM, the second son of Massasoit and sachem of the Wampanoag, who inherited the title and position. Known to the English as Philip of Pokanoket, or King Philip. For nearly ten years after he became chief he devoted himself to preparing for the hostilities he knew were inevitable with the white settlers. In 1675 the war broke out, and although great losses were suffered by the colonists the Indians were almost exterminated. Over fifty towns and villages had been attacked, and twelve were completely destroyed. Everywhere the Indians exhibited almost incredible bravery, and had it not been for treachery among the tribes the colonists would undoubtedly have been completely wiped out. The decisive action of the war was the attack on a palisaded town in a swamp in Rhode Island on August 12, 1676. Practically every Indian was killed, among them King Philip, whose head was cut off and placed on a pole at Plymouth, where it remained for twenty years. His wife and children, together with the other prisoners, were sold as slaves in the West Indies.

KINTPUASH or KEINTPOOS, commonly known as Captain Jack. A subchief of the Modocs of the Oregon-California border and leader of the hostile Modocs in the so-called war of 1872-73. The Modocs, unlike their peaceful kinsmen the Klamaths, were inclined to be a warlike, aggressive tribe, and were passionately fond of their ancestral home. They had been hostile to the whites up to 1864, when their chief, Sconchin, made a treaty agreeing to go upon a reservation on Upper Klamath Lake, where the Klamaths were already established. The majority of the Modocs objected strenuously to being placed alongside their Klamath enemies, and, led by Captain Jack, with about half the tribe, including seventy warriors, they roamed over the Lost River area, committing many minor depredations and terrorizing the settlers. However, in the spring of 1870 Captain Jack was induced to go on the reservation where the rest of his tribe, under Chief Sconchin, were already living. Soon after his arrival, Captain Jack called in a medicine man to cure two members of his family. The two died, and according to tribal custom Jack killed the medicine man. Orders were issued for his arrest, but he fled from the reservation to the Lost River country, and demanded that a reservation in his home area should be assigned to him and his band, as it was impossible to dwell in amity with the Klamaths. A few conferences were arranged, but without satisfactory results, and on November 27, 1872, Jack flatly refused to go on the reservation or to discuss the matter further. An order was then sent to Fort Klamath for the military to place him under arrest. When an attempt was made to do so the Indians resisted, killing or wounding eight soldiers and losing fifteen men themselves. The band then fled into the almost impenetrable lava beds across the California border, killing several settlers on the way. A number of civilian volunteers, as well as many friendly Indians of the Klamath and Modoc tribes, joined the small body of troops in an attack on the hostiles. But their position was so strong with its caves, rocks, and hidden passages that the attackers had no chance of accomplishing anything, and withdrew. A little later, Jack's band attacked a wagon train carrying ammunition and killed the drivers. An all-out attack was made on January 17, 1873, by Colonel Greer, with four hundred men and a howitzer battery. After an all-day battle, the force withdrew with a loss of nine killed and thirty wounded. The next step was the issuance of indictments for murder against eight Modocs who were alleged to have killed settlers. Then another conference was arranged by a peace commission consisting of General E. R. S. Canby, Indian superintendent, A. B. Meacham, the Reverend E. Thomas, an Indian agent L. S. Dyar. By agreement with Jack, the commissioners, together with Frank B. Riddle and his Indian wife Toby (Winema) as interpreters, met Jack and his fellow leaders on April 11, 1873. Scarcely had the conference started when Jack drew a revolver and shot General Canby dead while his comrades killed the Reverend Mr. Thomas and wounded Meacham five times. The others escaped, pursued by the Modocs until the latter were driven off by a party of troops. Following this murderous outbreak, Indian scouts were secured from the Warmspring tribes to track the renegades. A large body of troops equipped with field guns forced the Modocs from their hiding place, only to find safety farther along the shore of the lake. A few days later the Indians ambushed a force of eighty-five troopers and killed twenty-six, including both lieutenants in command, and wounded sixteen others. Other minor attacks followed, but by this time the Modocs were tired of fighting, many of Jack's men had deserted, and pursued by the soldiers he retreated for twenty miles to a new position. Finally, on May 22, 1873, sixty-five of the Indians surrendered. A little later others came in, and on June 1, Jack, with the rest of his band, surrendered to Captain Perry. Although he had had less than ninety warriors Jack had managed to successfully resist a military force of nearly one thousand regular troops, seventy-one Indian scouts, and a number of civilian volunteers. The Modoc prisoners were taken to Fort Klamath, and in July six of the leaders were tried by court-martial for the murder of General Camby and the Reverend Mr. Thomas. Four—Captain Jack, young Sconchin, Black Jim, and Boston Charley—were hanged. Bancroft the historian stated that "their brave and stubborn fight for their native land and liberty, was in some respects the most remarkable that ever occurred in the history of aboriginal extermination." Another contemporary stated that it was "started by a murder by a common ruffian and ended in a hanging." The truth lies between the two. Undoubtedly the Modocs could have been appeased and hostilities averted if the white authorities had placed the Indians on a reservation in their home area. But even the most pro-Indian person cannot overlook the treacherous murder of General Canby and the commissioners when at a peace conference. The Modocs who survived were not permitted to rejoin their people on the Klamath reservation, but were transported to Oklahoma, where a few still survive.

LA FLESCHE, FRANCIS. A son of Estamaza or Joseph La Flesche, chief of the Omahas, born in Thurston County, Nebraska, December 24, 1857. Attended mission school on the reservation and advanced rapidly in education, and accompanied Standing Bear as interpreter when the Ponca chief went to Washington to present his story of the mistreatment of his tribe. At subsequent meetings he was given a position in the Office of Indian Affairs. In 1893 he was graduated from the National University Law School. Engaged in writing an ethnological history of his people. Various papers on the Omahas' folklore and the story of his youth and schooldays, have been published in leading magazines. Has made valuable collections of ethnological specimens for various leading museums in this country and Europe. A member of the American Association for the Advancement of Science, and the Anthropological Society of Washington. In 1906 he married Miss Rosa Bourassa, a Chippewa.

LAPAWINZE. "Gathering Food." A Delaware chief who was among those induced to sign the "walking purchase" treaty of Philadelphia in 1737. This granted the whites all land for as far as a man could walk in a day and a half. When a survey had been made, the governor of Pennsylvania had a road built and employed a trained runner. The Indians naturally declared this a fraud and cheating, and as a result many joined the hostile Shawnees.

LEATHERLIPS. Sha-teiaron-hia, or "Twin Clouds." A Wyandotte chief of the Sandusky tribe of Ohio. In August 1795 he signed the treaty of Grenville in behalf of his people. His honorable character and friendship for the whites aroused the jealousy and anger of Tecumseh, who ordered him killed, accusing him of being a wizard. The execution was assigned to a Huron chief named Round-head, and he was notified of his condemnation by his brother, who sent him a strip of bark on which was drawn a picture of a tomahawk. The execution took place near Leatherlip's camp on the Scioto River in the summer of 1810, in the presence of a number of white men, among them a justice of the peace who had made an attempt to save the chief's life without success. Having chanted his death song, the chief knelt by his grave and was tomahawked by a fellow tribesman. The Wyandotte Club of Columbus, Ohio, in 1888 erected a monument to his memory in a small park within a stone wall that encloses the spot where Leatherlips died.

LITTLE CROW. Chetan-wakan-mani, or "Sacred hawk that comes walking." A chief of the Kaposia division of the Midewakanton Sioux, which, under his father Little Crow and his grandfather Little Thunder, had its headquarters at Kapozha on the west bank of the Mississippi about ten miles below the mouth of the Minnesota River. In 1846 while intoxicated he was accidentally shot and wounded by his brother. This caused him to forbid drinking among his band, and to ask the Indian agent at Fort Snelling to send a missionary to his village. As a result, the Reverend Thomas S. Williamson was sent. Although he had signed the treaty of Mendota, Minnesota, on August 5, 1851, by which the Indians ceded most of their land to the United States, Little Crow claimed to have been hoodwinked into signing the treaty, and that the terms had been misrepresented. As a result, the previously peaceful tribe became resentful. After they had signed the treaty the Kaposias had been placed on a reservation in upper Minnesota, and were on friendly terms with the white settlers until on August

18, 1862, they rose suddenly, spreading over a frontier of more than two hundred miles, and killed every white man, woman, and child they could find, a total of over one thousand. Led by Little Crow, the Indians then attacked Fort Ridgely, Minnesota, August 20-22, 1862. They were driven off, and Little Crow was wounded. In September 1862 the Indians were again defeated by General Sibley at Wood Lake, and Little Crow with about 250 followers fled to the protection of his kinsmen farther west. He was killed by a settler named Lampson, July 3, 1863, near Hutchinson, Minnesota.

LITTLE RAVEN. Hosa, or "Young Crow." An Arapaho chief who was the first to sign for the southern Arapaho the treaty made at Fort Wayne, Colorado, on February 18, 1861. Later he joined in the treaty of Medicine Lodge, Kansas (1867), after which all his energies were devoted to keeping his people at peace with the whites and leading them to civilization. Through his influence the Arapahos remained at peace even when their former allies, the Kiowas and Cheyennes, went on the warpath in 1874-75. He died at Cantonment, Oklahoma, in the winter of 1889, after maintaining for twenty years a reputation as the leader of progress in his tribe and an unwavering friend of the whites.

LITTLE THUNDER. A Brûlé Sioux chief who took part in the Grattan massacre at Fort Laramie in 1854, and took command when Chief Singing Bear was killed. He also took part in the battle with General Harvey at Ash Hollow, Nebraska, in 1855, and remained a chief until his death. He was a gigantic Indian, over six feet six inches in height, heavily built and very muscular, and had the reputation of being exceedingly intelligent. He also had the reputation of being an honorable and magnanimous foe, who admired and respected bravery on the part of his enemies.

LITTLE TURTLE. Michikinikwa. A Miami Indian chief born at Eel River, Indiana, in 1752. His father was also a chief of the Miamis, but his mother was a Mohican. Under the tribal clan system he was thus considered a Mohican, and gained no prestige because of his father's rank. Yet because of his talents and prowess he was made chief when scarcely more than a youth. He was the leader of the Indians who defeated General Harmaron in October 1790, and General St. Clair at St. Mary's on November 4, 1791. Together with Blue Jacket, he was among the leaders of the Indians in their battle with General Wayne's army in 1795, although he had tried to induce the Indians to make peace with the "chief who never sleeps." After their defeat at this battle, Little

Turtle joined in the treaty of August 3, 1795, saying, as he signed it: "I am the last to sign the treaty and I will be the last to break it." He kept his promise and remained at peace and friendly with the whites until his death. In 1797 Little Turtle, his brother, and Captain Wells visited President Washington in Philadelphia, where he met Count Volney and General Kosciusko, who presented the chief with a pair of beautifully mounted pistols. He died at Fort Wayne, Indiana, July 14, 1812.

LOGAN, JOHN. Indian name Tah-gah-jute, "Looking through everything or spying." A famous chief of the Cayugas whose father was a white man known to the English as Shikellamy, who had been taken prisoner in Canada and adopted by the Indians. He was made chief of all of the Indians living at Shamokin, Pennsylvania, where Logan was born about 1725. In 1774 a number of the Indians, including some of Logan's family, were brutally murdered by the white settlers at the mouth of Yellow Creek. In retaliation Logan declared war on the whites, and perpetrated fearful barbarities. After the resumption of peace Logan took to drink, and became a confirmed drunkard. During a drunken brawl with his nephew he was killed in 1780. His wife, who was a Shawnee, survived him. A monument to Logan stands in Fair Hill Cemetery near Auburn, N. Y.

LONE WOLF. Gui-pa-go. A Kiowa chief who was one of the nine signers of the treaty of Medicine Lodge, Kansas, in 1867, by which the Kiowas first agreed to be placed on a reservation. In 1872 he headed a delegation to Washington, but the murder of his son by a Texan in 1873 so embittered him that he led his tribe in an outbreak against the whites in 1874. On their surrender in the spring of 1875, Lone Wolf and a number of others were placed in military confinement at Fort Marion, Florida, for three years. Soon after his release in 1879 he died, and was succeeded by his adopted son of the same name.

LOWRY, GEORGE. Agin-agi-li, "Rising Fawn." A Cherokee, cousin of Sequoia, and second chief of the eastern Cherokees. He steadily opposed all attempts to force his people to move from their eastern lands, and when this had been done he was chief of the council held in 1839 to fuse the eastern and western Cherokees into the present Cherokee Nation.

LOWRY, JOHN. A Cherokee chief commonly known as Colonel Lowry. He was in command of the Cherokees who aided General Jackson in the Creek war of 1813-14, and with Colonel Gideon Morgan and four hundred Cherokees surrounded and captured the town of Hillabi, Alabama, on November 18, 1813. He was conspicuous in the battle of Horsehoe Bend on March 27, 1814, and for his services was commended and given a commission. He signed the treaties of June 7, 1806, and March 22, 1816.

MAHTOIOWA. "Whirling Bear." A Brûlé-Teton Sioux chief. While the Brûlé, Oglala, and Minneconjou Sioux were camped near Fort Laramie, Wyoming, in 1854, where they were awaiting presents from the government, one of the Indians killed a derelict steer belonging to some Mormon emigrants. The chief offered to pay a fair price for the animal, but the owner demanded twice what it was worth and the commandant demanded the surrender of the offender. In response, Whirling Bear indicated the tipi of the guilty Indian, telling Lieutenant Grafton that he might arrest him. Grafton, however, insisted that the chief should bring the man out and deliver him. When Whirling Bear refused to do this, Grafton, in a fit of temper, ordered his troops to fire a howitzer at the tipi in the center of the village. A shell killed an Indian and wounded some of the women, and instantly eighteen soldiers fell riddled with arrows. Only one escaped, by the aid of an Indian friend. The Sioux then besieged Fort Laramie until the garrison was relieved. During this action Whirling Bear was killed. This was the beginning of the Sioux War, all the result of the avariciousness of a white man and the hot temper of a tenderfoot lieutenant. Whirling Bear was succeeded by chief Little Thunder, (which see).

MANGAS COLORADAS. Sometimes written Mango Colorado, or "Red Sleeves." A chief of the Mimbreño Apaches who pledged friendship to the Americans when General Kearney took possession of New Mexico in 1846. At that time the Mimbreños were centered near the Santa Rita copper mines in southwestern New Mexico, where they had killed a number of miners in 1837 in retaliation for a treacherous massacre committed by white trappers. The latter invited a number of the friendly Mimbreños to a feast and murdered every one in order to obtain the bounty of one hundred dollars offered by the governor of Chihuahua, Mexico, for every Apache scalp. When the boundary commission reached Santa Rita there was friction over the taking of some Mexican prisoners held by the Mimbreños and the Americans' refusal to hang a Mexican who had murdered an Indian. The Mimbreños then stole some horses and mules belonging to the commissioners, and when the latter left on their survey for another area the Indians thought they had driven them away. About this time

Mangas Coloradas was brutally beaten and maltreated by miners of the Pinos Altos gold mines. Furious at the indignity, he gathered a band of Mimbreños and became the scourge of the white settlements for years. He formed an alliance with Cochise to repel the Californian volunteers, and was wounded in a battle at Apache Pass, Arizona, that resulted from a misunderstanding over the ownership of stray cattle. His men took him to Janos in Chihuahua and left him in care of a surgeon, who was warned that if Mangas were not cured the town would be destroyed. Shortly after his recovery he was taken prisoner by the Californians, who prodded him with a hot bayonet and shot him down on the pretext that he was trying to escape when he tried to evade the red hot iron.

MANUELITO. A famous chief of the Navajos. When, in 1859, the Navajos were surrounded in the Cañon de Chelly by the United States cavalry, a force of Ute mercenaries and a number of civilian volunteers, all under command of Kit Carson, the allied Indian chiefs could not decide what course to follow and made Manuelito supreme chief. The Navajos, numbering about ten thousand, greatly outnumbered the besiegers and probably could have wiped them out, but it would have been at a terrific cost to the Indians. Moreover, practically all their cattle, horses, and sheep had been killed by the whites, leaving the Navajo without means of subsistence. The whole trouble arose over the Navajos' refusal to be transported for several hundred miles to a reservation, and when Kit Carson pledged his word that if they surrendered he would promise they would be returned to their ancestral home later, Manuelito surrendered. In 1869 the Navajos were returned to their cañon home, and the government gave them thirty thousand sheep and two thousand goats, as well as cattle and horses. During their long march to and from the reservation and during their stay there the Navajos had suffered greatly, many had died of disease and other causes, and barely two thousand of the original nine to ten thousand returned to the Cañon de Chelley. However, they increased very rapidly, and today the tribe numbers between thirty-five and forty-five thousand—the largest tribe in the United States, about one-twelfth of all our Indians. After peace was firmly established in 1872, Manuelito was chosen by the government to command the Indian police. He died in 1893.

MASSASOIT. Woosamequin, or "Yellow Feather." A principal chief of the Wampanoags of the vicinity of Bristol, Rhode Island, and who, together with Samoset, welcomed the Pilgrims at Plymouth in 1621. He was pre-eminently the friend of the whites, and was a chief more renowned in peace than in war. Notwithstanding the fact that the English helped themselves to the Indians' lands and punished them severely on the slightest pretext, Massasoit's friendship never faltered, and while ill in 1623 he was well and kindly treated by some of his white friends. He died in 1662, and one of his sons, Metacomet, became famous as the hostile King Philip, who led the Indians in the long and bloody war.

MAZAKUTEMANI. "Shoots gun as he walks." A Sisseton Sioux chief famed for his friendship for the whites. Born in 1827. In 1850 he was a member of the Sisseton and Wahpeton Sioux delegation to Washington, D. C., and a signer of the Traverse des Sioux treaty of July 23, 1851. He was converted to Christianity when twenty years of age, and thereafter was an ardent supporter of the missionary work of the Reverend Stephen R. Riggs. In the spring of 1857, when the Spring Lake massacre by Inkpaduta's band occurred, Chief Mazakutemani proved his friendship for the whites by following the murderers and rescuing Miss Gardner, who was the sole surviving captive. When, in 1862, he received word of the Sioux outbreak, he used every effort to stop the massacre, and entered the hostiles' camps to rescue their white captives. He was always the chief orator and speaker for the Sisseton Sioux in their negotiations with the government. He died in the latter part of the year 1879.

MENEWA. "Great warrior." A half-breed Creek and second chief of the Lower Creeks in Alabama. Born about 1765. In early life he became noted for his daring and was known as Hothlepya or "Crazy war hunter." Each year he crossed the Cumberland to rob the settlers of horses. A murder committed in the vicinity was charged to him and his band, and the people of Georgia burned one of his villages in revenge. Later it was found that McIntosh (which see) had committed the murder in order to stir up trouble between the whites and his rival. When Tecumseh formed his league against the whites, Menewa joined in the conspiracy in order to guard against an attack by McIntosh and the Americans. He was the first to start the Creek war and was the war chief of the tribe, the head chief being a medicine man. Depending upon a prophecy by the latter, Menewa made a mistake in placing his warriors at the battle with General Jackson at Horseshoe Bend. With his own hand Menewa slew the false prophet and then dashed from his breastwork at the head of his men into the midst of the Tennesseans. Of his 900 warriors, 830 were killed, and all but one survivor were wounded. Menewa was left for dead on the battlefield, but revived during the night, and with other survivors reached a camp hidden in a swamp where the women and children were waiting. When they recovered, the wounded Creeks all surrendered voluntarily. Menewa's village was destroyed and his cattle, horses, and pelts, as well as trade goods, were confiscated. When he had recovered he resumed authority over the remnants of his band and opposed further cedings of lands to the whites. As McIntosh was in favor of the treaty, he was denounced as a traitor and was put to death by Menewa. In 1826 he went to Washington with a delegation to protest the treaty made by McIntosh by which the entire Creek country had been ceded to the government. He proposed that some of the area should be allotted in severalty to those Indians who chose to remain in their homeland rather than to emigrate to a strange region. This was agreed to by the government, but by an arbitrary allotment Menewa was deprived of his own land, so he sold the parcel he received and bought land in Alabama. During the Seminole war Menewa led a force of Creeks against the hostiles, and in recognition for his services he was given permission to remain in his native land, but nevertheless was transported, with his people, beyond the Mississippi.

MIANTONOME. A noted chief of the Narragansets and nephew of Canonicus, he was friendly with the whites and in 1632 visited the governor in Boston. Because of his friendship for Roger Williams and the theological hatred of the Pilgrim church for the Quakers, Miantonome was accused of disloyalty despite the fact that he helped the English in battles with the Pequots. In 1643, war broke out between the Narragansets and the Mohicans, and Miantonome was taken prisoner and was delivered to the English at Hartford. He was tried in Boston in September 1643 by the Court of Commissioners of the United Colonies of New England, who referred the matter to the Convocation of the Clergy, which in turn condemned him to death at the hands of the Uncas. The sentence was most barbarously carried out by Wawequa, brother of Uncas, in the latter's presence. He was buried where he died, and the spot known as Sachem's Plains was marked by a monument erected in 1841.

MIKANOPY. "Head Chief." A Seminole chief who was among those who resisted the government's effort to move the Seminoles to Indian Territory. He owned large herds of cattle and horses and over one hundred Negro slaves, and stood by Osceola and the majority of the tribe, who were determined to remain in Florida.

Although an aging man, he was a leader in the Seminole war, and in the annihilation of Dade's command on December 28, 1836, Mikanopy shot the commander. After that he took no further part in the hostilities. Short, stout, indolent, and self-indulgent, he had none of the qualities of a leader.

MOANAHONGA. "Great Walker." A Iowa warrior commonly known as "Big Neck." His Indian name was given him because of his habit of taking long trips alone and depending upon his prowess and his gigantic strength. Of lowly birth and not eligible for chieftainship, he was very ambitious, so he built a lodge apart from the others and gathered a band of his friends and admirers, over whom he acted as chief. In 1824 General Clark induced Moanahonga and Mahaskah to go to Washington and there sign a treaty that purported to convey title of all lands in Iowa within the borders of Missouri for an annual payment of five hundred dollars for ten years. The government representatives, through their interpreters, grossly misrepresented the terms of the treaty, and Moanahonga, amazed to find settlers taking possession of what he supposed was Indians' land, went to St. Louis to complain to General Clark. On the way a party of whites met the Indians, plied them with liquor until they were drunk, and made off with the Indians' horses, blankets, and provisions. When they recovered their senses one of them shot a hog for food. This provoked the settlers, sixty of whom rode up to the Indians and ordered them to leave the country immediately. To avoid trouble, Moanahonga moved camp for fifteen miles to beyond what he thought was the state boundary. When the whites followed him he went to meet them smoking his pipe as a sign of peace. As he extended his hand in greeting the whites opened fire, killing his brother and an infant. The Indians dashed for their weapons as a second volley from the settlers wounded Moanahonga's sister. Although the whites outnumbered the Indians two to one they were driven off, leaving the man who had shot the chief's sister a captive. He was sentenced to death and burned at the stake. The United States troops were ordered out and, obtaining hostages from the Indians, returned to their barracks. Although Moanahonga and several others were tried for murder, justice for once was done and they were acquitted. After this affair, Moanahonga resumed his friendly relations with the whites, but always kept his face blackened because, he said, he had sold the "bones of his ancestors." He was finally killed in a hand-to-hand struggle with a Sioux chief.

MONTEZUMA, CARLOS. A full-blooded Apache known to his people as Wasajah or "Beckoning." Born in 1866 near the Four Peaks of the Mazatzam Mountains of Arizona. In October 1871 he was taken prisoner, together with eighteen other children, including his two sisters, during a night raid by the Pimas while the men were absent on a mission of peace. The prisoners were taken by the Pimas to their *rancherias* on the Gila River. At the end of a week Wasajah was taken to Adamsville and sold to Mr. C. Gentile, an Italian who was prospecting in Arizona. Some months after the raid the boy's mother, who had escaped, heard of him through an Indian runner. Determined to regain him, she applied to the Indian agent for permission to leave the reservation and upon being refused stole away secretly. Later, her body was found in a mountain pass where she had been shot by an agency Indian scout. Wasajah was taken by Mr. Gentile to Chicago, and was renamed Carlos Montezuma—Carlos after himself and Montezuma from the so-called Casa Montezuma ruins near the Pima villages. Young Carlos entered the public schools in Chicago in 1872, graduating in 1875, and continued his education in the public schools of Galesburg, Illinois; Brooklyn, N. Y.; Urbana, Illinois, and in the University of Illinois. In 1884 he entered the Chicago Medical School, graduating in 1889, and receiving an appointment as physician in the U. S. Indian School at Stevenson, North Dakota. From 1890 until 1896 Dr. Montezuma served as physician at the Shoshone agency in Nevada, the Colville agency in Washington, and at the Carlisle Indian School. In 1896 he resigned from the service of the government and settled in Chicago, where he practiced medicine and surgery and taught in the College of Physicians and Surgeons and in the Post Graduate Medical School. He is the author of a number of articles and stories about the Indians.

MUGG. A chief of the Arosaguntacook Indians of Maine during the late seventeenth century. He had been seized by the English when treating for peace, and had been taken as a prisoner to Boston, although soon released. Drawn into the war by the ill treatment he had received from the English, he attacked Black Point (now Scarborough), Maine, with one hundred warriors. While the officers in charge were parleying with Mugg most of the whites managed to escape, leaving only a few of the officers' servants, who were taken prisoners and kindly treated by the Indians. Mugg was killed at Black Point on May 16, 1677, in a subsequent attack on the fort.

MURRAY, JOHNSTON. The fourteenth governor of Oklahoma. Chickasaw on his mother's side. Born in Indian Territory, Oklahoma, July 21, 1902.

NACHE. A Chiricahua Apache warrior, second son of Cochise and the hereditary chief after the death of his brother Tazi. His mother was the daughter of Mangas Coloradas. He was the leader of many raids that decimated the white settlements of Arizona and New Mexico as well as northern Mexico, many of these being attributed to Geronimo. Actually Nache was the leader of Geronimo's band. He was captured by General Miles and was sent as a prisoner to Florida, Alabama, and finally to Fort Sill, Oklahoma, where he lived until his death. He was reported by the officials as a very honest, trustworthy man, and was placed in charge of other prisoners.

OSCEOLA. Asi-ya-holo, or "Black drink singer." A noted Seminole leader, but never a chief. His real English name was Powell, after his white stepfather, who married Osceola's mother after the death of her Indian husband. His grandfather was a Scotchman. He was born in Creek County, Florida, in 1803, and led in the Seminole war of 1835. The war resulted from the refusal of a portion of the Seminoles to go to Indian Territory, although many of the tribe already were there. Osceola was famous for his reply at a conference with the whites when he stated, "This is the only treaty I will make," and drove his knife into the table. Together with Cooacootche, "The Wildcat," and others, he was treacherously seized while the Indians were under a flag of truce, and cast into prison. Cooacootche starved himself until thin enough to squeeze through the bars, but Osceola died in prison at Fort Moultrie on January 1, 1838. He was noted for his bravery, his strong personal magnetism, and his military strategy.

OURAY. (The Ute pronunciation of Willie, the name given him by a white family who adopted him when a boy.) He was born in Colorado in 1820, and became chief of the Uncomphgre Utes. When battling with the Sioux, his only son was captured by the enemy. In 1863 he signed a treaty with the United States, and he made a second treaty in 1868. He was famed for his unwavering friendship for the whites, and often protected them from the Indians when trouble arose. He restrained his tribe from joining the outbreak of 1879 when N. C. Meeker and others were killed, and women made prisoners. Ouray ordered a cessation of all hostilities, and for his services was granted an annuity of one thousand dollars for as long as he remained chief of the Utes. He resided in a well-furnished house on his large farm, where he died on August 24, 1880.

PARKER, ELI SAMUEL. Hasaconda, or "Coming to the front." A Seneca chief of the Wolf Clan, grandson of Red Jacket. Born in Tonawanda, N. Y., in 1828. When he became a chief he was named Deionin-Hoga-We ("Holds the door open"). He studied civil engineering and became the engineer on government buildings at Galena, Illinois, then the home of General Grant, who became his close friend. He joined the Union Army, rendering distinguished services at Vicksburg, and was made a staff officer May 1863 as Assistant Adjutant General with the rank of captain. Later Grant made Parker his secretary, and on April 9, 1865, he was made Brigadier-General of Volunteers. In 1866 he was first lieutenant of cavalry in the Union Army. In 1867 he became successively captain, major, lieutenant-colonel, and brigadier-general. At the surrender of Lee, Parker prepared the engrossed articles of capitulation signed by Grant. Parker resigned from the Army in 1869 to become Commissioner of Indian Affairs. He retired in 1871 to practice engineering at his home in Fairfield, Connecticut, where he resided until his death August 21, 1895. He was the author of *The League of the Iroquois,* 1851.

PONTIAC. An Ottawa chief born in Ohio in 1720. His mother was a Chippewa. He commanded the Indians who defended Detroit against the hostiles in 1746, and led the Ottawas and Chippewas in Braddock's defeat. In 1760 he met Major Roberts, who had been sent to take over Detroit on behalf of the English. He agreed to help, and prevented an attack by the French and Indians. The encroachments of the whites and their treatment of his people caused him to become hostile, and he planned a general uprising. He allied most of the tribes west of Ohio, and intended to make a concerted attack on all the towns and forts at the same time. Very soon the Indians had captured many forts and settlements, the defenders being killed, but Fort Pitt and Detroit successfully repulsed the tribesmen. This was a severe setback for Pontiac, and all hope of success was abandoned when he received a message from M. Neyon, the commander of Fort Chartres, ordering Pontiac to stop all further warfare, as peace between France and England had been arranged. He signed the peace agreement at Detroit August 17, 1765, and in 1769 he was killed in a drunken orgy by a Kaskaskia Indian at Cahokia, Illinois.

PUSHMATAHA. Apushim-ahtaha, or "The sapling is finished for him." A Choctaw born in Mississippi in 1764. He died in Washington, D. C., December 24, 1824. Before he was twenty years of age he distinguished himself on an expedition against the Osage west of the Mississippi. During the fight he disappeared, and upon rejoining his band he was jeered at and accused of cowardice. He replied, "Let those laugh who can show more scalps," and exhibited five Osage scalps he had taken in single-hand conflict. He won the name of "Eagle" and a chieftainship by his prowess. He was a great influence for peace with the whites and other tribes. After he had moved to Texas he led an attack on a Tonakwa village, and personally killed seven warriors and fired the village. When Tecumseh visited the Choctaws in 1811 and tried to persuade them to join in the war against the whites, Pushmataha refused. In the war of 1812 he joined the Americans, saying: "The Creeks were once our friends. Now they have joined the English and we follow different trails. When our fathers took the hand of Washington they promised that the Choctaws would always be friends, and I cannot be false to that promise. Now I am ready to fight against the Creeks." During the war he and his five hundred braves took part in twenty-four battles and accompanied General Jackson on his Pensacola campaign. In 1813 he joined General Clairbone and distinguished himself in the defeat of the Creeks in Alabama. So rigid was his discipline that his men became orderly, efficient troops, and he became known as the "Indian General." In 1824 he went to Washington to sign another treaty. He became ill while visiting Lafayette, and died a few hours later. He was buried with full military honors, including a procession of two thousand military and civilians led by General Jackson. He was buried in the Congressional Cemetery, where his grave is marked by a shaft with the inscription: *"Pushmata, a Choctaw chief, lies here. Died in Washington December 24, 1824."* Jackson stated that he was "the greatest and bravest Indian" he had ever met. Deeply interested in the education of his people, Pushmataha had given two thousand dollars of his annuity for fifteen years to the Choctaw school system.

QUANAH PARKER. The son of the Kwahadi Apache chief Nokoni and a white woman captive. He became a chief, and was noted as a savage fighter and enemy of the whites. In 1874 he refused to sign a treaty; organizing a confederation of the Southern Cheyennes, Kiowas, and others, he led an attack on Fort Adobe Walls in the Texas Panhandle, but was driven off. He continued to carry on the war for a year longer, when the majority of his force surrendered. Parker, however, kept his own band on the Staked Plains for two years more before surrendering. He at once adapted himself to the changed conditions and became the most important factor in leading his tribe to adopt civilization. He advocated education, encouraged building comfortable houses and developing agriculture, and frowned on dissipation of all kinds, although still holding to tribal ceremonies. All his children were educated, and his daughters married well-to-do white men. He was the most prominent and influential figure of the three tribes in all leases and negotiations with the government, and favored leasing lands to obtain income to support the schools. He made numerous trips to Washington and elsewhere. He was a very successful farmer and rancher, and lived in a large comfortable home near Fort Sill, where he was highly respected by his white neighbors. The town of Quanah was named after him.

RAIN IN THE FACE. So called because of the paint washed from his face and body by a heavy rain while on a foray. A full-blooded Hunkpapa Sioux born in 1835, died 1905. A brother of Iron Horse. Not of the chieftain line, he won fame and prominence by his own efforts and his courage and prowess. He was many times on the warpath against the Gros Ventres, Crows, and other Indian enemies, but his first affray with the whites was in 1866 at the so-called Fetterman Massacre at Fort Kearney, Wyoming. In 1868 he took part in the battle at Fort Totten in Dakota and was wounded. Arrested by order of Col. Thomas Custer, he was accused of killing a surgeon and a trader of the General Stanley expedition. He pleaded guilty and was imprisoned, but managed to escape, and joined Sitting Bull's band in 1874, vowing to kill Custer and eat his heart. He was a leader in the battle of the Little Big Horn, and was reputed to have killed Custer, although the other Indians all declared Custer committed suicide and hence was not scalped. Rain in the Face was badly wounded during the battle and was permanently lame, yet he followed Sitting Bull to Canada, where he remained until 1880, when he surrendered to General Miles at Fort Keogh.

RED CLOUD. Makhpiya-luta. ("Red Storm," or "Red Tempest.") A famous Oglala-Teton Sioux of Pine Ridge, Dakota. One of the most famous of all the Sioux chiefs. Born in Nebraska in 1822, he died at Pine Ridge in 1909. He was a member of the Snake family, and rose to fame by his own efforts and personality, as he was not of the chief line, the hereditary chief being "Young man afraid of his horse," or, properly translated, "They fear his horses," who was a more conservative and peaceful man than Red Cloud. Red Cloud's father died from drinking vile liquor obtained from the whites, which was one of the main causes of his animosity. In 1865, when the government tried to build a road from Fort Laramie, Wyoming, to the gold fields of Montana, Red Cloud opposed it, arguing it would drive off the buffalo essential to the Indians. The first party sent to start work on the road were captured by Red Cloud and his band and held prisoners for two weeks before being released by Red Cloud, who feared his young braves might kill them. Later he refused to listen to any arrangement with the road commissioners, and on June 30, 1866, at the council at Fort Laramie he angrily refused to consent to the road, recalling the promises in treaties that the area should remain Indian land. While he was still speaking, troops under General Carrington arrived, and when Red Cloud was told they would open the road by force the chief seized his rifle and shouting defiance left with his men. When the troops started to rebuild forts and open the road, Red Cloud with two thousand warriors surrounded the whites and prevented any supplies from reaching them. When, in December 1866, eighty-one men under Captain Fetterman were wiped out despite having been warned by friendly Cheyennes, and several smaller engagements had been fought, without a wagon passing over the road, the commissioners decided to try once more to win Red Cloud's consent. Finally an agreement was reached by which the boundaries of the Sioux territory were clearly defined, but Red Cloud refused to sign until the garrisons of all forts had been withdrawn, thus winning a complete victory. The treaty was signed November 6, 1868, and Red Cloud kept strictly to his promise of peace and took no part in the Sioux War of 1876. Realizing it was impossible to stop the encroaching whites from flocking to the Black Hills, Red Cloud ceded land to the whites and bowed to the inevitable. At the time of the Sioux outbreak of 1890-91, Red Cloud was almost blind and took no part in the uprising, even threatening to act against the malcontents. In the hope of helping his people he enlisted the sympathy of Professor Marsh, who was collecting fossils in the west, and with the scientist he went east, visiting Washington, New Haven, Connecticut, and many other cities. The results of his trip were better relations and aid for the Sioux. Red Cloud never had more than one wife. As far as known, he never personally killed a white man. He was a courtly gentleman and honorable, never known to lie or break a promise. Blind and decrepit in his declining years, he lived in a well-built house given to him by the government.

RED JACKET. Octitiani, also known as Wassha-goi-watha, or "He who makes them stay and listen." A famous Seneca orator and sub-chief. Born in Geneva County, N. Y., in 1756. Famous more for his oratory than for his prowess in battle. His main troubles were the white missionaries and the continual ill feeling between the Christianized Indians and Red Jacket and his pagan followers. Although he incited hostilities, yet Brant and other leaders accused him of evading actual fighting. On one occasion he was found butchering a cow in secret while a battle was being fought. Despite his oratorical ability, he was a man of very vascillating character. When his wife became a Christian, Red Jacket swore he would desert her, but later returned and aided her. In late life he became dissipated. He died at Buffalo, N. Y., January 20, 1830. He was buried in the Forest Lawn Cemetery, where other Seneca chiefs had been interred.

SACAGAWEA, or "Bird Woman." The Shoshone woman who accompanied Lewis and Clark. She was the wife of Toissaint Charnonneau, and was living among the Hidatsas. She was engaged as guide and interpreter by Lewis and Clark, being anxious to return to her tribe, from whom she had been kidnaped when fourteen years of age. The explorers had only the highest praise for her fortitude, her services, and her ability. When the expedition's boat was upset in the Missouri, she risked her life to save the priceless records. During the trip her baby was born, and for much of the journey she carried the infant on her back. Her brother, the Shoshone chief, enabled the expedition to cross the Rocky Mountains. When, on the return journey, the party was lost in the mountains of Montana, she guided them to safety. She remained in Wyoming, and when the Wind River reservation was established she resided near Fort Washakie, where she died April 9, 1884, at nearly one hundred years of age. A bronze statue of Sacagawea stands in Portland, Oregon, and her grave is marked by a brass tablet. There is also another statue in Bismarck, North Dakota.

SAMOSET. A Wabenaki Indian chief of Pemmaquid, Maine, who appeared to the Pilgrims at Plymouth in 1621 and, much to their amazement greeted them in English: "Welcome, white men." It really was no mystery that the Indian should speak excellent English, for in 1605 George Weymouth had visited Maine and had kidnaped Samoset and four other Indians, whom he took back to England, where they remained for several years. While there they acquired an excellent knowledge of English, and had learned much of English life and customs before they were returned to Maine.

It was fortunate for the Pilgrims that Samoset and his friend Squanto or Tasquantum, who was another of the five kidnaped Indians, had been well treated in England and were friendly, for the Pilgrims at that time were on the verge of starvation. But, guided by Samoset and Squanto, a party of the men journeyed to Pemmaquid and obtained all the corn and other provisions required by the Plymouth colony. Moreover, Samoset and his fellow tribesmen taught the Pilgrims how to cultivate maize and other vegetables strange to them, and kept them supplied with food until the whites were able to carry on by themselves. Then, as usual, the whites turned on the Indians and waged a war of extermination. Fortunately Samoset and his tribe were not within easy reach of Plymouth, and the settlers in Maine, being of a different stripe from the Pilgrims and Puritans, dealt rather fairly with the Indians, buying their land instead of seizing it. The first land purchased was at Pemmaquid, and was sold to John Brown of New Harbor by Samoset.

SATANTA. Set-tain-te, or "White Bear." A Kiowa warrior and chief born in 1830. Committed suicide in prison October 11, 1878. He was noted for his keen sense of humor and his remarkable oratorical ability. Although he was known to be hostile, yet he was personally liked by the Army officers. Often known as the "Orator of the Plains," he signed the 1867 Medicine Lodge treaty agreeing to go on a reservation. The band, however, delayed until attacked by Custer, who seized Satanta and Lone Wolf as hostages. Because, so it was alleged, Satanta had stated he had taken part in a raid in Texas in 1871, he, Big Tree, and Setangya were arrested and held for trial in Texas. Setangya was killed while resisting a guard, but the other two were sentenced to life imprisonment in Texas. After two years they were released on condition of good behavior of the tribe. In 1874, when the Kiowas again went on the warpath, Satanta was rearrested and taken back to prison, where he leaped to his death from the upper window of the hospital. He was a man of magnificent physique and impressive bearing, and was described as princely even in prison garb. He was regarded by the Kiowas as one of their greatest men.

SEQUOIA. Sikwayi. An eastern Cherokee who is famed for having invented the Cherokee alphabet. Born at Taskigi, Tennessee, in 1760. Died at San Fernando, Tamaulipas, Mexico, in August 1843. Son of a white father and a Cherokee mother who was the daughter of a chief. Sequoia was also known as George Gist (or Guest), the family name of his father, believed to have been a German trader. Sequoia grew up in the tribe knowing nothing of English or of civilized ways, and became a hunter and fur trader. He was also a skilled silver worker, an ingenious mechanic, and with strong inventive tendencies. Owing to an accident while hunting, he was crippled for life, and devoted himself to carrying out his many ideas. Greatly impressed by the white men's writing and printing, he determined to devise means to enable his people to read and write, although ridiculed by the Indians. In 1821 he submitted his results to the tribal councilors, who approved it and began studying the newly invented alphabet and the words written with it. In a few months thousands of the tribe could read and write Cherokee, and in 1822 Sequoia visited Arkansas to introduce his alphabet and writing to the western Cherokees. He took up his abode there and had portions of the Bible printed in Cherokee. In 1828 the *Cherokee Phoenix,* a weekly, was first printed in Cherokee and English. Sequoia was sent to Washington in 1828 as envoy of the western band, and it was his influence that led to the unification of the tribe as a united nation in Oklahoma. He visited a great many tribes trying to work out some form of universal language or "Indian Esperanto," but was unsuccessful. He also endeavored to locate a "lost" band of Cherokees, and while on this quest in Mexico he lost his own life. His alphabet of eighty-six letters is considered the most complete and perfect in the world. It is still used in printing Cherokee papers, magazines, and books.

SHABONE. ("Made like a bear.") A Pottawattomie chief, grandnephew of Pontiac. Born at Naumee, Illinois, in 1775. Died July 17, 1859. His father was an Ottawa who fought under Pontiac. When a youth Shabone moved to Michigan and became a lieutenant of Pontiac, and was by the latter's side when he was killed at the Battle of Thames. Incensed by the ill treatment of their Indian allies by the British, Shabone and others joined the Americans. A man of magnificent presence and almost gigantic stature, he was chosen peace chief of the Pottawattomies and was their spokesman at the Chicago Council in 1836. During the Winnebago and the Black Hawk wars Shabone saved many settlements by warnings. When in 1827 the Winnebagos rose, he kept the Pottawattomies from joining in the uprising. He was made a prisoner by the hostiles at Geneva Lake and was threatened with death because of his friendship for the whites. Black Hawk appealed to him personally to join him, but Shabone refused, and tried to convince Black Hawk that his revolt would end in disaster. Finding this useless, he and his men went to Princeton, Illinois, warning the settlers of the outbreak, and continued to Chicago in time to warn the inhabitants. In revenge the Sauks and Foxes tried to murder Shabone, and succeeded in killing his son and a nephew. In 1836 he went west beyond the Mississippi. Although he joined his tribe, he pined for civilization, and in 1855 returned to lands at Pawpaw Grove that had been given him by the government, only to find that they had been declared abandoned and sold. The citizens of Ottawa, Illinois, then bought him a small farm near Seneca, where he lived the rest of his life, receiving a government annuity of two hundred dollars and contributions from friends. He was married three times and was succeeded by his grandson, Chief Smoke. There is a monument to his memory in Evergreen Cemetery at Morris Hill.

SHAHAKA. She-he-ke or "Coyote." A Mandan chief commonly known as "Big White," and principal chief of the Mandans on the Missouri. Born in 1765. He was friendly toward the whites, rendered valuable services to Lewis and Clark on their expedition, and was given a medal by the government. He was mild and gentle in disposition, and with skin almost as fair as that of a white man, hence his popular name of "Big White." When Lewis and Clark were on their return trip they induced Shahaka to accompany them to St. Louis and to visit President Jefferson, who had invited Lewis and Shahaka to see his collection of Indian objects. The chief remained in the east for a year, leaving St. Louis for his home in May 1807 with an escort of eleven troopers and two officers, the Mandans and Arikaras being at war. While they were ascending the river a party of Arikaras opened fire on the boat killing one Sioux member of the party and wounding a white man and Shahaka's interpreter. The chief refused to attempt to proceed overland because of the presence of the women and children and the wounded. The Missouri Fur Company then promised safe conduct to the Mandans' home, and in the spring of 1808, with an armed escort of 150, they left St. Louis and arrived safely at their destination to find peace between the tribes. Shahaka's stories of his experiences among the whites in the east seemed so incredible to his people that he fell into disrepute as a prevaricator. He was killed in a hand-to-hand battle with a Sioux warrior.

SITTING BULL. An Oglala Sioux chief. Was one of the signers of the treaty of 1867 by which the government established the Sioux reservation and promised that the land would belong to the Sioux "as long as the grass shall grow and the waters flow"—a promise completely broken a few years later. He was always friendly with the whites, and on one of his visits to Washington, President Grant presented him with a rifle that is now in the Museum of the American Indian, Heye Foundation, in New York City. He died a short time before the Battle of the Little Big Horn. Often confused with Sitting Bull the Hunkpapa Sioux medicine man, but not even a distant relation.

SITTING BULL. Tatanpka Ho-tan-ka, "Waiting Buffalo Bull." A Hunkpapa Sioux warrior and medicine man but never a chief, although a leader. Born in South Dakota in 1834. Son of Four Horns, a subchief. First known as Jumping Badger. At ten he showed his hunting skill by chasing and killing a young buffalo. At fourteen he was on the warpath with his father against the Crows, and counted one coup. On their return his father announced his son had won the right to use his own name, but changed it to "Waiting Buffalo Bull" when he made medicine in 1857. He won recognition as a peacemaker in the tribe and as a great medicine man. He took part in the wars of the 1860's, and first became widely known in 1866 in the raid on Fort Buford. Almost constantly on the warpath from 1869-76 against whites, Crows, or Shoshones. He refused to go on the reservation in 1876, which led to the campaign that resulted in the Custer battle. At the time he was in the mountains making medicine and had no part in the battle. He claimed to have foretold it and its result. The Sioux separated. Sitting Bull, in command of the western party, was attacked by Miles and routed. Many surrendered, but others with Sitting Bull reached Canada, where they remained until 1881, when all surrendered at Fort Buford under promise of amnesty. He was a prisoner in Fort Randall until 1883. Although he had surrendered and had gone on the reservation, he remained unreconciled, and influenced the Sioux against land sales in 1888. At his camp at Standing Rock and by his invitation, Kicking Bear organized the ghost dance, the first on the reservation. The authorities ordered his arrest on the grounds that he was inciting trouble through the dance and a promise of the coming Messiah. During an attempt of his men to rescue him he was shot by two Indian police sergeants, Red Tomahawk and Bullhead, December 15, 1890. His son Crow Foot and others were also killed, as well as six Indian police. Largely famed for his "medicine" powers, foresight, organizing skill, observance of natural phenomena, and uncanny ability to understand the inner natures of both Indians and whites. Well regarded by his people for generosity, his quiet disposition, and steadfast adherence to Indian ideals and causes. He left two wives, one of them called "Pretty Plume," and nine children. The oldest son, Louis, attended Storrs College, Connecticut.

SPOTTED TAIL. *Sainte-galeshka.* Brûlé Teton Sioux. Born 1833 near Fort Laramie, Wyoming. Not a chief by heritage, he rose to be a chief by his fighting prowess. He took a leading part in the destruction of Lieutenant Grattan's detachment in 1854 when they tried to arrest an Indian who had taken an old, seemingly abandoned cow. After the massacre of innocent Indians by the soldiers, Spotted Tail and two others marched into Fort Laramie in full dress, chanting their death songs to give themselves up to save the tribe. He regained his freedom and became chief of the Lower Brûlés in 1865. When the government tried to get a right of way through Montana, Spotted Tail favored it, but Red Cloud opposed. Other chiefs signed the treaty on April 29, 1868, accepting a Teton reservation covering all of South Dakota west of the Missouri River and agreeing to the construction of the roadway. The government recognized as unceded sections of Wyoming and Montana north of the Platte River as far west as the Big Horn Mountains, abandoning the road to the mines and Fort Kearney, where Fetterman was killed, and Fort Reno on the Powder River. When gold was discovered in the Black Hills, Spotted Tail and Red Cloud arranged to go to Washington to negotiate the sale of mining rights. To learn the facts Spotted Tail went to the Black Hills area and hung around the prospectors, and mines, and decided they were very valuable. The Commissioner sent to negotiate the sale found Spotted Tail, and the Indians asked sixty million dollars for their rights. This was thought to be so high that all efforts to buy ceased for a year, and troops were sent to protect miners going to the Black Hills across acknowledged Indian lands. This caused all the young braves to go on the warpath. Red Cloud was accused of disloyalty, but actually had no part in it. In the course of the campaign Spotted Tail was made chief of all the Sioux of both agencies. He negotiated the settlement that made Crazy Horse (his nephew) surrender in 1877. Always trying to arrange peace and amity, he won the enmity of the others, and for this was shot and killed by Crow Dog near Rosebud Agency August 5, 1881. Throughout his life he was a friend of the whites when possible. Again and again he prevented young warriors (as well as chiefs) from entering into hostilities.

STANDING BEAR. A Ponca who was, perhaps, the greatest factor in causing our government to change its Indian policy. When arrangements were made to move the Poncas from Nebraska to Indian Territory, Standing Bear found they were to be placed on Sioux area and refused to consent. When the officials refused to take them back home, the Indians started afoot, with only a few dollars and a blanket each. In forty days they traveled five hundred miles, only to be arrested. Meanwhile, over a third of the tribe had died from hardships and exposure. Standing Bear's son having died, he took the bones and with followers started north for his old home, arriving destitute in March at the Omaha Reservation. Borrowing land and seeds, the band were about to put in a crop when soldiers appeared with orders to arrest Standing Bear and his followers and take them to Indian Territory. On the way they stopped near Omaha and Standing Bear was interviewed by T. H. Tibbles, a newspaper correspondent, and the story was printed in the newspapers. Citizens were aroused, and had the chief repeat his story in a church meeting. Poppleton and Webster offered their services as lawyers and issued a *habeas corpus*. The United States denied the Indians' rights, considering them "not persons within the law." On April 18th Judge Dundy decided that "an Indian is a person within the meaning of the law," and that "no authority exists for forcibly removing any of the prisoners to Indian Territory," and then ordered them discharged from custody. Standing Bear and his band returned to Nebraska. In 1879-80 with two interpreters he visited the east, where he related his story and won such widespread sympathy that thousands of letters were sent to the President and to Congress, all protesting the unjust treatment of the Indians and demanding that something be done to right the wrongs. In 1880 the Senate appointed a committee to make a thorough investigation, and a satisfactory adjustment was arranged. Better lands were allotted to the Poncas, who chose to remain in Indian Territory; full payment was made to those who had lost property, and a home was provided for Standing Bear. He died peacefully in September 1908 when seventy-seven years of age.

TECUMSEH. Teksem-thi, or "The one who springs," so called because he was a member of the gens of the Great Medicine Panther or Meteor. Often referred to as "Crouching Panther" or "Shooting Star." A famous Shawnee chief born near Springfield, Ohio, in 1768. Son of chief Cornstalk (which see.) Brother of Tenskwatawa or "The Prophet." When still a youth he distinguished himself in the many border wars. He was noted for his humanity, and forced his people to cease torturing prisoners. He and his brother were strongly opposed to the advance of the whites, and denied the right of the government to make treaties with and to buy lands from any one tribe, claiming that the land belonged to all tribes in common. Convinced that no one tribe could stop the inroads of the whites, Tecumseh determined to form a confederation of all the tribes from Florida to the Great Lakes and west to the Missouri. With this purpose in view he personally traveled over the entire area and held conferences with the chiefs. Although not wholly successful, some tribes refusing to join the confederacy, he managed to make allies of more tribes with a greater number of warriors than ever were united in the history of Indian warfare previously. Had their plans been carried out they undoubtedly would have swept the whites from most of the middle west, but Tecumseh's plans were spoiled by the Prophet's premature attack on Tippecanoe, November 7, 1811. Then the War of 1812 still further interfered with his plans, for some of his allies sided with the British, while others joined with the Americans. Tecumseh and his tribe supported the British, and he was given a commission with the rank of brigadier-general in command of two thousand warriors. Although the Indians fought valiantly, and in numerous battles saved the day for the British, yet again and again they were defeated and forced to retreat until Tecumseh, declaring he would retreat no farther, made a final stand on the Thames River near Chatham, Ontario, October 5, 1813. In the terrific battle that took place the Indians were defeated and Tecumseh was killed. Before going into battle he had discarded his uniform in favor of buckskins, stating, in words to that effect, that he would "not be found dead" in garments of the white men. Some historians have stated that Tecumseh was, in their opinions, the most extraordinary Indian in our history. This, however, is far from being the case. He was unquestionably the greatest of our Indian organizers, as well as a military genius and a famous orator, but also he was an idealist and placed too much faith in the prophecies of his brother and other medicine men. Moreover, he abhorred shedding the blood of noncombatants, which was essential if his plans were to succeed.

TWO MOONS. A Cheyenne chief and associate of Dull Knife (which see).

TWO STRIKES. Nomkopa, or "He killed two." A Sioux chief who won his name in a remarkable manner. Regarded by the other youths and by the men as of little account as a hunter and of a far too peace-loving nature, he was challenged by his father to kill a buffalo with a single arrow. To his father's amazement the youth drove an arrow into a cow, killing her almost instantly. At almost the same time a bull, wounded by the boy's father, had turned on him, knocking over his pony. Knowing he hadn't a second to spare, the boy pulled the arrow from the dead cow, fitted it to his bowstring, and drove it through the heart of the wounded bull. The feat won the praise of everyone, and when, later, he proved his bravery and prowess as a warrior, he was made a full chief. He was a natural-born comedian, inordinately fond of practical jokes and forever acting the part of a clown, falling off his horse, tripping on some imaginary object, or performing sleight-of-hand tricks. On one occasion his buffoonery saved his life. In a brush with a party of Crows he pretended to be mortally wounded and dropped from his racing pony. The Crow nearest to him dashed up as his comrades sped by, and bent down to scalp the supposedly dead Sioux. Two Strikes' feet shot up, hitting the Crow's belly and knocking him backward. The next moment Two Strikes had wrenched the knife from the other's grasp and plunged it into his throat. Stripping off the Crow's scalp, he leaped on his victim's pony and rode to safety. Although he repeatedly proved his valor in warfare, yet Two Strikes was naturally of a peaceful nature and inclined to be friendly with the whites. As far as is known, he never took an active part in any of the battles between the Sioux and the whites.

UNCAS. A Mohican chief and warrior made world-famous by Fenimore Cooper's *Leatherstocking Tales* and other novels. In these works he was pictured as the epitome of all that was noble, a magnificent character in every way. In reality, if we are to believe contemporaneous accounts, Uncas was selfish, jealous, tyrannical, grasping, and untrustworthy. One writer who knew him well stated that "he was unrelieved of a single trait of magnanimity," and that "his habits were bad and he was addicted to every vice of the white man and some others." Also he was strongly anti-Christian. He sided with the English against the Pequots, from whom he had been banished because of a quarrel with Sassacus and his attempt to assume control. Although Uncas and his Mohicans are always pictured in history as staunch allies of the whites, whereas the Pequots are invariably vilified as archenemies and fiends incarnate, yet the two tribes had been one and the same until about fifty years before the landing of the Pilgrims, when tribal jealousies and struggles for control led to the division of the nation. The Pequots were foes of the whites because the Mohicans were their allies, and the Mohicans were friends of the whites because the

Pequots were hostile. Had the English seen fit to ally themselves with the Pequots by attacking the Mohicans, the early history of the colonies would have been very different.

WALKING TURTLE. Nawkaw. A Winnebago chief born in 1735. Died in 1833 at ninety-eight years of age. His home was at Big Green Lake, Wisconsin. He first became famous at the battle of the Thames in Canada, October 5, 1813, and was beside Tecumseh when the latter was killed. He was active on behalf of peace and devoted the remainder of his life to this ideal. He signed numerous treaties, which he always kept. One of his most notable deeds was preventing his Winnebagos from joining Black Hawk in 1832. In order to keep watch on them he camped close to the government agency and aided in getting the surrender of Red Bird and his accomplices in the murder of Gangier. Having induced them to surrender, he went to Washington and personally appealed for and won clemency for them. However, the pardon for Red Bird arrived after he had died in prison. Walking Turtle was a huge man, standing well over six feet, very stalwart and muscular, with a broad, pleasant face, but with an immense lower lip hanging to his chin. He was very sagacious, intelligent, firm, upright, peaceful, always true to his promises, and was highly respected by the whites.

WHITEFEATHER, HENRY. Quapaw. Timber expert. Probably no living man had a wider, more intimate knowledge of commercial timber than Whitefeather. He made many expeditions to South America, Africa, Asia, and the Pacific Islands in order to study tropical woods in the native habitat. He was familiar with the qualities, properties, and suitabilities of every known commerically valuable wood for various purposes. Often consulted by architects, boat-builders, yacht designers and cabinetmakers in regard to the woods best adapted to certain conditions and requirements.

INDEX